THE HEALIUM WAY

THE ART OF BEING *EXTRA*ORDINARY AND LIVING WITHOUT REGRETS

PART 2 *of* 2

JIM PEERA

The views expressed herein are those of the author alone and should not be taken as professional advice. As an unconventional transformational guide, the author believes in being an equal opportunity critic — delving deep into the multifaceted human experience without excuses or reservation. The information presented comes in a raw and un-sanitized package based on the author's personal experiences, anecdotal evidence, facts, real stories and events. It is intended for informational purposes only. The reader is responsible for their own actions.

In honor and celebration of all the unconventional movers, shakers, lovers and peacemakers...

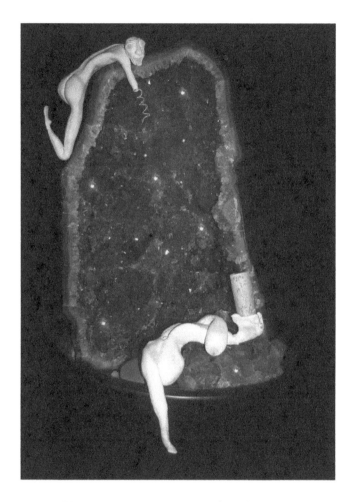

"Uncork my world" Artist: Jim Peera

Table of Contents

No Risk, No Reward

In Part 1 of The Healium Way, I wanted you to know how my life's story influenced my own transformation and why I give a damn about being *extra*ordinary and living life without regrets. By sharing my personal stories and traumas without filters or masks, you came to understand the real person behind The Healium Way. Hopefully, you also gained some insight into the power of the creative and healing arts: our Divinely gifted medicine within us. In Part 2, we turn the narrative and focus on you, the reader. The mirror is now flipped towards you and the journey inward is where you will discover the better, the more *extra*ordinary you. As we've established earlier, I offer no magic pills or quick fixes — but rather a very practical and common-sense guide that you can incorporate on your own path. Your job is to remove all excuses, distractions and take action by doing *something* each day to improve yourself. Using the 21 Principles I've identified as being transformational to personal growth, you will guide yourself and test each Principle at your own pace and leisure. Consider it a template for creating a healed life.

Before we get into all the fun however, it's important to do a couple of exercises to clear and focus your mind to receive the information and knowledge as optimally as possible. So first I will share with you a daily "I AM" (4 P's) mantra that I created for myself. It does wonders for me, and I say it over in my mind each morning. It's a universal affirmation that will help you focus on your positive traits and clear away any doubts and negative thoughts you may have about yourself:

"I AM POWERFUL. I AM PROTECTED. I AM PROSPEROUS. I AM PEACE."

To make my point, close your eyes and repeat these words in your mind to yourself three to four times right now. Take a deep breath between each pause and repeat the process with both your hands on your chest. You will notice an immediate difference in your energy as the cells in the body begin their regeneration. Words are powerful in ways we can't imagine. Positive words can make you, while negative words can break you — not just emotionally but physiologically. Sending a dose of uplifting verbal signals to our brain on a regular basis is an essential practice toward an improved mood, a positive attitude and overall mental wellness.

Let's dissect this special mantra. You are *powerful* because you are a Divinely empowered being who battled a million other sperm to get here for some purpose. Have faith in your personal power and don't let anyone drain it out of you. Think it, believe it and act on your higher self at all times and you will stay empowered. You are *protected* because you are part and parcel of the Divinity you emanated from and that always watches over you. Stay connected to this Source and you'll learn to protect yourself from destructive energy from people and be protected from undue harm (unless your earthly time is up). You are *prosperous* because you have an abundance of valuable human capital that no man-made form of financial capital can buy. Keep investing in yourself and spread your human prosperity everywhere. You are *peace* because it is the only sustainable condition for yourself and your coexistence with others. Always fight for it and never deviate from it. It's your life's default position for your mental wellness. This 4 P's mantra is my personal empowerment daily practice, but feel free to make one of your own to suit your needs.

Next, you will need to get your mind focused toward your higher vibration stream of consciousness with clear intention.

Take time to set your intention to make desired positive changes manifest for you. This is the InManTra exercise I wrote about in Part 1: (INtention, MANifestation, TRAnsformation). The intention can be as simple as:

"I wish to be a more fun and loving person" or as detailed as *"I must come clean and be authentic with people in my work and home.", "I desire to be a more balanced person and live my life without regrets.," "I wish to manifest good health"* and so on.

Write your intention(s) in the box below:

Remember, the intention you just wrote down is not so much a demand, as it is an "ask" from your higher self to the universe, with you in charge of manifesting it. The Healium Way's definition of intention also holds you accountable and keeps you honest. Because the ask is useless if you don't follow through with an action plan that matches that intention with commitment. For instance, having an intention to break an unhealthy drug addiction is disingenuous if you replace your cocaine habit with an opioid one. The intention is also meaningless if you don't stick to a consistent plan. I've witnessed this condition frequently at our Center. Often, we either suffer from the paralysis of analysis or we're too lazy to do the work and prefer to outsource it to other people and conveniences. It's a classic case of absolving our responsibility. Most of us fail at manifesting what we want because we are afraid of failure.

We get stuck in a feedback loop; we hear that little voice in our head that stops us short of taking the first step into the unknown. We set ourselves up to fail because our expectations are too high. So don't go down that path. Instead, just be realistic with your intention and be content with any positive incremental results. The most successful people are not only focused — but are doers. An honest person will not brag about being honest, he just *does* honest things. A great leader seldom bangs the drum on how great he is, he just *does* great work. No one is grading you, but you're only as good as your actions. The Healium Way works in the same manner and is best when activated in real life situations. If you don't convert your thoughts into action, you get nowhere. By not allowing yourself to feel pain, you'll have no appreciation of pleasure. When you stop taking risks, you won't be rewarded. And none of it matters if you don't believe in yourself.

1
The Principles of The Healium Way

T his scene is a great metaphor to meditate upon before I
introduce you Principles of The Healium Way.

There's a dead tree trapped
between the rocks. It's stiff, lifeless
and stuck with nowhere to go. It's
been suffocated by the rocks. It feels
trapped and lonely. Now look at the
other trees around. They're healthy,
flourishing and very much alive. The
soil and climate conditions are
exactly the same, yet we see
different outcomes. Can you relate
to it? What do you think has
happened to this dying tree? Take some time to process the image and
reflect on your own life. Which tree's condition bears similarity?

The fate of the dying tree is in the hands of the tree. In The
Healium Way of understanding this dichotomy, we look to nature
again to show us human parallels. The dying tree is devoid of joy
and the fullness of life, which is similar to a person with a vacated
Soul who's suffocating within. The rocks mirror our fear, rigidity,
ego, resistance, busyness, greed, stupidity, etc. These negative
forces are always there to impede our growth — as are the various
inclement conditions in nature. The healthy trees, though, choose to
get smarter and creative by not attaching to the life-sucking

conditions. They're focused on reaching up to the sky, kissing the sun, sharing their limited water supply with each other, and keeping their roots healthy. No matter what it takes or how hard it gets, the healthy tree is always self-correcting and doing something "extra" past the ordinary or conventional, while the unhealthy tree is rigid and thus cannot adapt or change.

So what separates people who feed their Soul from those who don't? Our own intentions, choices and actions do. Also our own resistances and attachments. It's our own doing and undoing. Once again, nature shines a mirror on us. If you're looking at the decaying tree, most of us can see some part of ourselves — dying or dead in a similar fashion. Don't make the mistake of thinking that this is not about me. Or to camouflage the truth with material riches, toys, ambitions, work habits and a multitude of addictions. In reality, those imbalances or crutches just impede our road to realignment and cause a domino effect of more damage down the road — often cascading into other generations. Now look at the choice between the lifeless tree and the surrounding healthy ones. Which one is for you?

KISS OF LIFE

If you're like me, you want to be a healthy tree until you croak. As a 60-year-old man, with hair growing in places I don't like and falling out in others, I may not be as virile and youthful as I used to be. But I'll be kissing the radiance of life — not the doom and gloom of death — until my last breath. I want to be dancing on my way to the grave, not crawling to it with fear and trepidation. It's the only way to be. The white hair and wrinkles on my face will be my reminder of a life well lived with all its twists and turns, valleys and mountains — to honor, to be proud of and to celebrate — not to be ashamed of or to hide behind a mask.

Not surprisingly, I've talked to many adults at our Center and in my travels who have surrendered to the notion similar to our dying tree above. To all of you in this category, I can assure you that age is only a number and although your limbs may be weak, your outer shell may be decaying, your hair may be balding, your mojo within still has the ability to kick ass in life and rekindle unbound joy. That is, if you so wish. You need less blue pills to ignite your sexual libido and more time appreciating the blue skies and blue waters each day. Because your fountain of youth comes from having a balanced and an uplifted mental attitude emanating from your everlasting Soul, not your temporary decaying shell.

It is never too late to look at the metaphor of the healthier trees around and be inspired to regrow and strengthen our roots. The soil is forgiving and ready to see you flourish again. And by taking some baby steps along The Healium Way path, the time is right to replenish your Soul and water the dying tree inside. The real stories I've recounted in Part 1 of The Healium Way have hopefully inspired you to unpeel your own personal situations and experiences. I believe by now you are a lot less resistant and more open to take some risks and do some practical exercises. You're also ready to make a lifestyle change and be that *extra*ordinary person. Now, let's begin exploring this exciting journey together!

There are **21** Principles (or roots of a tree) that help to strengthen and ground you in The Healium Way :

1. **Knowing the importance of U**

2. **Removing our resistances**

3. **Fusing the creative and healing arts**

4. **Solving every problem creatively**

5. **Mastering detachment and resolving conflicts**

6. **Avoiding being sheeple**

7. Unleashing the magic of humor

8. Honoring your emotions

9. Learning to self-care

10. Resisting the art of replicating

11. Understanding the power of surrealism

12. Being a participant of life

13. Keeping the inner child alive

14. Opening the communication door

15. Activating the heart of hugging

16. Using the magic of spontaneity

17. Being an instrument of peace

18. Knowing the value of adaptability

19. Leading by example

20. Practicing soul, body and mind balance

21. Staying consistent

These Principles are your prescribed medicines to administer and to make yourself better today than you were yesterday. They're not set in stone, or designed for one time use. Think of them as your booster shots to give yourself each day you're alive. The Healium Way, like life, is in itself a paradox. It is not a fixed way, but rather a loose set of proven Principles that each person can custom-tailor for themselves and plug into their busy lives at their own pace. I'm sure you can add your own Principles on top of it, as you see fit. So in effect The Healium Way is *your better way*. These Principles are also not novel. In our man-made hustle and bustle, we've simply misplaced and buried many of these common-sense applications.

Now I am unearthing them for you with a fresh twist. As I said in Part 1, these Principles are not about upending your ways or forcing you to break out of your many man-made boxes, as they are about inspiring you to have an open mind, stay curious and have a willingness to test them out in your own life. Ideally, I'd love for you to make them all a part and parcel of your life's regimen. Once each of us understands how to reattach these Principles into our lives, we can begin to forge a new path to our more joyful and higher self — devoid of man-made confinements.

Kerala, India. Photo: Jim Peera

KEEPING THE PILOT LIGHT ON

I've always preferred attaining contentment to happiness. Many of us conflate the two, but I view being happy as a temporary condition, such as the feeling one has by going out on a hot date with someone. Whereas being content is keeping that flame alive by having a deeper and lasting relationship with that individual — working towards attaining satisfaction, gratitude, joy and inner peace. Of course, a healthy life can include both happiness and contentment. Typically, people who seek only happiness are shortsighted and impulsive, whereas those who seek contentment are more patient and willing to go the distance to get the long-term benefit. For this reason, contented people are rarely disappointed, as they've done the work to be firmly rooted and self-empowered; whether it's living with themselves or with their chosen life companion. As a married man, it is my conviction that this disposition is a result of being in rapport with making the most of the present while not taking the tomorrows for granted. Specifically, it is about having three important conditions met:

1. **Having *someone to love*** (our sharing).

2. **Having *something to do*** (our purpose).

3. **Having *something to look forward to*** (our aspiration).

If you have all of these three conditions at any given time and you're healthy, you're a fortunate person who will also likely stay young at heart at all times. You have absolutely no reason to complain, feel dissatisfied or be depressed operating each day in this alignment. Even if you're not financially well off. That's because our definition of joy and contentment is not concerned with the accumulation of material possessions.

In order to have *someone to love*, we must first love ourselves unconditionally and be willing to share part of our Soul, body and mind with others in similar fashion. This has been a critical lesson in my own life as a perfectionist and someone who is always in pursuit of improving everything and everybody. It took some work on my part to start loving the parts of myself that I disliked and not try to impose similar treatment on others. When I did this, I found it easy to attract and retain someone I could love in my life. This 'someone' must be human (not a pet or a robot) as it's vital we don't dilute our human Spirit — or even worse, give up on homo sapiens as our intimate sexual partners.

In order to *have something to do,* we must be willing to give meaning to ourselves and find purpose. This second condition is ever-evolving as we all shift from different stages of our life cycle. What's important is to understand the value of connecting to something that you feel passionate about (for yourself) and offering it to the world in your own unique way. For couples, this means not living in the shadow of your spouse; but for your own pleasure and identity — to keep your Soul alive. When you get this condition right, you will boost your self-esteem and not be seduced by or be easily attached to low vibration forces.

In order to *look forward to something and aspire,* we must be willing to always improve our current state of being and not stop exploring and expanding. Although all three of the above-mentioned conditions must exist for us to find joy, inner peace and fulfillment, this third condition is the most fascinating to uncork. It is a feeling we get when we're anticipating going out to see a new movie or visiting a different vacation spot. There's a certain excitement and pleasure of discovering and experiencing something fresh. But rather than settling for a once-in-a-while temporary condition, we learn to create a sustainable lifestyle habit in this manner. Because in order to *look forward to something,* we must believe that our today will be better than yesterday, and our tomorrow will be better than today. In this way, we're not resting on our laurels, but recreating adventure and keeping our passion for life and flame from extinguishing. It's our new dawn moment. The anticipation of the rising sun is always more exciting and enticing than the afterglow of the sunset, as it offers an entire new day to look forward to — to explore and experience. Every single minute we're alive, we can only seize the moment of what's already here, and look forward to what's ahead, not what's been. We can relish in the beauty of the afterglow of the sunset, but we can never bring back the awesome power and energy of that day's sun. As we keep moving toward the next sunrise, we refrain from banging our heads with unnecessary couldas, shouldas, wouldas from yesterday. Our energy is best spent gearing up for tomorrow with new knowledge, vigor and wisdom. A second lesson is to understand that we have some grander purpose ahead to motivate us, even when we think we've done our best work.

When an interviewer asked Paul McCartney what he had left to do in his life after all his iconic musical success, he said, *"To keep working towards my best album yet — or otherwise why would I even want to get up in the morning?"* Legendary songwriter Barry Gibb affirmed a similar penchant of the Gibb brothers' amazing career composing more than 1,000 songs: *"We always found a way to keep the hunger alive and not rest our laurels on our success."*

The Healium Way translates this to mean that we must always keep our creative pilot light on within, and to never stop being motivated to become better at whatever we put our minds to — be it in a vocation, a relationship, a community endeavor, a humanitarian project and our own self-improvement. For me, this aspirational mindset is also about giving ourselves permission to expand into unchartered areas beyond our career or known talents by letting go of the familiar and comfortable habits.

LETTING GO

For many of you, the outlined Principles will entail *letting go* of your many resistances. Much of our risk-averseness and inactions can be attributed to the obstacles of fear, ego, judgment and pretense that clog our flow of experiencing self-liberation and untapped possibilities within us. We will discuss in the following pages how to reduce these resistances and become more open to experimenting, exploring, adventuring and participating in life's wonders and hidden treasures. At our Center we've found how people start letting go effortlessly when they're made aware of these resistances, many of which are programmed in the brain but we're not always conscious of.

When we understand each of the 21 Principles in detail, we will start seeing the benefits almost immediately. Life will begin to feel more joyous, connected and in a healthier balance. We'll discover our enlightened Spirit within and regain our true power. We'll love ourselves and love others. We'll become a better parent, a more loving spouse, a gentler boss, a more respected citizen, an empathetic leader, a person who can look in the mirror and be proud of what they see. It is about each of us waking up in the morning and seeing that on the one hand we're grateful to shine a light on ourselves for what *we* have. And on the other hand, not stopping short of spreading our own light onto others, and being happy for what *they* have — no matter what label. This latter point must be mastered in order to shift from an ordinary to an *extra*ordinary condition.

The Healium Way of life also liberates us from any restrictive or myopic thinking about people, cultures, food, places, beliefs, philosophy etc., since it does not favor any one type of ideology. For example, instead of simply liking jazz, you'll appreciate ALL genres of music. Instead of just loving Jesus, it encourages you to appreciate other prophets and enlightened beings. Like the metaphor of being akin to the roots of a tree, the idea is to be unafraid of seeking new opportunities and taking new risks. In this manner, we move from small shrinking minds to more open, curious and expanding ones and we become more resilient in our thinking. This in turn makes us stronger and more grounded, which makes it easier to stay in a healthy balance in all aspects of life. Not surprisingly, the most critical aspect is to take action and apply as many of these Principles into our life in order that we can make the best possible lifestyle changes for ourselves.

TAKING SMALL STEPS GOING UP

You'll achieve the best results by taking small bites and baby steps of The Healium Way each day for a year, rather than binge eating the Principles in one week and being overwhelmed by them.

An Army drill or a cold turkey approach aren't effective methods in the healing arena. We prefer slow, steady and consistent growth. Otherwise, we will not achieve long-lasting effects necessary for a sustainable lifestyle transformation.

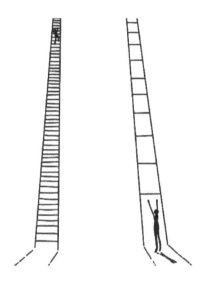

Taking the baby-step ladder of self-improvement

COMPETE WITH YOURSELF

It is difficult telling an American to be a steady and consistent turtle, rather than an impulsive fast-moving hare. That's because our society rewards those who are speedy, competitive, financially successful and taught the value of winning. In today's America it seems that everything is based on competition, material accomplishment and exceptionalism. In business, competition can be a positive trait to improve quality and prevent monopolies from forming. In sports, competition is the prerequisite to measuring human strength, speed and agility. One can also make the case that material accomplishment and exceptionalism is part and parcel of a for-profit entity.

But the shift from ordinary to *extra*ordinary is not to apply the same metric to our social behaviors and human connectivity. If you want to compete with anyone, compete and compare yourself to yourself. It is a better and more accurate measure, as you know your own idiosyncrasies. This is a more effective motivator and a litmus test to help you become a better person today than what you were the day before. That is one of the critical missions of The Healium Way. We must avoid pitting one person against another and rate "the best" in fields of endeavor, because then we'll normalize separating and devaluing people based on subjective metrics. Yet, we do it all the time! The Healium Way is aware of this reality and as a result it only focuses on helping you, the individual, who is in control of their own destiny and is ready to get to a healthier place of balance.

MENTAL SCHMENTAL

I cannot prescribe to you The Healium Way Principles without mentioning my personal view of America's looming and pervasive mental crisis. Borrowing from my Jewish acquaintances' Yiddish pejorative term, it's what I call a *mental schmental* game. Don't misunderstand me, Americans are definitely way more mentally unhealthy today than they have been in recent memory. We've seen clear evidence of it at our Center before the wrath of Trumpism and Covid-19 pandemic exposed it even further. We went from a society that stigmatized mental illness and hid it under the rug to one that labels anyone who is unruly or outspoken as being "mentally unstable." We can blame our lack of priorities and a dozen other excuses, but it doesn't explain why America's mental crisis is so pervasive, chronic and becoming normalized.

The answer is of course, money. What's the incentive or benefit in holistically solving any mental condition for a "profit-over-people" consumer-based society? None whatsoever! Would mentally healthy people buy as many unnecessary goods that line the pockets of money-hungry corporations and vulture-capitalists than mentally unhealthy consumers? America loves its crazies and it conveniently exploits them — as it does the stupid, the obese and the ignorant. This 'land of opportunity' is a land of opportunists. Many who wake up each day to prey on the uneducated, the naive and the most vulnerable. There are billions of dollars being made every year by keeping you sick, fragile, disempowered and even divided. It's quite a racket. And it's a self-fulfilling prophecy. Mental health experts make money by confirming to you that your mind is unhealthy. Then the news media, gun sellers and social media wring their greedy hands to feed this unhealthy mind labeled as depression, anxiety, bipolar disorder, fear, loneliness, etc., with more fear and garbage content. Soon the professional drug pushers such as physicians and pain clinics milk your insurance company by prescribing your unhealthy mind with a cocktail of chemicals, they call medications. And to ensure that you don't harm yourself or society, Big Pharma gets you hooked on them for the rest of your life. You quickly go from visiting the doctor's office complaining about your sleep apnea to becoming a full-blown functional drug addict. As Michael Jackson's ghost would probably say to you, *"You got hit by a smooth criminal!"* referring to a society's drug con-game on its own people.

Many Americans are already in an emotional and financial straitjacket, and caged in a cuckoo's nest called America — they just take more substances to forget about their reality! And this genre of substances, often containing toxic man-made chemicals, is layered on top of the other crutches many Americans use to cope, i.e., alcohol, religion, money, work, social media, fast food and a plethora of other bad sh*t. It's taking an ugly truth, mixing it with an inconvenient truth and turning it into a shameless mindf*ck. And we're all paying for it — individually and collectively. As a landlord, I've witnessed perfectly healthy tenants in their 20s collecting government disability checks for a condition known as 'anxiety disorder'. I know they were playing a scam because I've seen them sitting at home all day watching porn and playing video games. In many cases, these thumb suckers misappropriated their taxpayer-funded money and were often late paying rent and at risk of being evicted. At some point I wondered if I too qualified for the same disorder being a stressed-out landlord with high bills and dead-beat tenants to throw out!

If any of what I am saying, sounds like your life or someone you know, The Healium Way is here to help. This self-induced mental timebomb is your slow destruction that you cleverly manage and keep under control with superficial pacifiers and enablers. It's time, though, to wake up and invest in your reconstruction by taking charge of your own mental health, by self-diagnosing and then self-prescribing smarter alternatives. The Healium Way Principles are your ignition keys to improving your mental wellness and get you started on a more sustainable path to your transformation.

So let's begin the journey!

"Untitled" for YOUR interpretation

(Clay, Acrylic Mixed Media) Artist: Jim Peera

Principle # 1
Knowing The Importance of U

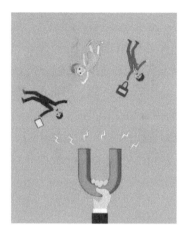

YOU ATTRACT WHAT U ARE. NOT WHAT YOU WANT.

When I created the Healium logo, the U was highlighted in bold red to emphasize the importance of putting YOU in charge of your own transformation. With this intention, the U is a call for self-responsibility that turns into a self-fulfilling prophecy — akin to a magnet. When you're real, you will attract real people in your life. But this first Principle of The Healium Way can be confusing as it appears to be implying that if you are seen by others as a jerk, butthole or lowlife then that is your true self. Quite the contrary! This first Principle sets the stage for all others as it establishes the idea of not just authenticity but *Divine-inspired authenticity,* upholding the ideals of the higher self.

The U by this definition refers to the notion of investing in you by *doing you,* (connecting to your true higher self), *by you* (taking self-responsibility) and *for you* (self-love). Our goal is to be in alignment with all three of these conditions. Accomplishing these ideals becomes easier by having a transparent awareness of how far you've deviated from your Divinity by claiming and owning who you are.

OWN IT

Your man-made and flawed self is your mirror of truth. Look at yourself honestly, without any filters and see the person within for who you really are today. Do you like yourself? Can you look in the mirror each morning and be proud of your character? Do you see yourself as fitting in the "leaves, branches or roots" analogy that we discussed in Part 1? Or are you a combination of them? Wherever you place yourself, your careful analysis of yourself will reveal something interesting. The U that you're walking around with every day as an adult may not be the best version of you. Your higher version of yourself may be buried somewhere underneath your man-made cover. And you must shine a light on it from the inside out. As an example, if you're a narcissistic person, it's not the transparent Divinely authentic U that gets conveyed to others, but an opaque low-vibrational outer-version of you. It's a convenient mask for you to hide behind your truer self. Sure, it may be your outward personality and character, and it may have served you well in your unhealed vessel, but it is detached from your higher self. That's all quite normal, though.

After all, narcissistic people were not born self-absorbed jerks. They acquired this condition growing up, often in a survival mode. And when no one had the courage to call them on their unhealthy way of being, they took it as permissible behavior. That behavior superficially numbed them from journeying deeper, and over time they attracted more unhealthy traits and drifted further from their higher self. Think of them as Divine beings trapped in a man-made version of themselves, stuck in a low-vibrational box. The real U and higher self is waiting for you to unearth it and expose it to the world. You also may not want to; it's definitely your prerogative. For the purposes of The Healium Way, I am not encouraging you to hide your low-vibration self as much as I want you to see it for what it is and be aware of its damage to yourself and others around you.

When you own your man-made self with all its flaws, you're in essence bringing it to the surface for honest observation. Those unhealthy components are now in your hands to prune and dispose of when you're ready. Your Divine-inspired authentic and unique self appears when you consciously undo the undesirable layers of your man-made you. It's not perfect by any means, but it mimics the energy field of your Creator by resonating love over hate, hope over despair, light over darkness, faith over doubt, joy over sadness, courage over fear and so forth. For many, living in this Divine-inspired state is difficult and scary, especially when it's weighted against the pressures and pretenses of the real world. But it is the condition achieved by *extra*ordinary and enlightened beings. And it's not a utopian philosophy. It's where we simply harness our best self by not being ashamed to visit our less desirable attributes and improving on them. Being the best U is your ultimate reward, because it's where you are liberated from the shackles of a disillusioned state of conformity, religious dogmas, strict traditions and other crutches that can shape and permanently mold your life. Your true self exposes your unfiltered, unmasked, honest and imperfect human self, not the labels that you attach on yourself or have been given to you by others from childhood. Those of us who go through life without peeling off those unhealthy layers are setting ourselves up for an unfulfilled life, and living in the shadows of others. Instead of honoring the center of gravity within you, and aspiring to be a *roots*-type person, you resign to a lower-vibration version of yourself. *"But what if I like being a leaf or a branch, and I am perfectly happy with this state of being?"* you ask.

That's your prerogative and acceptable too. Then you're asked to aim toward the higher version of the leaves and the branches. This is the teaching philosophy of The Healium Way. But as you get further down this path, you will likely tire of being a flake, fragile, rigid, fickle, self-centered, selfish and so on. That's because as you grow within, you will start to attract people who will parallel your behaviors and characteristics. Just like a magnet. And you won't understand why. In fact, you'll go around trying to figure out why you're not making any progress in life, why people don't like you, why you're lonely and why you have an unfulfilled life. It's your karma and your own doing. I've seen many cases at our Center where people complain they have a difficult time finding good soulmates and life partners. I always suggest that they work to figure out who they are, rather than put on a superficial mask or emulate others. When we deviate from our true selves, we deviate from our higher selves. Your homework is to evolve from this self-defeating state into a more Divine-inspired condition. We will be revisiting this subject in later chapters and the many exercises presented will help you reveal your better self. When you're kind, loving, generous, honest, courageous and sincere, you will attract those types of people in your life too. It's not rocket science.

BEWARE OF THE SEEDS OF REGRET

One of the greatest regrets in life is to be what others want you to be rather than being yourself. I call it the *"Seeds of regret."* Sometimes our loved ones want us to make the best choices for ourselves and plant a fertile crop for our future. It's all well-intentioned, but not always in our best interest. And when we have a strong conviction of our career path, we have to respond with fortitude and truth — as I did. When my family elders asked me after my high school graduation why I was choosing to pursue a career in fashion design (instead of going to medical or law school), I told them because I wouldn't be happy in any those professions.

I knew my talents and that medicine and law weren't for me. Why pursue something I wasn't passionate about?

Using The Healium Way template of transparency and honesty, I told them that they didn't have to worry about me, because whatever profession I chose to undertake, I would be the best at it— and be a success pursuing my ambitions. What I also meant was that I would plant my garden to harvest and enjoy — on my own terms. And I did! Although I didn't become a rich and famous fashion designer as I had envisioned, I pivoted and became highly successful in other endeavors. The elders witnessed my determination, drive and ascent and never questioned my decisions again, as I didn't disappoint my family or myself.

"If I cannot do great things, I can do small things in a great way."
— Dr Martin Luther King

WALKING LIFE'S TIGHTROPE

Knowing the importance of U is therefore about doing the best and most unfiltered version of you by reconnecting to your Divine path without excuses or crutches. When you're in rapport with that intention, you'll also inspire others in your circle of influence to do the same. Because it's also about being straightforward and upfront with people. This includes voicing your honest opinions and being afraid of giving constructive criticism. It's a healthier proposition and necessary for living authentically. As an example, if you're direct with your partner, boss, friend, relative or a stranger about something you don't like in them, you will likely get an upfront opinion and a critique back about you, too. Now each party is an honest broker with the other and releases the truth from their chest without pounding someone else's, with lies and fake distortion —

that festers to do more harm. Therefore, by being the best version of you, you get the best version from others. It's a win-win proposition that encourages personal growth, self-expression and self-transformation.

The transformation from ordinary to *extra*ordinary is not a straight upward line, but a rather jagged, slippery and often a scary premise. It's definitely not a quick process, but requires a slow and consistent commitment. The good news is that we have the ability to straighten out the bumps, and walk the tightrope of life with the right attitude and mindset. I've been there many times, and I will share some of my own examples in upcoming chapters.

Principle #2
Removing Our Resistances

"Money can't buy life."
— Bob Marley

As we get on our path to becoming a more *extraor*dinary individual, there are four impediments we've found at our Center that always seem to get in the way of our self-improvement. These are the four hooded horsemen that show up as guardians of our resistances: *fear, ego, judgment and pretense.* These resistances act like an obstruction in our plumbing system impeding our natural flow. Often, they're our convenient filters that we use to justify sitting in our various boxes. They latch on to our brain receptors with great success to give us a false reading of our higher and true self. In fact, when people enter our place, we remind them to be aware of these low-vibrational traits, and to consciously leave them at the door. These four main culprits are interrelated and coexist with each other seamlessly.

Once we understand that we all carry them as defense mechanisms in some manner, we can work to reduce their prevalence in us. Notice how I am not suggesting that we work to totally eliminate them, because as flawed beings, we will never be able to do that. It's idealistic thinking. There will always exist in us some element of ego, fear, judgment and pretense. So let's not put a big burden on surgically eradicating them.

For the purposes of The Healium Way, our goal is to be realistic and work toward looking at these four negative elements in the face and say: *"I know who you are, I know what harm you cause, and I will do my best to not let you get in my path of transformation and balance."* Nothing more, nothing less.

Fear is a natural and primitive human emotion. It has its purpose as a warning signal for us to self-correct and avoid harm, such as to stop us from jumping off a high rise or to avoid stepping in front of a moving train. But for the most part, it is a disempowering characteristic. It is without doubt the most corrosive trait to creativity that can hold us hostage. Fear's antidote is courage, which helps you detach from its low vibration energy. The trick to being courageous is to have the willingness to confront pain, danger, uncertainty or intimidation; the triggers of fear. Fear can also be dimmed by not inviting doubt into our minds. But feeling uncertain about something is one thing. Being afraid is another. Without discounting its societal erosion in mental health such as anxiety disorder, post-traumatic stress disorder, chronic phobias and so on, we must learn to minimize fear's damaging effect on us. I've witnessed fear's wrath on all types of people. From religious zealots to real estate wannabe investors and everything in between. Some people even allow fear to manifest into paranoia and other behavior disorders. Fear yields a variety of responses: to fight it, to numb it, to avoid it or to justify it. What's fascinating to me is the ability of some people to justify fear and succumb to inertia. After all, overthinking and inaction is what separates the risk takers from the risk-averse and fear-driven individuals. As a result, the less we think and analyze a fearful situation, the less we have a stuttering or paralytic condition. This in turn liberates us from fear and allows us to take more risks. The more risks we take, the more we accomplish and experience; as the saying goes "practice makes perfect."

READY, AIM, FIRE

Specifically, what separates most successful people from the not-so-successful ones is the act of pulling the trigger. In a simpler militaristic analogy, it's to be *ready,* to *aim* and to *fire.* Without the firing, none of it matters; be it in business, personal relationships or life's adventures. My wife recently jumped off a 30-foot cliff into a freezing cold lagoon for the first time in her life — a personal bucket list for her. She made it look easy, but that jump was decades in the making. Her *firing* would not have been possible without deliberately living an adult life of fun and adventure (traveling, experimenting, taking risks, activating her inner child, etc.) — all important conditions to get her *ready* for that milestone moment. This is a great lesson for all adults to take life by the horns and just ride it! Since she knew how to swim, her fear factor was lower than mine, and she took the calculated risk; the *aim* and *fired* herself without hesitation into the blue lagoon. But not all of us take swift action with everything, especially when we're over-analytical or have unpleasant past memories. I know of people who sat beside me at real estate seminars who charged thousands of dollars on their plastic cards to learn how to flip houses — and two years later had not made one single deal. It's quite astounding. When I asked them what their reasoning was, they never mentioned they were afraid to fail or lose money. Because that would make them seem weak. So, they simply justified it with a plethora of excuses — cleverly crafted to camouflage their true emotions wrapped up in uncertainty and doubt.

TURBOCHARGED FEAR

When fear is wrapped in a cloud of uncertainty and doubt, it's called FUD (Fear, Uncertainty, Doubt). FUD is prevalent in times of crisis, such as wars, pandemics, recessions, financial market meltdowns, and even destabilizing political regimes. It often shows up when money is at stake, especially when we can't stomach the idea of losing it. Often a self-fulfilling prophecy scenario ensues, as people flee in panic out of fear of losing their investment. Sometimes it has the opposite effect. For example, during the early stages of the Trump era, I avoided investing my money in the stock market or real estate.

My logic was that having an unstable leader with divisive policies would rock the property and financial markets. But I was wrong, as both markets thrived and hit historic highs. FUD got an unhealthy grip on me, and I lost out on four years of a bull market. Many of us go through temporary FUD periods and come out of it, but others are held hostage to it throughout their lives. Looking at my own fears and FUD, I am less afraid of losing money than I am of heights and of drowning. The embedded childhood trauma of seeing my friend fall to his death in Africa and almost drowning as a child in the Indian Ocean, has resulted in double-barreled fear. In order to help me overcome these two fears, I designed the *six-step fear-reducing method* for those who can't just 'fire away!' on certain fears. It has helped me. I hope it can benefit you too.

Six-step fear-reducing method:

1. **Express** your fears freely with others (visually, verbally or artistically).

2. **Assess** the fear impulse objectively by not over-analyzing it or inviting doubt.

3. **Visualize** the positive payoff or reward by embracing the feared subject.

4. **Befriend** the fear by emotionally connecting to it.

5. **Act** to engage with the feared element.

6. **Reward** yourself afterward for "partnering" with the fear and taking the risk.

Let's deploy these simple steps by showing a personal example of my own fear of drowning. I know it emanated from a childhood incident when my eldest brother threw me in the deep ocean in Africa. He thought he'd help me learn to swim, but it backfired and I was terrified of water for decades. I've tried taking swimming lessons but they've not helped. Now I just accept it as an inconvenient limitation that I can get creative with. Since I love water and spend many of my vacations on beautiful beaches in places like Costa Rica, I don't let my inability to swim stop my fun. As a result, I deployed the six-step process to help me cope with my fears and enjoy life in the water, the jungle, the mountain or any outdoor adventure.

Each time I go out to the sea, I start out by *expressing* my fear of drowning with my family and friends and tell them about my limitations. This helps me stay authentic and have someone keep an eye on me who can swim in an emergency. If I'm alone, I will move on to the next step. In the second step, I *assess* the depth of the water and stay in shallow water up to my waistline. I then *visualize* in my mind the pleasure of being in the water and take small steps to get in it. While in the water, I *befriend* it, as opposed to running away from it — by respecting it and connecting emotionally with its energy and power. Often, I will chant the Sanskrit sound mantra "OM" (symbolizing the essence of consciousness) a few times to synchronize my energy with the water. Reciting "OM" (aka, A-U-M) is known to reduce stress, relax the body and bring down blood pressure levels. It does wonders to calm me down. Then I *act* to engage with the element — such as boogie boarding, snorkeling, jet skiing, rafting, canoeing or just floating in it with pool noodles. This action stage is where you detach from any low vibration thoughts of the subject and partner with c o u r a g e. When I'm done, I'll thank the sea for the experience and *reward* myself with some ice-cold adult beverages! I do this same routine in a lake, river, a waterfall or in a swimming pool.

NO RISK, NO REWARD LOOP

I have a brother who could definitely use all of these steps to improve his fear and FUD. He's a chronic case of both of these conditions that affect his economic livelihood. I believe it stems from seeing my father lose all his hard-earned fortune in Africa. He is great at getting ready, aiming and collecting all the data and knowledge on investing in a particular asset, but has a stuttering brain and a "paralysis of analysis" to act decisively; similar to the many real estate wannabes I've met in my life. He even admits his apprehension. In a typical situation, he starts by complicating the subject at hand. What follows are excuses and justifications for not pulling the action trigger. His vocabulary is preset with defensive words like *"I know, I'll think about it and I'll see."* He then closes up his emotional receptors and inhibits his natural ability to express freely or honestly. It's cleverly camouflaged by saying he doesn't like confrontation and arguments. What predictably follows is his loss of self-confidence that manifests in not being able to stomach failing. Alas, he stops taking uncomfortable risks in other aspects of his life as well. When he's trapped himself in this fear box, he drowns in a fountain of scarcity rather than swim in a sea of abundance. Any time he encounters a source of abundance, he freaks out, distrusts it and digs up evidence to dog it. He soon enters a nasty *no risk, no reward loop*. It's a debilitating state to be in, because on one hand he hates not taking risks, yet on the other hand, he does nothing to fix his paralytic condition.

I believe that this self-defeating loop is a symptom of a deeper underlying issue for individuals mired in this condition of fear and FUD programmed behavior. Could it be that this type of person is bad at facing and resolving their childhood traumas, demons and shadows for fear of not being able to handle some ugly truths? Is it possible that this type of individual uses fear as a crutch to justify their inactions? Is it an issue of not valuing or loving themselves? Could it be that this person prefers to wallow in a fear and scarcity box because it's just easier, and a lot less work than getting out? Do you know someone who fits this profile in your family or circle of friends?

PRACTICE REDUCES FEAR

There's a dichotomy in the importance of striving to be the better or best you. If our ugly truth is that we are flawed beings, then we must not be afraid of unearthing our past traumas or discovering our flaws. And paradoxically, fear is a type of an emotional flaw that holds us hostage to our self-improvement. Studies show that 90 percent of our fears never materialize, but yet most of us will simply work ourselves into anxiety and succumb to a paralysis of losing courage and not taking risks. The fact is, that when we stop fearing fear, we liberate ourselves from the shackles of conformity, stagnation and weakness. By looking at fear as a disempowering trait that serves no useful purpose except holding us confined to a low-probability outcome, we are able to defeat it. After practicing The Healium Way steps on removing a particular fear, each subsequent time becomes less burdensome and easier to deal with. Soon you'll find yourself going into an automatic *fearless* mode of dealing with any one kind of fear. Because your mind sees more merit in the reward than the risk and adjusts itself. But each of us will deal with fear differently and there is no magic formula. Taking the first step toward the unknown and trusting that you'll be OK does the trick for most of us. It's important not to anticipate any predisposed result and just surrender to the outcome. Using step #3 in my six-step fear reducing process, visualization helps me go from a state of anxiety to a position of calm.

I've gotten rid of many of my phobias this way. As an example, I fear the sight of blood. So instead of getting worked up about having blood drawn out of my veins at the doctor's office, I simply visualize the blood already in the vial and offer my arm to the nurse with a smile. If you fear heights, imagine yourself already on top of a mountain looking down at the beautiful view. Then take a cable car to the top of the mountain. Eventually you'll be able to take a chair lift up that mountain and not freak out. I've done this many times. If you have stage fright speaking in front of a large audience, start by practicing in front of a small group of people you know. Soon, you'll find you have the needed confidence to speak in front of larger crowds without being afraid. I overcame all the above fears doing exactly that. The last one was the most challenging.

"Fear of the unknown is a great creative partner."
—Alejandro Gonzalez Inarritu

Jim speaks to a large crowd at Healium Center.

FU*K FFFEAR

As a child-acquired stuttering speech impediment (induced by my many traumas in Africa), I've had to work hard my whole life to overcome the fear of public speaking and not deny myself the right to voice my opinions. By not allowing myself to retreat into a fear-based mindset, I have trained my mind to say what I want regardless of how it comes out. If I stutter while I am making an important point, so be it. I don't get too hung up on it. I keep moving with my thoughts and am seldom self-conscious of it. The idea is to speak your mind because for a person with a speech stammer, the substance is held hostage to the delivery. And it shouldn't be. In many cases, the substance is my weapon of inspiration, education and transformation. Building self-confidence, breathing correctly and not being intimidated has made a huge difference to overcome the delivery. An unusual inspiration came when I heard Elton John's song "Bennie and the Jets" with the stuttering lyrical chorus line. It helped lighten the stigma and get me to laugh at myself when I stuttered. Today, I've licked much of my stuttering and I give credit to the medicine of the arts and applying many of the Healium Way Principles. I'm not the only one who has done this. Joe Biden was a bad stutterer in his youth and by his own admission got rid of most of it by writing and reciting poetry. Mel Tillis, a famous country western singer/songwriter (1932-2017) known as *"stutterin' boy,"* had an extreme case of stuttering and learned to talk normally simply by singing. He could not put two sentences together without stuttering — until he discovered that singing his words out loud stopped his stutter. Studies have shown how music and singing expand the right side of the brain while suppressing the left brain that controls speech. Once a stutterer becomes more confident, he becomes less fearful and doesn't hold his voice back. As a real estate investor and developer, I've used my voice to change laws, stop racial injustices, rezone land assemblages and fight for property rights for myself and others in public settings and courts. I was often nervous, but always fearless in my intention to accomplish my goals.

NEVER UNDERESTIMATE THE POWER OF THE LONE WOLF

A great case in point is how during the writing of this book and the pandemic period, I put on my fighting gloves to battle my neighborhood association, the city's Planning & Zoning department, a councilman and more than 75 property owners during a

Zoom video meeting. You could say I was the lone wolf in a den of sheep. This story is not just about being fearless but about being creative, self-confident and courageous to stand up to the truth — no matter what the odds. I didn't ask for the fight, but I had to get in the ring to defend and protect the property rights and freedoms of many people in the community; whether they appreciated it or not. This is The Healium Way to help protect the forest – not just save your own tree.

The controversial issue involved a rezoning change that the white-dominant neighbors wanted to legislate that negatively affected the land Healium Center sits on. It was a terrible proposal that was fear-based. A handful of neighbors were jealous and disgusted with developers profiteering and overbuilding million-dollar duplexes on their block. The concern was quite petty and illogical being that we're in a high-demand in-town area that has a shortage of quality housing supply. So instead of crafting the bill to address the specific issue and incentivize smaller units to be built to fix the problem, they set out to throw the baby with the bathwater and down-zone the properties, eliminate new affordable for-sale housing in the community, attract McMansions, eliminate many duplex lots and negatively affect property values by up to fifty percent. You'd think that if the property owners knew these facts, that they would not support it. But something interesting happened. The all-white committee that initiated this idea camouflaged and packaged the bill of goods so cleverly with inaccurate facts and confusing zoning lingo that the tribal neighbors blindly followed like sheep without questioning the details. Using the manipulative trick of showing an apple and calling it a banana worked well as all the six dozen neighbors supported the ill-fated and discriminatory proposal — not knowing their land values would be driven down. This majority-favored neighborhood vote became politicized and influenced the councilman and city planners to support it. There was no fact-checking of the poison pill embedded in the bill and like the "leaves" on a tree, everyone swayed in the direction of the prevailing strong winds. It was quite shocking to see how the spark of fear from a handful of racist neighbors fanned the flames of ignorance of the actual facts and spread it like wildfire.

No one had the spine to speak the truth, and the lies became the truth. And so, this is where I came in — to set the record straight. I was appalled at how the destructive proposal had been allowed to advance so far without common sense or logic. I wrote to the city how the bill was a hypocrisy to their own progressive affordable housing initiatives and how the gentrified community of the affluent white homeowners were doing a disservice to the entire city by pushing the bill for approval. Six months passed and after repeated emails arguing my case, my pleas went nowhere. Soon I got a notice that a final rezoning hearing was set for approval of this application.

Knowing I'd have a fighting chance of hiring a lawyer, I contacted one of the best real estate attorneys in town and paid him a handsome consultation fee for some advice. He told me the bill had too much momentum of support and that I had *no case* getting a favorable outcome. Specifically, he gave me many examples of similar "lost causes" and reiterated that I had a zero chance of stopping the ill-fated rezoning into law as there was unanimous approval from all sides. It was disappointing news and there was nothing I could do. Or was there? Sure, there was. We do it The Healium Way! I took the 'no' as a *"What do I have to lose, yes"* and geared up for the fateful meeting. I put the Principles into practice by looking at the big picture (the forest from the trees), being creative and staying in an empowered fear-free alignment with my higher self.

Instead of admitting defeat, I would swing for the fences. I had nothing to lose except a serious devaluation of my property's land value. Not to mention living with a coulda, shoulda, woulda regret of not trying. I got ready, put on a positive mental attitude and was anxious to unleash my arguments at this critical meeting.

I prepared a short factual presentation to vocalize in front of the online attendees. As our case was called, the neighborhood association, the city planner and the homeowners all voted to support the discriminatory and dangerous legislation. When the meeting chairman invited all those in opposition to speak, I was the only one to raise my hand. I was the lone wolf. But I was ready to speak my mind. I was relaxed and not expecting to have any attachment to a particular outcome except to be on record that I was strongly opposed to the insidious legislation. I smiled, greeted everyone and eloquently fired a seven-minute round of facts to refute the proposal. I didn't make the issue about myself as much as about the entire city and its residents. I told the audience they were making a huge mistake passing this bill and should remove the most dangerous item that would destroy property values and affordability in the community. When my time was done, I noticed a long pause and pensive expression on many attendees' faces. It appeared I had opened some minds and uncovered the lid on the inconsistencies that were cleverly disguised. Within seconds there were a couple more people who came on board to speak in opposition and agreed with my prevailing points. Soon, the seemingly "cut-and- dried" case was beginning to get messy with deeper questions and investigation from the voting board. The proponents continued to double down on their disinformation and untruths, but alas I couldn't correct their falsehoods. My microphone was muted by the meeting administrator the entire time they were debating the rebuttals of the application. It was quite frustrating and unnatural. I wanted to call out their lies and bullsh*t. In the unapologetic nature of The Healium Way, I got creative. Since my camera was on, I decided to use my body language and facial expressions to communicate with the panelists. They watched my colorful mannerisms attentively. I showed two big thumbs up and smiled when I heard the truth and two thumbs down and shook my head if I heard nonsense. Many long minutes passed as the panelists volleyed their views back and forth, as I clenched my teeth. Soon I got a sense that my arguments were sinking in with key individuals on the voting panel. One by one, the opposition grew. It was quite impressive. As the discussions ended and the legislation came up for the final vote, all three board members voted to amend the bill in my favor. It was quite a surreal and a jubilant moment for me. Against all odds, I had just won a major victory for preserving affordable housing and property values in our community. In addition to arresting a domino effect in the city of Atlanta at large. It was a significant victory for the truth and keeping politicians and leaders honest and accountable. In a way it reminded me of the Montgomery ordeal, only it was less about corruption and more to do with tribalism, fear, gentrification and common sense.

For me, creativity, confidence and courage are always the default weapons of choice in resolving differences. No matter how big or small they are. The above example is a testament of the power of being fearless and speaking out. We all have the power within to not fight *against* the light but to fight *for* the light. The low frequency and dark condition of fear can only be conquered by exercising unfettered courage and staying in the higher frequency of light. I know many neighbors are secretly thanking me for sticking my neck out and protecting their property values. But I am not waiting for gratitude. I am happy to have done the right thing, as I've done many times before without seeking validation. Being the warrior-type personality, I always have to make sure I only fight the battles worth fighting for. Although we're not going to prevail in all dispute cases, at least we'll have the satisfaction of putting up a good fight and speaking truth to power. It's about making the *extra* effort and showing the ordinary opponent what *extra*ordinary looks like.

When the virtual meeting was done, I jumped for joy, thanked my guardian angels and Divine Spirit and celebrated the evening with a cigar and an ice-cold glass of gin and tonic. *"Great job, honey!"* exclaimed my wife with a big smile, as she turned to congratulate me, *"You prevailed against the dark forces again!"*

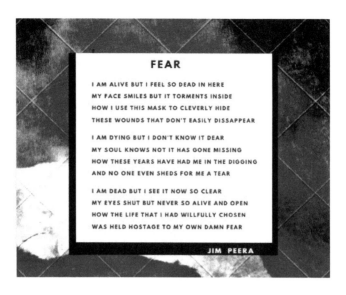

Practice The Healium Way

FEAR RELEASE EXERCISE: List your top three fears (losing your job, being broke, dying, etc.) Pick ONE and use it to experience your detachment and release. Then do the following art activity. Visualize this fear in your mind and draw a large circle and dump all the words that you associate with this fears into this circle. On a separate piece of paper write down all the emotions and sensations you are feeling in your body as you think about this fear: racing heart, uneasy stomach, sweaty palms, etc. Now using either a pencil, pen or crayons, ARTiculate what you feel (negative emotions) on a third piece of white paper. Don't worry how the drawing looks, just freestyle it and unleash what you see. It can be stick figures. Use as much time and just let go. Play some soft relaxing music while you do this. Once completed, take all three pieces of paper and put them in a metal pot. Take a glass of water with you and go outside. Now safely burn them. This is your release ceremony of your particular fear. As your drawing is burning, say these words, "*I no longer fear you.*" *I am not attached to you.*" Now put out the flames with the water. It's an effective mind-over-matter exercise that can be practiced at home by yourself or with a group of people.

Combine it with my *six-step method* and see if it helps reduce many off your fears, one at a time, in the real world.

Ego is when you attach yourself to the following unhealthy value system: I am what others think of me. I am my achievements, my possessions and my reputation. I am special and am separate from everyone. Buying into this parasitic condition gnaws away at your very essence by luring you in with the man-made temptations of material success, superficiality, power, control, dominance and greed. *"I am a self-made millionaire"* is a good example of an egotistical individual who fails to give credit to all the people in his environment that helped him on his upward journey. This proposition detrimentally affects your health, relationships and spiritual upliftment. Slowly but surely, the "I" stops defining your higher spiritual values and becomes a separate entity that takes over your life. It becomes your perfect weapon of resistance from the higher self. But you don't realize it until you start showing symptoms such as comparing yourself to others, being jealous of more successful people, blaming others when things don't go your way, having to be right, feeling good for others' loss, valuing outward appearances, never being satisfied, etc. Ego is one of those low-frequency human characteristics we all have but need to constantly tame. I have it, you have it, we all have it. Having traveled to many countries around the world, I am always curious of how ego manifests in different cultures. Since egotistical people come in all shapes and sizes, this resistance beast has universal attachment to people who love making and hoarding money and are often insecure. Since money and power are once again the common denominator, the ego falsely directs you to be seduced by and openly flaunt your material riches — at the expense of your balance, being authentic and disconnecting from your Source. In modern history, the Taj Mahal, Las Vegas hotels, and the entire city of Dubai were built on inflated egos. Sometimes we tend to confuse ego with high ambition or drive. But they're not the same as ego often lives on fear and lack, and copes by being blind towards feeding the Soul. In this context it will get in your way and give you a false positive by manipulating you to attach to what makes you feel good, not what needs to be done. Here's one good example: a person who throws expensive parties to show off their status rather than connect with their own free spirit and inner child that fuels fun and joy. You will seldom see this type of individual dance, play musical instruments and authentically engage with the crowd. This person is usually more interested in impressing the world than experiencing it without their egotistic filter. Ego separates them from their true spirit and they willfully allow it. In the healing and creative arts community I've seen ego manifest itself within people who separate themselves due to their degrees and higher level of artistic training or expensive education. Take the following case of a part-time artist who has showcased at our Center and who displays a good example of this type of egotistic filter.

THE P-DEGREED

KP is an intelligent and professionally trained painter whose visionary/expressionistic style allows him to use his art form to express his emotions on a more mystical and spiritual level. In many ways, KP has already opened the creative porthole of unbound possibilities and used his artistic talent to help him improve his mental wellbeing. But he's still stuck in the shadow of his ego that separates him from his higher self. He's quite competitive with other artists, especially when he finds out they're not holding any art credentials like he does. I call it the *"P-degreed"*: people who walk around with a conceited attitude due to their various degrees/training and/or preppy upbringing. Sadly, many highly educated folks operate in their little bubble worlds and are disconnected from common sense and humility. These types of people exist all around the world, and I've seen the evidence of it in artists, too, who often develop an elevated opinion of themselves. KP is a good example to demonstrate this condition. It's easy to notice his traits of jealousy, judgment and competitiveness by his body language and behavior. I know when artists are egotistical because they'll seldom compliment other artists' works and will even resort to derogatory comments and pass judgment. Sometimes they're introverted and expose their insecurities by not engaging with other fellow artists. There's a certain snobbery that you can detect in their overall energy as many are standoffish. Some are extremely protective of their art and don't allow anyone to take pictures or film videos of their works. These folks often sit in their little boxes of self-adulation and exceptionalism thinking they're *special.*

Although I was aware of KP's tendencies, I experienced this *ugly truth* manifest one day in my own clay sculpture gallery. KP often showcased his art at our art exhibitions and would pop his head inside my personal gallery and walk away without any comment. One day when he came to see me for a business meeting, he saw my open gallery with my picture and name on it and had a stunned look on his face. He turned at me and asked if I had anything to do with those sculptures. I told him I had created all those pieces over 16 years. He took a deep breath, patted me on the back and chuckled, *"Wow Jim! these are pretty cool. I didn't know you had it in you to do such good work."* When I went on to tell him that I was self-taught in sculpting, he rolled his eyes, scoffed and changed the subject. This was KP's ego in firm control of his uncanny behavior. He just couldn't fathom that a self-trained artist, like myself could produce such high-quality and captivating works. KP is also the type of person who doesn't value freestyle artistic self-expression as we do in The Healium Way. Instead of looking at it as a powerful therapeutic release without judgment, he'd often comment to me that people should take proper art classes, attain credentials and learn the many drawing and painting techniques taught in art schools. This artist's ego conveniently forgot to remind him that structure and technicality in art will strangle the Soul if you don't first connect with your inner creative freedom. It's a lesson for all creative beings. If you look at KP's paintings, they may be technically great and beautiful, but they don't have the raw emotional impact of many paintings created by regular participants at our Open Studio workshops.

I've encountered quite a few "KP" types of people in my life, and interestingly the majority of them live in America. Why do you think that is? Take a minute to think about this. How does your own ego control your actions? Do you always talk about yourself or money around friends? Do you walk around with an elevated opinion of yourself? Are you always dominating conversations with people? Observe your behavior and see if you can reduce your competitiveness. Instead of imposing your ways on others, allow them to take center stage and lead the way. And if you're degreed, graduated from a preppy school or come from a high society upbringing, be aware of the ego beast that's shaping and controlling your character. It's separating you from your higher self and disconnecting you from your true spirit. You must work to do better.

Practice The Healium Way

EGO-TAMING EXERCISE: Are you in the process of buying something you really love and want? It could be a big item such as a house, a car, a new TV, laptop, etc. Get a few of your friends together and tell them to talk you out of it. Get each of them to give you reasons why it's *not* a good idea to purchase the item. Don't interfere or influence them in any way. Write down all the reasons they give you on a piece of paper. Now carry that paper with you and read it each morning and before you go to sleep. Make a few copies of it and post it around the house as reminders. You'll be surprised how much your egotistic beast is controlling you and how by using this exercise you can adjust your buying behavior.

JUDGMENT is a universal condition of our human nature. Far too often it is woven into the ugly fabric of our society in malicious ways such as the caste system and racism. Often, it's automatic learned behavior from ancestral programming that becomes a mind virus in the subconscious brain. But whether it's human to have implicit or unconscious biases towards others is a subjective argument depending on who is benefiting from the practice. What's undisputed is we all are guilty of it whether we're willing to admit it or not. The word prejudice means to prejudge and is derived from the noun "judgment." As a result, many would argue that it's totally normal to prejudge and often it's a harmless form of social behavior. But it's inhuman and destructive to do it to harm or devalue others. As an example, judgment can be as subtle as sizing up a man's penis in a men's locker room or as damaging as denying a black business owner a loan because of their skin color. Dr. Wayne Dyer often stated that *"when we judge others, we define ourselves."* How true! Judgment therefore simply justifies our insecurities; it doesn't deal with them. In order to truly manifest our higher self, we must remove the urge to judge. For many of us this is a difficult task, especially when we are constantly stereotyped and influenced by our environment — conditioned by our highly competitive nature. We use judgment quite frequently to make us feel more superior in relation to others. Many harmless personal biases can become pernicious if we don't practice non judgment as a daily mantra — unless we are willing to experience a boomerang effect on our own autonomy.

In my travels I've had multiple experiences from airport security to hotel staff using various forms of judgment to single me out and treat me with prejudice. After 9/11, I was extremely annoyed at being racially profiled and targeted by white people. This was during the pre-Trump era when the only tolerable and "non-threatening" brown-skinned people were Hispanics. And so I toned down my Indian accent and added a southern Mexican one. I wore Spanish slogan caps,

Walmart jeans, plaid shirts and avoided growing a beard. I thought I had disguised myself as a Latino quite well. But I got nailed anyway!

HOMEY DEPOT

It was a busy Saturday fall morning in Atlanta, Georgia. The leaves were turning their beautiful gold, red and brown autumn colors, and everyone was out beautifying their homes. I had just picked up my usual labor help guy to help me renovate a rental house I had just purchased. Somehow on that particular day I left my Mexican attire at home and instead looked like myself. As I was leaving Home Depot after buying several items, the security alarm blared. The cashier realized her error and rushed out to apologize to me. She'd forgotten to scan the security tag off on one of my items. So she had me re-enter the store and repeat the exit process. The alarm sounded again. This time a tall, heavy-set white guy in his fifties, wearing blue denim overalls and a red cap akin to a 1980s "Hee Haw TV show character who approached me and yelled in a heavy Southern drawl: *"Hell, if you'd take off that bomb vest you're wearing, maybe you'd stop the darn thing from going off!"* Both the cashier and I were stunned at the man's remark and she ran back in the store looking flustered and scared. As I stood there in the heat of the moment, he kept on rambling racial slurs. He paced back and forth near the exterior sidewalk area and got louder with this vitriol. He was trying to provoke me, but I wasn't scared. With my heart racing in astonishment, I looked the pudgy red-faced guy straight in the eyes and quickly fired back; *"Hey, aren't you that man who got arrested for molesting kids in school?"* I am not sure how I came up with that line, but it was a counterpoint comment to make him think about his judgment of me. Looking back, this was the time when some prominent white Catholic priests were in the news for sexual misconduct of underaged school boys. The angry white man looked at me in confusion and said, *"Now what the hell is that supposed to mean?"* I replied; *"Well sir, you stereotyped me, and so I stereotyped you! How does that feel?"* The guy shook his head, gave me a dirty look and asked me if I believed in Jesus. At that point I decided to ignore him and continued to load my van with my purchased items. But he was adamant and shouted a few more racial slurs in my direction, then said, *"Y'all sons of bitches gonna go straight to hell!"* as he proceeded to eventually walk away. The cashier, who was a 40-something white lady, brought a security guard with her to contain the commotion, but I was already loading my van with my helper and eager to leave before the man returned and got more violent. As I composed myself, took a big breath and got seated in the van to drive off, my work assistant who was a black Southern man looked at me without much surprise and chuckled, *"Hey homey, that sure was some crazy dude man, but you sure handled him well."* He patted me on the shoulder and exclaimed, *"So now you know how us 'niggers' feel!"* My jaw dropped and my heart sank. I was speechless and dazed at his truthful but disturbing comment. I had just experienced the unhealed wounds of racism from the mouths of an ignorant and angry white man and a slavery-scarred black man. It was quite surreal to be caught in the middle of the raw crossfire that emphasized the danger of judgment, especially in arsenic situations like this.

Looking back, things could have turned out a lot worse had I reacted differently and given fuel to the man to inflame his vitriol. This example is just one of many that I've faced my whole life as an immigrant living in a white-dominated society surrounded by unhealed individuals. At Healium Center, the test of every participant is to refrain from first judging themselves and their creation. This is turn gives people good practice not to judge others' work. Unlike being in a competitive setting for an acting audition or applying for a job, freedom of self-expression is best activated without rules, grades or judges. This freestyle prescription removes a huge amount of pressure off most people to not just relax and have more fun but to journey deeper within their Souls. By not judging people, their labels, process or their end product, we spend our energies delving into individual stories that are more interesting and relatable to our own. Often being unaware of people's personal, religious or political characteristics can be a blessing and a catalyst for unity. I recall the following situation at The Center that dramatically proved this point.

THE POWER OF ART

Four individuals who arrived separately at our Open Studio event and did not know each other, sat at a table to paint and socialize. Each one was radically different in their spiritual and religious beliefs. Soon, they picked up their canvas, a palette of acrylic paint, some refreshments and began their freestyle creative journeys. While the evening progressed, I noticed how this particular table was more vocal with louder outbursts of laughter, jokes and uninhibited fun. As I approached the group to investigate, one of the participants, who was Jewish, got up in excitement to hug me and declared: *"Isn't this insane and amazing Jim! Can you believe I am sitting on the same table with a devout Muslim here, a Jesus-freak there and a Satan worshipper right beside me! And we're all having the most awesome time making art and not hating on each other. Thank you for creating Healium."* My spine tingled and with a big thumbs up, I smiled and replied: *"See this is what happens when we stop judging, labeling and stereotyping. We just start living and being one. This is the power of art guys!"*

The above disparate but powerful stories help us see all the possibilities within each of us to expand our minds. When we stop the urge to judge, we begin to see people without a harsh critical eye or man-made filters and are able to be more compassionate, loving and forgiving beings. How uncomplicated, beautiful and *extra*ordinary is that!

Practice The Healium Way

JUDGMENT EXERCISE: a) If you're a shopper at any of the large big box discount retailers, try experiencing a trip at a luxury boutique shop or to an affluent part of town. Or vice versa. Dress the same way as you normally do and just have some fun. You will be tempted to judge your new uncomfortable environment and people, but don't. Keep your head up, look people in the eye and just be nice. Try engaging with a sales clerk and compliment her/him. Crack a joke or two. Buy something even if it's small to connect with your new setting. b) If you're a white person, try visiting a predominantly colored community and immersing yourself in that environment. Walk the streets and eat the food you typically would not. Take public transport like a bus or a train and experience the journey. You'll be amazed to notice how others treat you. Don't be tempted to judge, simply see everybody as a part of you and appreciate the diversity as a beautiful quilt with unique, colorful patches.

Pretense is as American as apple pie. Americans are taught early in life the value of *"Fake it until you make it"* as a means to showcase and flaunt an illusion of what they don't have. It's America's self-deceptive packaging that gives it its overrated status to the rest of the world. But don't scoff, it has its merit. There's this phenomenon called the placebo effect, that partners with a pretense-based mindset to build confidence and even shifts your brain to a more positive state of mind to attain your goals.

In real estate, I've found it often necessary to use this tactic to appear more successful and capable to get bigger deals done. I went from catching small fish to hooking whales using this mind-over-matter philosophy. Even the Law of Attraction sees a value to *acting as if you already have it*. You visualize your future successes and achievements and manifest the behaviors necessary to get you there.

Often metaphysical holistic treatments are more effective due in part to their mind-over-matter placebo effect. Healing modalities like crystal stone healing and faith healing are prime examples. So, yes, faking the mind for the right reasons can provide you benefits. But that's when we need to not conflate it with living a life of lies or having a smokescreen personality. Getting this condition wrong can create all kinds of problems with trust, transparency and keeping friends. Pretense acts like a drug to keep our acting skills polished, but it tarnishes the essence of our true self. By design it conditions us to avoid negativity, always focus on positive things and not train our emotional receptors to deal with dark emotions. In fact, it has us bypass our harsh and authentic realities, which make us stronger and more resilient. In some situations, people cleverly hide their internal pain by putting on a happy exterior facade that further postpones their path to healing. Therefore, living pretentiously has detrimental effects as it makes us weaker, fragile and depletes our coping skills. What's worse is when it becomes a functional addiction and you live and breathe a lie. Because pretense is a highly effective weapon in providing you with a tool of resistance from the higher self. Often, it's a defense mechanism that hides your insecurities and jealous tendencies — a little box that you conveniently step inside to avoid looking at your true self with all its flaws.

Perhaps counterintuitively, faking it the right way isn't actually about being fake. It's about changing your behavior and trusting that your feelings will follow suit. The dangerous side of being a pretender starts quite innocently in social circles as a way to fit in, but it slowly engulfs us and rules our daily life. A pretentious person is akin to a leaf person who is easily swayed with the wind and by the whims of others. Not surprisingly, these are the same people who have fake money, showing off to the world material riches they don't have or have borrowed to the hilt to acquire expensive cars and homes. Being pretentious is a self-inflicted derived disease that feeds off validation and acceptance of others. Sometimes this condition traps a person into being people pleasers and opening their heart to everyone they meet.

I've met many individuals at The Center who easily attach to people due to their craving for validation or love from others. This particular type of individual is an undercover pretender, who is probably masking a deeper underlying issue. The fact is, when you're constantly trying to please others — you are avoiding to please and love yourself. You elect to normalize your superficiality, which is the modus operandi of a pretender. Therefore, the only path to avoiding a pretender's condition is to look in the mirror and change ourselves rather than trying to change how others see us. But it's not that easy. Vanity is rampant in our society, costing American women nearly a quarter of a million dollars in beauty products during their lifetime, according to a Groupon survey. That amounts to an average of $225 per month. We'll spend thousands of dollars to look younger and prettier on the outside, yet a fraction of that to fix our ugliness and emotional pain within. When we surveyed 100 random people at our Center, we found that on average they spent $400 per year going to arts-related activities. That figure comes to 1 percent for someone earning $40,000 per year. If we add a suggested 10 percent of income to religious contributions, we still fall well short of a healthy investment in mental and spiritual health. We see plenty of evidence of this imbalance in our society. When you add the validation-feeding machine of social media, we notice how people are held hostage in a bubble of superficiality and pretense on a daily basis.

ISOLATION THERAPY

One of the most common telltale signs of pretentious individuals we find at The Center revolves around the taking of selfies and posed pictures with friends during set periods of creative activity. Then, when these smartphone users do participate, they're so consumed by what others think about their creation, they don't display any real emotion in their work. I can usually tell within a few minutes of meeting pretentious or fake people.

Most of them arrive in a group rather than alone. They're codependent individuals who crave friendships for their own sense of stability. It's their drug.

To combat this tendency, we isolate them from their group in what I call *isolation therapy,* which aims to get them free of distractions so that they can sit with their own thoughts. They are then exposed to our surrealism art galleries and its dark, emotional art. This is the truth serum that takes pretenders into skin-deep territory. I get the person to pick a piece of art that disturbs or provokes them the most and to engage with it freely. It's quite remarkable how often I've seen a spark ignite within their dormant emotional receptors. This spark can be a game changer. Once their veil of illusion is penetrated, they become more inspired by other art works and are ready to express themselves on their own. Some will even soak up the vibes in the Zen room for a few minutes. Once they are comfortable in a safe space like Healium, they'll discover a part of them they've lost for a while and have deeper connections within. Others will experience a flash of personal awakening and we won't see them for a long t i me.

I had this experience with a woman named Vanessa; a middle-aged attractive woman who arrived with a good-looking younger man akin to a model. They could have been in a Botox commercial. Vanessa appeared quite snobby and pretentious at first encounter and she felt uneasy entering a place where everyone was being themselves and even walking barefoot. *"Yes, we're a bunch of urban hippies here. And we're totally harmless!"* I joked as she entered, wide-eyed. I offered them some wine and took both on a tour of The Center. The boyfriend said he played the guitar so I insisted that he stay in the basement and jam with others on stage. He agreed without any pushback. This was my "isolation" intention. I took Vanessa into the art galleries and she was speechless as she entered my personal surreal sculpture gallery. It was too raw and honest for her comfort, but it was exactly what she needed.

She asked about a piece I had done 13 years ago when I celebrated my 25th wedding anniversary. Her eyes lit up in amazement and she asked me how my wife and I still looked this good and happy. I told her that it all came down to balance. That we dialogued a lot and kept our relationship real and playful. As she turned to look at other pieces, she was particularly fixated on one called *"In Search of Love."* that I had created a few years prior. It depicted woman looking down an amethyst mountain reaching out for an object of *love* that is unattainable and caged.

"IN SEARCH OF LOVE"

(Amethyst, Clay, Mixed media) Artist: Jim Peera

She stared at it for a while and teared up. She told me that she could really relate to the art. Vanessa went on to reveal how she found it difficult to find real people to fall in love with and to settle down. I told her that in life we don't attract what we want, but what we are. We spoke for about half an hour and she smiled, hugged me, wiped the tears off her face and complimented me on creating a great place. I left her to attend to other participants and she enjoyed the evening interacting with a variety of people.

I didn't see Vanessa again for about a year. When she returned to our Center, she gave me a long, warm hug and told me how spending that one evening at Healium had been the catalyst to her much-needed self-awareness and transformation. She revealed to me that she had to do a lot of work on herself and in the process got rid of her circle of friends who were enablers and fake. She told me how the surrealist-style art in our galleries opened her Soul and made her a better observer of her own flaws. What happened for Vanessa was not unusual for Healium Center, where we've had many similar stories. There are also countless cathartic stories like hers across all facets of human experience. Vanessa not only found inspiration through art to remove her low-vibration resistances, but she had a heart-to-heart dialogue with total strangers who could relate to her story. Surrealism art removed her veil of illusion about herself and was the trigger that she needed to break out of her unhealthy pattern of behavior. Once she became an unfiltered observer of her behavior and actions, it was easier to open her portal of self-love, express it freely on a piece of canvas — and talk about it with others. Her experience at The Center was a mirror on herself. As she broke through the barriers of self-induced pretense and embraced her true self. She was able to guide herself back into a healthier balance. Vanessa was no longer afraid of cutting her ties with her disempowering, needy and so-called "friends." She was now self-empowered to take the risk and the necessary action to retrieve her lost Soul. When I asked her about her love life — she said she was dating a man and had never been happier. *"You'd like him Jim, he's real and funny, just like you!"* she remarked with a big smile. *"Now, just be sure you give yourself the necessary time to heal and stay consistent on the course of your path,"* I replied.

So how ready are you to look at your own authenticity? Do you see yourself as being vain or pretentious? Are you preoccupied with your physical appearance when you're at work or in social settings? Do you constantly take selfies and post them on social media sites for validation? Do you go to a nice restaurant with friends and spend more time using your cellphone and being distracted instead of enjoying your food? If you're not comfortable letting the world see you as you are — the dark and the light, the sweet and the bitter — you are living a lie. And it is not sustainable. When your youth and looks are gone and your circle of enablers you call "friends" are not there to validate your deceptions, it may be too late. What's worse is, like an incarcerated person in prison who upon being freed commits a crime and is thrown back in prison — your illusive reality will hold you hostage to your own suffering. In order to be real, it helps not to try too hard. As an adult, you've already figured out what you like about yourself. It could be your personality, your physique, your intellect, your talents, etc. What I am suggesting you do is to put a magnifying glass on those attributes and use them as your branding and your image to highlight your authentic side. By focusing on those traits that you love, as opposed to those you hate about yourself, you'll reduce your insecurities and jealous tendencies. You won't be afraid to be yourself, which will in turn stop you from being a pretender.

Practice The Healium Way

REMOVING YOUR MASK EXERCISE: Take a good look at yourself before you go to work. Your attire, your attitude and your sense of self-esteem. Do you feel good about your job? Are you happy with what you're doing there? Do you feel you're well compensated? Do you like working for your boss or supervisor? Are you wearing the clothes that you like? If the answer to any of those questions is "No," but you keep complaining about work, you're hiding behind a mask. It's time you stop pretending and start being truthful. The longer you wait the harder it gets. You're not giving an authentic signal to your boss of your discontent. If you're a woman, put into action another layer of this exercise by not wearing makeup in public one day. How does it feel to not care what others think of you or not wear your superficial physical mask? Let the world see you and love you as you are, with all your perfect imperfections.

Principle #3
Fusing The Creative and The Healing Arts

All the arts are medicinal and healing. They've been used and studied as a wellness regimen for thousands of years. In this Principle, we'll look at how The Healium Way masterfully fuses the creative arts with the healing arts in one seamless fashion to help us achieve a more healed life. First, I define the "creative arts" to mean the *visual arts, music, drumming, dance,* and *poetry.* When I say the healing arts," I am referring to *sound vibration healing, meditation, yoga, storytelling, tai chi, laughter healing, breathwork,* etc. Arts like cooking and gardening were not specifically studied at Healium Center, but are also important to our overall wellness. I know when my wife cooks or bakes, the process improves her mood and induces happiness.

I've also heard my gardener friends say that getting their hands dirty makes their brain "happy." Scientists have proven that the mycobacterium in the soil boosts the chemical serotonin in the brain and lifts moods and improves function. What is fundamental to understand is how interacting in nature, being creative in the kitchen and engaging in the various categories of the arts, in either a personal or group setting, are medicinal and beneficial to our body, mind and soul balance. They all have the ability to slow us down from our busy minds, embrace curiosity and open our imagination. Having successfully experimented with this methodology at our Center, I've seen firsthand the arts' power in uplifting and healing people from the inside out. When administered without rules or parameters, the inner creative takes us beyond conventionality and into limitless possibilities for our personal growth and mental wellness. The most fascinating and powerful of all the arts are the ones that take us inward to help us heal our various psychological scars and wounds. These arts are the emotional-release tools that allow self-expression to flourish and ultimately heal us from the inside out. Since we all have embedded emotional scars that need to be healed, we must become aware of their long-term damage if left unresolved. The idea of calming the mind with the healing arts and then expressing the underlying emotions via creative artistic expression is highly effective and powerful, as we've seen time and time again at The Center. Yet this road is much less popular than the highly marketed, profit-over-people one of medicating the mind to numb the emotional pain. A visit to the therapist is an obvious choice to address embedded traumas, but for many people this path is prohibitively expensive, intimidating and seen as a last resort. Others choose to consult mental health social workers in their community. That option is viable — but can be cumbersome, highly clinical and best suited for people medically diagnosed with mental illness. But for those millions who are not tagged as mentally ill, and are longing for some help nursing their mind and soul, the most popular choice is attending a local neighborhood worship center. Many find solace and a sense of redemption there. But an unhealed person cannot be expected to effectively transform into a more healed person using tactics of damnation, judgment or repression. We all need free will and unconditional freedom to do the job correctly. There must be hope without fear. Perhaps an unconventional approach is the solution.

THE FUTURE OF WORSHIP IS HERE

It is for this reason that I believe the future of worship centers (churches, mosques, temples, etc.), will look more like Healium Center — serving more freestyle thinking activities, incorporating pluralism, opening dialogue, expanding spirituality and offering the creative and healing arts in an interactive format to connect with our true unbounded spirit. It is not so much a place of worship, as it is a philosophy — an unconventional sacred space of self-discovery, finding balance and attaining inner peace. This can be accomplished in a group setting at your home or at a dedicated center. It is where true connectivity, upliftment and empowerment with oneself, with others and with our maker takes place, nurturing the body, mind and soul. It is where the shift from ordinary to *extra*ordinary is manifested in each participant by heart-to-heart and soul-to-soul connectivity.

For this reason, I'm a skeptic of an all-virtual method of spiritual congregation. There are some things that modern technology cannot replace and this area is one of them. As of this writing, I'm noticing the insurgence of online subscription apps to help busy minds meditate, help fix depression and reduce mental illness in America. Does it surprise you that a profit-over-people society would try to satisfy a complex human need with a click of a smartphone button? But texting your way out of your problems will not provide effective and sustainable benefits. The Healium Way is open-minded about technology's role in improving our wellness, and offering long-distance methods and modalities of personal healing. Reaching vast amounts of diverse-minded people around the world is powerful indeed. But social dis-connectivity is not the answer; we need a more balanced approach. When it comes to more traditional worship in brick-and-mortar places whose healing methods extoll fear, guilt and submission, they will become a thing of the past. We're seeing the dismantling of the old restrictive ways with interfaith ministries gaining in popularity across the globe. People, especially millennials, are tired of attending worship places that traffic in guilt, judgment and mind-conditioning. Whether they're denominational or not, many religious institutions often handcuff us to a particular belief system that is restrictive and suffocating. In this confined state, freedom of true self-expression with authentic emotional release and Soul repairing cannot happen. For those believers who practice blind faith, the mind gets re-wired to accept imprisoned conformity as God's will. But there's nothing godly or willful about preaching separation. Instead, they overlook our true Divinity and upend our self-autonomy. Once again, it's the man-made version of God that gets in the way of true and unbiased healing that resides within each of us.

Interestingly, we seldom question this ancestral mind-conditioning. We're afraid of rocking the boat of organized religion. By not having faith in putting the power in our own hands (as opposed to a chosen religious leader, theology or deity), we fall short of discovering our own healing power. This power is accessible by tapping into our dogma-free spiritual realm and allowing it to fuse with creative tools that work to penetrate our external superficialities. The existing group worship programs of preaching, lecturing, praying, singing, chanting and other forms of cultural traditions may get us to a state of bliss and inspiration, but fall short in a critical way — they're all wrapped conveniently in a box filled with predisposed conditions and only provide temporary respite and relief. Often, they're layered with a sin- repentance approach of worship using confession booths and other man-made contraptions that give a false sense of hope and validation.

By contrast, The Healium Way inspired spiritual sanctuary removes all such obstacles and opens the floodgates of limitless possibilities in each of us. By using the seeds of the creative and healing arts that God has already planted in us as intended, we're able to reach deeper inside of ourselves without any gimmicks, money-hungry self-righteous middlemen or strings attached. By actively engaging in these offerings, people can cultivate their own beautiful garden of unconditional love and freedom. They will harvest these two powerful medicines in conjunction with imparting new knowledge, learning from the stories of the ancient deities, journeying into the metaphysical realm, teaching healthy eating habits and even experiencing plant medicines to create a more healed and balanced you. How *extra-*ordinary!

THE MASOCHISTS

My eldest brother is a textbook example of a person who has resorted to self-prescribing organized religion to find solace and comfort in his golden years. Although he takes care of his body by exercising, eating well, doing yoga and meditation, he's deficient in the many Principles of The Healium Way that would help him stitch up his open emotional wounds. In his case, those unhealed wounds have manifested in the form of chronic psychosomatic ailments such an inexplicable body-trembling resulting from his wife's untimely death, from breast cancer 15 years ago. My sister-in-law, Lydia was a smart, pretty, dedicated and very hard-working Filipina woman. In many ways, she was a superwoman who wore herself out juggling a teaching career, being a mother to three children and satisfying a patriarchy-modeled man. She was an avid meditator who swore by its power and benefit. But meditation only bought her more working time, as she literally worked herself to death. When she was diagnosed with late-stage cancer, I created a piece of art titled "Hanging on", to help her heal. It depicted a woman flying like Superman at the top of her career (symbolized by the driftwood mountain) who was trying to hang on — as Spirit was taking her away (depicted by the drifting breast).

She told me she liked it, but she was afraid to die and it made her cry. We must have spent a couple of hours chatting on the phone about the piece as she found herself bearing her soul and releasing a sea of raw pent-up emotion — a very untypical occurrence. After she passed, my brother returned the artwork saying it was too painful to look at it. I understood his sentiment.

"Hanging On"
(Clay, Driftwood, Rock) Artist: Jim Peera

As a person tormented internally with guilt and regret for not being fully present during his wife's prolonged illness, my suffering brother is not fully present for his one and only son. The son, a successful doctor in his mid- 40s, has opted to "cancel" his father and not forgive him for those long-ago misdeeds. Both father and son are mule-brained and sit comfortably in their respective self-righteous boxes, filled with pride, resentment, crutches and excuses. Hopefully, before it's too late, one of them will be inspired by my own repair story with my daughter to bury the hatchet and stitch up the wounds. It's taking the *extra*ordinary path and living without any regrets. The antidote for this emotional cancer is the powerful act of forgiveness and uninhibited self-expression — which can be accomplished creatively using The Healium Way. The irony is, most of my siblings are masochists and can't see the value of the arts as medicine. So I don't impose that on them, and can only hope they'll break out of their unhealthy boxes when they're ready.

READY TO TAKE THE MEDICINE

But not all adults are masochists or too closed-minded to see the benefit of the arts as beneficial medicine. Some of them come to The Center ready with a set intention to heal. And they don't have time to waste.

Take the case of a young man named Ken who became a frequent participant after he experienced a breakthrough moment. One day as I was manning the reception area, he arrived in frantic demeanor and couldn't utter a complete sentence without stuttering profusely. His body was shaking, his face was flushed and he appeared to be having an epic anxiety attack. *"I aaaaaammmm sssssorry Jjjim, bbbut I am haavvving a tterrible dday."* I looked at him in astonishment as I had never seen him act in this way. *"What's wrong dude, what's going on with you, are you OK?"* I asked. *"I rrrreallllly nnneed to gggo jjjam rrright nnnnow!"* he said. *"You need to go jam?"* I asked. Without wasting any time or collecting his entrance fee, I escorted him to the basement music stage area and left him to join the Open Jam session. I told my wife and other volunteers about the perplexing incident and to keep an eye on him. About an hour later, I walked to the jam area to check on him and he was sweating heavily and zoned out playing the electric guitar. He mustered a smile and kept on strumming. It was quite surreal. When the song was completed, I approached Ken on stage and asked him what had happened to him. He went on to explain that he was a total wreck from work with stress and anxiety and needed to come to Healium to get his music medicine. *"Man, you have no idea how badly I needed to play today! I feel so much better now."* he said without any stutter. He apologized for his uncanny behavior, thanked me for being sympathetic, and offered to pay his entry free, but I told him it was on the house.

Ken was one of the fastest transformations I had ever witnessed in a participant. It was quite amazing to see how playing music relaxed his nerves and restored him to a normal state of mind. It was his healthy drug, so to speak. From that day forward, I never saw Ken have any breakdowns or even stutter. It's quite remarkable how this young man was able to control his anxiety attacks by simply self-prescribing the powerful medicine of music. Yet, it's not unusual to see individuals have similar benefit in other areas of creative expression.

For most people; however, it takes time to activate their creative receptors. Take the case of a young couple named Josh and John who came to our Center for the first time to experience a creative night out at our *Open Studio & Open Jam* weekly event. One was working in the IT department at a large firm, and the other was pursuing an engineering degree. Both were extremely excited and curious about Healium, and on this occasion I, the director, was free to have the pleasure of giving them the obligatory tour for first-time participants.

EXPERIENCING AN *EXTRA*ORDINARY SANCTUARY

Healium Center is housed in a large freestanding 110-year-old brick and granite stone purpose-built church. It has two floors plus a basement totaling about 12,000 square feet. The main sanctuary on the top floor has 16 foot ceilings and is often leased out to churches, while the other two floors below are dedicated to Healium activities. From the outside, the building looks rather unpretentious and conventional; to match The Healium Way philosophy of keeping a low-profile. But the moment you step through the double kaleidoscope-stained glass doors, you know you've come to a creative sanctuary, unlike any other. As you enter a fiery red lit reception area, the scent of lavender aromatherapy fills your senses as New Age music from around the world permeates your Soul. The high-spirited energy of smiling and happy people infects you immediately as you become inducted into the Healium creative family.

A pair of white laced closed curtains teases your curiosity at the hallway entrance. Above it, the symbols of four religions; Islam, Judaism, Hinduism and Christianity welcome you to an all-inclusionary sanctuary. As you open the curtains, you discover a one-of-a-kind healing place. The burnt orange expansive six-foot wide hallway caresses you with love and warmth. This sacral chakra color of creativity, abundance and sexuality reaffirms your arrival at an unconventional creative home. You will feel the urge to sit on raw, hand-carved red oak benches as your eyes drift to the walls filled with captivating local works of art. As you walk down the hallway, dozens of floating white clouds dangle from the 10-foot ceiling while at the end of the long hallway, the words *ART HEALS* drape over a doorway of a room filled with people having fun painting their masterpieces.

You're excited and want to see more. Soon you encounter two art galleries filled with more thought-provoking art that stop your heart and pique your curiosity. In another room, local craft vendors await you in a Moroccan-style seated den, draped in colorful Indian saris, with the ceiling filled with canvas paintings created by participants. If you are daring, I will give you a personal tour of my private, black- draped "forbidden" surreal gallery with more than 50 mind-bending clay and mixed media artworks. Soon you are escorted back out of the front entrance and taken to an intimate music and dance basement room lit with LED lights and "stars" from floor to ceiling. The stage is filled with musicians jamming and people ecstatically dancing on the floor. Finally, you will check out the outdoor lawn and drumming circle area with fiery torch lights and a 10-foot chalkboard to draw and create art as you please. This Center is intoxicating and vibrating full of life and positive energy. People are dialoguing, creating, laughing and being inspired to celebrate their higher selves. On this particular night, I escort Josh and John back to our art galleries to get their creative juices flowing. I asked each of them to look at a surrealist piece of art and interpret it. At Healium, our unconventional thought process invites the viewer, not the artist of the artwork to tell us what the piece is about. It's much more interesting, fascinating and fun to watch. It usually takes folks a couple minutes to get immersed in the artworks and start writing or talking about it.

In this case, both attendees were stuck in their heads and kept looking at each other. After a few long minutes of silence and uneasy body movements, I asked what discomfort or emotion they were experiencing. Josh sighed and responded, *"I can't say I feel anything."* while John put his hands in his pocket and asked, *"What do you want me to feel, Jim?"* This blank-stare condition is not that uncommon at our Center. I've seen people freeze up when asked to interpret a piece of thought-provoking art or paint freestyle. It's quite normal for first timers. So rather than press them into something they weren't comfortable with, I took them both to our mesmerizing Zen room created specifically to relax people and dismantle this paralytic condition. The black light room intoxicates you upon entering with the aroma of lavender oil to clear your mind — as a transparent flowy white canopy cascading from the ceiling hugs you like wings of an angel. A gentle waterfall feature and meditation music permeate your Soul, as a jaw-dropping, two-foot violet crystal sculpture, burning candles, and the words *SURRENDER* highlighted on the wall welcome you. It's a Divinely inspired space that was designed for my wife, who is known in the healing community as Blue Thunder.

Josh and John were thrilled to be there and melted into the captivating ambience. This room, like all the rooms at The Center, is designed to make you feel at home and offers its own unique personality and charm. The couple got comfortable sitting on yoga blankets and laid their heads on throw pillows, as I had them close their eyes to chill and quiet their mind. I shut the door and left them alone to marinate and Zen out. About 20 minutes later, they both came out and went back to the gallery and revisited the art piece that they had trouble with before.

They now had an enlightened look on their faces; their aura had actually changed. Both these guys were ready and eager to talk about what they each saw. One of them got very descriptive and detailed and I noticed a remarkable difference in their energy as both began interpreting and connecting with many more artworks in the gallery. They were aligned with the beauty and inspiration all around them. Soon, they were ready to paint their own unique pieces. Neither had painted since high school but they were filled with ideas and excitement to create. I offered the gay couple some wine, which they accepted, and sat them at a table with a palette of paint, water and brushes. The studio was pretty packed with a diverse group of people. This indigo blue room is usually filled with art on the walls, a food vendor that serves gluten-free dinners, a chair massage person, a beverage table and an array of drums for anyone to jam. There's a projector screen that plays music videos from around the world, or ambient music with motivational quotes. Sometimes we'll have a live poet or musician who entertains the artists with a didgeridoo, violin, flute, hang drum, sitar, opera etc.

So Josh and John are pretty stoked to spend their four hours at a wondrous creative playground on this special night. But before they could partake in the other activities, they needed to complete their masterpieces. It took them about ninety minutes to turn their blank white canvases into something they loved, and they were eager to share the stories of their works with me. Josh had painted a stark, gray sky with a fiery red heart dripping down among the smaller dangling black hearts. He told me he had gone through a lot of bad relationships. Meanwhile, John used his fingers to paint rainbows with the shadows of two people in the background. In his case, he had not been accepted by his parents for being gay. Both had journeyed deeper with their creations and were happy to express themselves authentically. *"Wow, I can't believe I just painted this Josh!"* John exclaimed in a burst of emotion to his partner.

It was beautiful to see their Souls blossom and emotions flow freely in such a short period of time. Healium had done its job drawing out the *extra*ordinary in each of them!

PASSIVE-ACTIVE HEALING

There are many people like John and Josh out in the world who are shut off from their emotional receptors. Males, overall, have been programmed by society to block and numb their emotions and put on a tough exterior facade. What's more, there are a dozen other factors from overworked environments to our technological revolution that are affecting millions of American adults. This shut-off valve is also keeping people from delving deep into themselves, as is encouraged at The Center. From the beginning, we saw how some participants did not relate to surrealism-style art and preferred to stay shallow. They would just come to have a good time with friends, paint a pretty flower or replicate a picture and leave. Although there's nothing wrong with that, The Healium Way asks that participants to reach deep within for creative exploration, fulfillment and healing.

I knew the mind was the culprit that had to be quieted in a "theta" brain wave state before activating it with any deeper purpose. Soon Blue Thunder and I, brainstormed and created a powerful experience that combined meditative storytelling and sound healing followed by freestyle painting — a *passive-active healing session*. The idea is to fuse a unique mind-relaxing meditative experience prior to a creative activity to open people's emotional valve. It has worked wonders. A typical session holds a small group of participants in the intimate Zen room and allows people to soak their minds and open their Souls by mind-traveling into a wondrous metaphysical realm. Each original meditative story is created by my Shaman wife and includes the celebration and connection with multidimensional realms consisting of deities, angels and mythological entities. The precept is to temporarily disconnect you from the present reality and reconnect you to your better self by using powerful and inspirational life lessons. The meditative journey lasts about 30 minutes, and after the participants get relaxed, each person is able to use their mind's eye to open the Soul and pour out the contents of their hearts on a canvas. This passive-active combination is highly effective in prying open the portal of pain and embedded childhood trauma. The storytelling and sound-vibration combination when done correctly is a detoxifying catalyst to bring to the surface the wounds festering within. For some people, it is a life-altering and cathartic experience. The interplay of the creative and healing arts also allows for a harmonious soul-over-mind relationship, especially for the restless mind. The inner critic, blockages and other embedded mind viruses go on ice for a while, as the emotional receptors within release freely. The results are varied from person to person, but are always fascinating to watch.

I've observed stoic and sterile people come out of the room smiling and recharged. I've seen anxious people attain spiritual inner peace. And I've witnessed grown men shed tears. This healing process is beautiful and priceless. The passive- healing session is immediately followed by the active creative activity. There is no time pressure, and each person has free reign to create their masterpieces without limitation or rules. What happens during the following 90 minutes or so is quite remarkable.

We witness ordinary people without any painting skills open their third eye, unleash their imagination and release deep and dark emotions without holding back. They find the opportunity to uncover their "covers," and break out of their imprisoned minds, to turn their ugly truths into beautiful truths. They take the extra step out of their low-vibrational boxes by moving into the light of *extra*ordinary creative beings — similar to what Josh and John experienced that amazing night!

Participants experiencing a *'passive-active healing'* journey at Healium Center

Interactive Exercise:

STORYTELLING SHAMANIC JOURNEY BY BLUE THUNDER

In this exciting exercise, you will be experiencing a meditative journey into a different metaphysical realm and learn the powerful lesson of life. Use your **SMARTPHONE'S CAMERA** to take the ride!

Jim's wife, Blue Thunder

Principle #4
Solving Every Problem Creatively

It's 2 p.m on a frantic Monday in June 2020. More than 100,000 Americans have already lost their lives due to the Covid-19 pandemic, and to make matters worse, there's civil unrest against police brutality on the streets all across the nation. A black man named George Floyd was just murdered in cold blood by a policeman who choked him to death without cause. The entire incident was captured on a cellphone and broadcast to millions of people across the globe. America is waking up and its multiracial young population is displaying its unfettered outrage unseen since 1968. A few miles down from the riots in the city of Atlanta, sits Healium Center, which is temporarily closed due to the pandemic. And after having contracted the Covid-19 virus in March, my wife and I are not taking chances being in harm's way of either of these calamities. It's an unprecedented time in our modern history and in a serendipitous way, the pandemic is America's mirror on itself. It is revealing the country's existential fissures and ideological problems that are akin to a third world country. It's also a time of reckoning for a country mired in deep rooted racial divisions and inequality.

To make matters worse, there's a commander-in-chief at America's helm suggesting people ingest disinfectants and bleach to kill the virus. Once regarded as a well-respected world leader, America is now a world's laughing stock. But we reap what we sow and we've done it to ourselves.

By having an American exceptionalism mindset of being the bad ass and greatest country in the world, our hubris has boomeranged on us. And it is costing us dearly in a multitude of ways. By seeing ourselves as special, we've turned into a nation of unprecedented failures from a dysfunctional government to a disjointed people. While thinking we're the smartest, we've actually dumbed-down our society and fallen behind in education in comparison to the rest of the world. By touting our war machines and invincibility, we've created a nation of intolerant, fearful hate mongers who worship guns. By taking our freedoms for granted, we've imprisoned ourselves with an illusory reality that is unsustainable. By waving the flag of white supremacy, we've lost our respect for human dignity and morality. By worshipping capitalism, we've surrendered ourselves to unfettered greed and excesses. By relentlessly pursuing the American Dream, we've woken up to a nightmare of economic opportunities for the few and disillusionment for the many.

MAKING MARGARITAS OUT OF LEMONS

There's a saying that goes *"10 percent of life is what happens to you and 90 percent is how you respond to it."* As I write this book, I ask myself, will a life-upending event like the Covid-19 coronavirus pandemic be the tipping point and an overdue catalyst for people to take charge of their country? Or is this virus and our unreckoned imbalances the perfect storm that further weakens an ailing superpower?

What will post-pandemic America look like? Are people going to take this opportunity to get smart and make effort to rebalance the inequities or be in denial mode and further inflame the divisions? Is the self-fulfilling suffering temporary — or the beginning of permanent psychological and economic malaise for Americans?

In this Principle of The Healium Way, staying creative to resolve problematic situations has never been so critical. We look at creativity as jumper cables imbedded in the brain that each of us activates as needed to respond to life's twists and turns. Some of us, like myself utilize it automatically in everyday life, while others require a catalyst to tap into it. As respected leaders in our healing and arts community, my wife and I are creating self-care and inspirational videos to our Healium family subscribers during the coronavirus pandemic. We specifically suggest that they look at down times such Covid-19 as a glass half-full opportunity to *go within* and discover their true self — while practicing safe common-sense protocols. We reiterate to them that life is not fair, no one owes you anything, to ditch the victim/entitlement self and turn any crisis into a positive opportunity. It is by standing up tall, applying yourself to your best ability, using common sense, being creative and thinking unconventionally, that you can tackle any challenges. We remind people that there is a creative solution to every problem, and to reactivate the various tools of the creative and healing arts such as meditation, painting, music, dancing, creative writing, yoga, drumming and so forth, to help them stay mentally healthy. Once the mind is uncluttered, it operates more efficiently by focusing more clearly, having clarity and making unemotional and sound decisions.

This advice may seem unconventional to some people who prefer to pop pills, but these activities have been used for thousands of years as natural pathways to reduce depression, loneliness, anxiety and promote overall mental wellness. But I'm not preaching this practice. I am self-prescribing these creative medicines myself during this period to write this book and create art to help me heal. With a plethora of bad news breaking on the hour, a crisis or a downtime offers the perfect climate for us to release our pent-up emotions and get aligned with the all-abundant force of inspiration—turning lemons into margaritas! This is our opportunity to awaken our dormant artistic faculties within each of us as it is intended by our maker.

Check out Jim's Covid-19 inspired art: Clay mixed media:

"America's broken wings"   "Grabbing the last straw"

What is amazing is that I have not been professionally trained in many of these creative endeavors. And don't need to be, as you are coming to understand by reading this book. It is not necessary for me to be a society-validated artist, trained musician or dancer, accredited poet, etc., to reap the positive health benefits. These activities are done for my pleasure and need no one's approval or judgment. As a self-admitted perfectionist, it is often a challenge to keep this in mind, but I have to remind myself that I am not trying to monetize or make a professional career of it. I am simply trying to have fun with it, which in turn provides a therapeutic benefit that is powerful and lasting. Interestingly, activating our creative receptors rewires our brain to function better in stressful situations. It triggers the beneficial neurochemicals that liberate us from a mindset of fear and desperation to help us cope better. For me, once I administer this creative medicine as a lifestyle change, I not only lower my blood pressure and stress levels but am able to think a lot more clearly of the situation at hand. An interesting phenomenon occurs when we participate in our life's adventures in this way, as opposed to simply being observers; it's highly contagious. It transforms the energy of people around you, and can instill positive change in others almost instantaneously.

I've done some pretty bold and courageous things in my life as a result of thinking creatively.

THE LITTLE MAN THAT COULD

Having a creative mindset is not just about deploying a particular form of the arts in moments of distress, but rather it's about having innovative answers to ALL our life's issues. As I look at my own life, I realize that in many moments of difficulty or crisis, my brain always kicks into an automatic creative default position using unconventional means to attain the desired benefits. I acquired this habit early on in my life as a stutterer in boarding school who had to gain respect from the other boys by being more creative when facing my speech challenges. Instead of struggling with a speaking role in drama class, I studied the famous French pantomime Marcel Marceau and deployed miming routines in group skits to get around memorizing painful lines and be the butt of jokes. Rather than dealing with the fright of talking in front of a class on a 'show and tell' assignment, I learned magic tricks and impressed the audience with my newfound talent.

As a relatively small built male (comparable in size to actor Dustin Hoffman), I've always had to find innovative ways to get noticed and avoid being bullied. In order to beat the larger, more muscular boys in wrestling matches, I used my brain to psyche them out and win points by being quick and nimble around their oversized bodies. As an adult, I'd learn how to use my little stature to achieve big things, just by going the extra-mile, being courageous and always staying creative. As a fashion designer, my haute couture clothing and accessory collections were sold in luxury stores and turned heads from Los Angeles to London. I transformed a boring carpet-cleaning profession into a sexy and profitable business and became the coveted luxury brand serving Atlanta's wealthiest people and made my first $1 million in my 30's. In real estate, I went to seminars to learn how to flip little ugly houses with "zero down" techniques, but separated from the crowd by using the same knowledge to flip multimillion dollar deals and bring home six figure checks. Eventually, I turned the creative notch even higher by learning how to assemble land and be known by many local real estate professionals as an *"unconventional and fearless land developer with a vision."* In the art arena, I flipped the conventional model upside down by developing a creative playground for ordinary adults to prove how art heals and unites people. I don't consider myself anything special, though. I'm just passionate and driven about what I do, am not afraid to take risks and most important — I find *creative* ways to accomplish special things. That is my secret. And you can discover this secret too. You will earn a lot of respect by being creative. What's important to note is once you train yourself to find creative solutions to every problem, you also become unconventional in your thinking and fearless. And those three attributes are always part of your ethos in everything you do. They're forever etched in your DNA and take you from being average to better — from ordinary to *extra*ordinary.

DON'T TRY THIS AT HOME

Let me share with you a story of how my inner-creative default mechanism activated within me in the face of adversity. It's quite an exciting story to share that could have had me killed. So please don't try this at home.

I had just purchased an investment property in an urban Atlanta neighborhood known as Reynoldstown and was rehabilitating it with my handyman friend Mike for student-group rental. Today, the neighborhood is highly coveted with expensive homes, but in 2012 it was still a diamond in the rough with crime and undesirable elements. To many Atlantans, Reynoldstown was considered a "bad" neighborhood. Translated in the segregated American South real estate lingo, the "bad neighborhood" label is code for *there are many blacks in the area,* as opposed to a "good location," which means *there are fewer blacks in the area,* and a "great location," which is a totally gentrified area with *no blacks to be seen except for domestic help and workers* (aka, a "white- hot neighborhood."). The day prior to signing a lease with the students, I had Mike install a new air conditioner condenser for me. The neighborhood was experiencing a rash of robberies of A/C units at the time so I had the idea of securing it with heavy duty chains cemented into the ground. It was getting dark in the evening and as we were finishing up pouring the concrete, I noticed a tall black man in a sleeveless white shirt and tattoos attentively watching us from his back porch next door. I didn't think much of it at the time. Mike told me that the concrete would take a few hours to solidify with the embedded chain.

The following morning as I arrived to prepare for the college kids, I noticed the house was very warm. So I went to the backyard to inspect the air conditioner, but it was gone. I was furious! My immediate gut feeling told me that the man next door had taken it, as he was the only one who witnessed the installation inside our fully fenced yard. Yes, I was prejudging him, but no other rationale made sense to me. I called my wife about it and she suggested I call the cops to file a report. I told her that was useless as I had a couple hours before the students came to sign the lease. I abruptly hung up and without any hesitation briskly walked up into the driveway of the neighboring house. I knocked hard on the front door and a tall heavy set black man with a gun tucked in the waist of his pants front opened the door and confronted me. As he looked down at me in disdain, he tried to intimidate me by spitting something out of his mouth above my head. My heart was racing, but I was so pumped up in an adrenaline rush that I didn't realize the imminent danger I was in. *"Excuse me guys, but it is very rude for y'all as my neighbors to steal my freaking air conditioner unit! I got five students coming here in a couple of hours and how the hell am I gonna explain a hot-ass house with no A/C?"* were the angry words that rolled off my tongue. *"Man, get the hell on* *outta here before we f*ck you up! I don't know what you're talking about. And why did you call the cops on us?"* the man replied in a rage as he pointed his finger at a police car that had just arrived. Apparently, my wife had called 911. I turned around and rushed up to the young white officer who looked at me in bewilderment and asked if everything was all right. I told him what had happened and he quietly urged me to get back into my own driveway and not harass the neighbors. He advised me *"not to approach those people again as they were dangerous"* and to get inside my house. He looked scared. He told me there was nothing he could do for me and quickly jumped back into his police car and sped off leaving me alone to deal with the irate neighbors, who I now began to suspect were dangerous gang members. As I stood nervously alone on my porch, three of them walked up to me with their guns halfway tucked in their front underwear and pants. They were not happy campers. For a split second, I thought I was going to be shot dead but instinctively mustered a friendly smile and told them the cop had made a mistake and came to the wrong house. *"Everything's cool, guys!"* I continued explaining as they kept their silence, their piercing eyes directed toward me. *"So guys, I know you probably didn't steal my unit, but you know who did and can get it back for me right?"* Now as good neighbors, we all got to get along, so I got a proposition for you"* I said, then took out my wallet, slipped a hundred-dollar bill out of it, ripped the bill in half, and gave one half to one of the guys. I continued: *"Now look here, man, I don't have much time, but you go find me my unit and if you can return it before my tenants get here at noon, I will give you the other half of this bill."* They were just dazed. *"Man, this dude is a crazy motherf*ucker y'all, check this sh*t!"* I heard the guy say as he held up the torn bill. The other two gangsters just scratched their heads in dismay and confusion. *"So why don't y'all get busy now and go find me my unit and I will be waiting for you right here,"* I said, anxiously. Soon I noticed one of the guys holding a cellphone and talking to someone as all three guys rushed out my driveway. I turned around, walked toward my door and went inside the house.

CRAZY ASS GANGSTA

For some reason I wasn't as scared as I should have been and just wanted to get my A/C unit returned. My cellphone was totally dead at this point and I had no charger to call anyone. I wasted no time preparing the house for the new tenants and after about 30 minutes I decided to go back outside. As I looked to the street, I saw a black truck approaching my driveway hauling what seemed like my air conditioner unit on the back. And it was! It was quite a surreal sight. I was elated. The three guys waved at the driver to back the truck into my driveway. The unit was quite heavy and each of them helped unload the unit onto a hand truck and brought it to me. *"Here it is, man. Now where's the rest of the money?"* I gave the guy the other half of the Benjamin bill, he shook his head and told me I was a *"crazy ass gangsta"* as he left my property. My installer soon arrived and we had the house ready in time for rental. It was quite an exhilarating morning.

Later that year the gangsters' house was raided by the FBI and a large swat team arrested the men for theft, illicit drugs and illegal weapons. They were known as one of the most prominent crime gangs in Atlanta and masterminds of air conditioner robberies. Although I don't recommend anyone try what I did in the above story, it is important to view the example as a powerful lesson in finding creative ways to fix any given problem.

CHILDREN TEACHING ADULTS

Activating our inner creative spark, on demand and when needed, is a Healium Way skillset you will learn with practice, and even teach your children. Fortunately, our kids learned it simply by watching their parents use it in public settings. And they knew exactly when to deploy it, and turn an ordinary and ugly situation into a beautiful *extra*ordinary one. Here's one example of what I mean. We were returning from a family vacation in China a few months before the

2008 Beijing Olympics, and our jam-packed plane was stuck on the tarmac for several hours. We were informed that the delay was weather-related, but unknown to us, the captain and half the flight crew of Air China had left the aircraft a couple hours into the ordeal. The toilets were overflowing, the air was heavy and everyone was restless displaying their cabin fever. In this chaotic period, while the adults were complaining and pacing the aisle in rage, there was something quite remarkable that started taking place in front of us. Both our teenage kids began clapping hands, singing, making funny faces at people and uplifting themselves. They could have chosen to ignore their reality and put their headphones on, but they didn't. It was as if they were tired of being in their present reality and wanted to change it into a better one. Amazingly, it worked. My wife and I didn't stop them and joined them in their child play. Although some people were confused and frowned at us, we didn't care. Within minutes, we observed other kids in the adjacent seats begin to activate their own playful receptors too. Pretty soon, the heated temperament of the cabin fever began to cool off.

One by one the adults stopped fussing and just watched our kids and others start dancing, singing and 'make lemonade out of the lemons.' The joy was contagious and the entire energy of our surroundings was positively transformed. It was a delightful sight to see how the carefree and spontaneous attitude of two kids applying the Principles of The Healium Way raised the vibration of the entire plane and got us through the confining and horrid five hour experience. This could have been a frightful and discomforting experience in an unsympathetic communist country. But it seemed a lot less terrifying and hostile due to the enlightening spirit of these two "un-adult-erated" young souls.

"Do not fight against the light. Fight for the light."
— Jim Peera

Principle #5
Mastering Detachment & Resolving Conflicts

"The root of suffering is attachment."
— Buddha

I've come to the conclusion that all our habits and addictions result from our inability to detach from the many seductive elements to include *people, things, places, ideologies* and *outcomes.* Knowing how to reduce or entirely remove our grip on many of these attachments is the key to controlling our emotional suffering. The wisdom of the ages teaches us the destructive force of making negative attachments. Yet, we're all guilty of succumbing to this default position in every aspect of our lives. As difficult as it is to implement the concept of non- attachment in our human experience, it is a vital part of maintaining peace and being proficient at resolving conflicts. For one, it tests our resilience and willpower. Secondly, it frees us from the prison of our external and material reality. We know, for instance, how addicts suffer with their particular attachments, be it alcohol, junk food, drugs, work, money, dogma, smoking, love, sex, toxic people and so forth. For some, being able to quit cold turkey is easier than it is for others.

For many more, the process of detachment is often painful and requires professional help. If you are the observer, detachment is a tricky condition to handle. On one hand, you want to throw a lifeboat to save someone from sinking. On the other hand, you want to practice non-interference by allowing them to fall and get up on their own. But it's critical that they be ready and have the intention to change their reality. I know of people at our Center who'll teach by example by discreetly bringing friends to help them kick bad addictions. Conversely, I've witnessed individuals afraid of losing a friend to the truth, stay silent and become enablers. Sadly, the latter situations are more common in our busy grind and validation-based society.

It is also a fact that the deeper you love something or someone the more grueling it is to detach. As parents, most of us have probably faced situations with our kids where we've realized our over-coddling and overprotective habits with them. Often, we're only willing to admit that we've spoiled them when we get disrespected and underappreciated. In many ways, these triggers are our signs to unearth the skeletons in the closet and not be afraid to face them with fervor. A lot of our self-realization occurs after our children have moved out, as we have more time on our hands and are wiser and better observers of our past mistakes. As it did for me. During this self-reflection period, we realize the importance of setting boundaries in any relationship. Sometimes this awareness is necessary in detaching ourselves from a particular outcome and forging a healthier path forward.

BLURRED BOUNDARIES

Defining boundaries is a process of determining what behavior we will accept from others and what we will not. And visa-versa. It requires a lot of discipline and willpower to get it right for many of us. There are many types of boundaries including physical, emotional, financial, sexual and intellectual. Briefly defined, the physical boundary is about our personal space and privacy. The emotional boundary relates to our feelings. The financial boundary is all about money. The sexual boundary has to do with physical intimacy with another person and permissibility. While the intellectual boundary is about showing respect for different ideas and views. All of these boundaries are important to practice in our interaction with adults in everyday life (our partners, bosses, friends, siblings, strangers, etc.) As a married man and director of a community center, I understand its value and take it very seriously. Alas, I didn't get this memo raising my own children. My wife and I admit that we blurred the boundaries with our kids as we were both trying to make up for our own childhood shortcomings. It is critical to get it correct with children, as their brains are underdeveloped and they're looking at us adults to guide them. If not, we slip into murky waters that confuses the child and sets us up for problems down the road. I caught myself overcompensating with my son and daughter for not having the closeness to my own dad. I made the mistake of playing multiple roles as a father, boss, landlord, mentor, therapist and friend. By not having clear boundaries, my kids were confused, and I was trapped in a conundrum between earning their respect and expecting it unconditionally as the elder.

While it seemed like a functional idea while they were kids, it began backfiring on me as they got older. They were confused as to what role I played. Often, they got so comfortable with me as a "friend" that they talked to me in a condescending manner — not realizing that b e h a v i o r constituted being disrespectful toward their father. I knew I raised them well and was an above-average father in many ways, but because I did not set clear boundaries, they had a hard time appreciating each of my roles. If you're a parent raising a child, just be aware that you, not your child, is in charge of your actions. Therefore, learn to set tougher boundaries early on if you want to avoid stressful and often painful episodes down the road. If you're in the empty nest period as I am, understand that it is probably the best opportunity to clear the waters and patch up any old wounds with your grown children. It is never too late.

Personally, I have no problem diving head first into the choppy waters to save a relationship and mitigate the suffering, including my own, for my own peace.

A FATHER'S 30-DAY PEACE PLAN

Being a father of two millennial children, I can tell you about my own detachment story not too long prior to the pandemic. As an Eastern-mindset born and raised person, I was quite attached to my son and daughter, both of whom are Western raised and very independent-minded. My *hierarchy of expectation* bar (discussed in Part 1) is quite high for my kids — as it should be. They grew up privileged and were given all the attention and love any parents could possibly give them. They also had the best of birthday parties, vacations, clothes, toys, summer camps, extracurricular activities and more. Naturally, I expected them to respect me and be grateful for what I'd worked so hard to provide for them. When I didn't get a desired outcome from them, I noticed that I suffered. I'd often have images of the late comedian Rodney Dangerfield's famous routine, *"I get no respect!"* Sometimes a particular argument or issue at hand would take months to resolve and I'd develop stomach and heart pains in the process.

In one case, I had a nasty fallout with my daughter, where we ended up not speaking for several months. It all began one day while she was driving a car that I'd just purchased for her after her first car accident. She erupted in rage like a volcano for no particular reason and spewed vile wounds at me. As a strong and grounded father, I knew that I was her default "dumping ground" that day. But her highly charged unsettling emotional eruption almost got us all killed. She failed to apologize for her uncanny behavior and I was quite hurt and upset for quite a while. It was a top priority for me to stop my own emotional bleeding, and instead of seeing a therapist about it, I put The Healium Way into practice — one baby step at a time.

First, I went into a quiet meditative state and concocted a mental picture of the desired positive outcome. I visualized setting aside a realistic 30 days to remove all the resistances that I had justified for not contacting her. This was my intention. You can choose any time frame from two weeks to three months for most challenging problems. My clear goal was helped by retaining a clear photographic image of the desired intention and not having any hostility towards her. It's important to notice how my mission was not to change her, but to change myself. That change is the only thing in my control.

During this period, I had to be focused and disciplined. I began and ended each day with a prayer of gratitude. This sets the night and day bookend of being grateful and aligned with your highest self. During the week, I made a pact with myself to keep my mind cool by meditating regularly, smiling and randomly laughing as much as I could, even if I didn't feel like it. Laughter is an instant uplifting medicine that releases the brain's happy chemicals. I recalled how we had some great funny moments together, and began unpacking them, using old photographs and revisiting childhood videos of her with me. Then I made sure I ate well and my body got exercise with some nature walking, yoga, tai chi and going to the gym. Finally, I spent a lot of time activating my inner-creative self by sculpting, writing poetry, drumming, photography and dancing. These self-expression activities are my favorite creative medications to release pent-up emotions festering within. Often, I'd start out angry and end up with thoughts of hope, love and compassion. During this period I went through some pretty rough internal torment and openly surrendered to all my emotions, no matter how dark. There were days where I didn't want to wake up. But I knew I had to get motivated and take action if I wanted to stop suffering.

I also let loose of any inhibitions by singing in the shower and releasing my emotional and physiological pain, sometimes by crying. Yes, grown men do cry and it's highly therapeutic. I began allowing myself to experience each activity without resisting the waterfall of emotions. It was spiritually cleansing. I did this uninhibited balance regimen for a month in a consistent manner. Soon, I started to release and lift the beast of burden off my heavy chest and untangled my twisted stomach. Instead of having a rigid set of demands or an ideal outcome with my daughter, I became more pliable and compromising.

Rather than wait for her to connect with me and apologize for her unmerited and visceral outburst that felt like a knife slicing into my heart, I took the initiative to not get ugly. Instead of responding to her accusatory fiery texts in hate or angst, I threw ice on it with a compliment. This took courage but it was the necessary act of opening the portal of healing for me. I had no expectation except that it liberated me from the prison of my own suffering. Soon she wrote me back without an angry tone as she had done in prior texts. The reciprocal connection was a pleasant outcome and a great start to begin the repair. My intention was indeed manifested. I saw it as a baby step in the right direction, and best of all, I stopped holding the pain, sadness and disappointment within.

By not being attached to any predisposed outcome from both my children, I felt better. This detachment exercise has helped me forge a new pathway on a broader level. Now instead of being upset over insisting on receiving a conditional response, such as a *"Thank you" "I'm sorry"* or other expected actions, I find it's a lot easier to give to people (including my children) without any expectation of anything in return. Unless it's a personal loan or a business transaction, I try hard to remove three things out of any relationships with people: *condition, expectation and validation.* In this way, you are sending a one-way ticket gift without strings attached, freeing you from any set outcome to disappoint you. Once detached, you become in charge of your own emotions, actions and path. You cut the cord of attachment and you are in sole control of manifesting your road to healing. You feel lighter, freer and less f*cked up inside having unloaded all your resistances and excuses.

In other situations, it is about removing yourself from a toxic person who is taking your power and weakening you. When we take the time to work on ourselves in this manner and are rewarded with a particular positive outcome, we are then emboldened to fix other areas of our lives. My personal detachment exercise not only helped reduce the burdens of my emotional suffering but it had an unintended side effect: a physiological change in my overall health.

I started to smoke fewer cigars, drank less coffee, reduced my alcohol intake, increased exercise and had more sex. All of these are positive attributes, especially the last one! Once you master this art of detachment you will also inspire others to try it and do these activities for their own transformation.

WHITE LIGHT AND ROSES

If you are on the offensive end of the dispute and have thrown a temper tantrum or launched a hurtful verbal attack on someone in haste, it is as important to know how to do damage control. Usually, the quicker you throw ice on the inflamed remarks, the better the outcome. As actions create reactions, the flamethrower has a small window of opportunity to either retract the incendiary remarks by unconditionally apologizing or explain it with humor or other gestures of goodwill. Sadly, most of the time due to our self-centered and egotistical nature, we'll do neither and let the verbal bombs begin to instill pain and suffering on both parties for a protracted period of time. That's our human flawed nature in action. Interestingly, when we unleash the rabid dog within us, it is seldom as a result of a direct provocation and more to do with our own imbalanced emotional state of mind. Take for instance a situation in which you're having a bad day at work and unfairly dumping on your partner. This trivial annoyance has triggered you to lose your sense of cool. Your blood pressure is high and you're having an out-of-body experience that's exposing the ugliness within you. Instead of having an outburst of dark emotion on this person, stop and take a quick second to mentally switch places with them and observe yourself being pummeled with rage.

How does it feel? What emotions do you feel being the receiver of hostility? You'll find it's quite demoralizing. That's because you're disconnected from your higher state of being and we have to get you reconnected. Now, take a deep breath and visualize being showered by *white light with roses around you.* That is your invisible field of protection. Feel your invisible higher self, stepping in and getting you out of your low-vibrational mode. You will notice how quickly a confrontation can be avoided. At this point, you'll need to reverse the damage by apologizing for your out-of-place behavior and give that person a sincere hug. Afterward be silent and meditate for a few minutes and thank yourself for avoiding conflict and being creative to promote peace. This powerful exercise will help you stay calmer and connected in future heated situations. It is a healing tool that my wife taught me a few years ago and it has worked for me many times.

Practice The Healium Way

DETACHMENT EXERCISE: Is there someone you love who you're too dependent on? It could be your boss, your partner, a friend, your parents, etc. There's a certain attachment that you know is unhealthy but you're afraid to reduce. Now is this moment. Spend less time with this person. Take less goodies (advice, gifts, money, orders, etc.) from them. Imagine that they're no longer there. What would you do? By visualizing detaching yourself from the person, do you feel more or less empowered? If it's less, then you are dangerously attached and must get back into a healthier, balanced relationship with this person. You need to regain your own power. Alternatively, seek to reduce being attached to a set outcome from people. For instance, if you're feeling too dependent on getting the right advice on treating your health condition from your doctor, stop and use the internet to investigate various accredited sites for care and treatments. Put yourself in charge and reduce the propensity to rely on anyone or anything to have all the answers.

Principle #6
Avoiding Being Sheeple

"If you don't stand up for something, you will fall for everything."
— Alexander Hamilton

One of the most important outcomes of The Healium Way is being self-empowered. In order to do that, it requires that you avoid becoming part of a sheeple mindset, people who are easily led without having thoughts of their own. There is nothing more self-defeating to your personal growth and advancement than to allow someone to take your power away. Whether it's a boss, a lover, a dogma or a leader of a group, you must be careful not to outsource your power, because it will demoralize you and eventually enslave you to harmful levels and a low-vibrational state. Your higher self is a courageous fighter not a feeble sheeple. You have to not just fight for what you believe in, but get in the ring to fight for others whenever possible. By standing up for others, you learn to stand up for yourself, and not be duped easily by manipulative or intimidating tactics. Sadly, the sheeple mindset prevails not just in our society but in many other countries (developed and undeveloped) around the world. I am very concerned about this disempowering phenomenon that affects millions of people. I am not referring to simply a "follower" personality as much as a pattern of subtle brainwashing and robotic behavior that can manifest in not questioning authority, bullies and malice toward you. It boils down to conforming to rules as opposed to upholding ethics, morality and common sense. Some rules are necessary for a society to function properly. But unethical and radical rules can destroy us. Just look at the sheeple who followed Adolf Hitler, Idi Amin, Pol Pot, Robert Mugabe and so forth. These despots convinced humans to commit horrific crimes against other humans by following toxic rules. From little acorns grow big oaks, and much of this mind-conditioning begins with one person or a group planting a nonthreatening idea that grows into larger dire ideologies. It can germinate quite innocently at home or at work and replicate and manifest in other areas of your life. Think of how often we see a lot of sheeple in government positions, the military and other institutions who succumb to habitual rule of order and compliance. In more visceral political discord, it manifests in recruitment of extremist ideologies as is exemplified in terrorist organizations. Since the sheeple mindset is a weak one that just follows orders, it is indifferent in deciphering between the good or bad —by simply taking action from its set command or rule book. Quite often these unquestioned, dumb protocols germinate harmlessly, are not questioned and mutate into unnecessary and more insidious rules and harm the followers. It is not until someone questions those stupid rules that a change is made. Here's one example you can probably relate to: restaurants that enforce a mask-wearing policy during the Covid-19 pandemic, but allow you to remove it upon being seated — just a few feet away from other diners. How stupid is that, I said to myself! I was so annoyed on one occasion that I confronted the waiter and made a scene proving my point: *"This is such a nonsensical rule, dude. Think amigo, think! Does Covid only exist at your entrance area, but not anywhere else in the restaurant?"* I asked him in frustration. He looked at me stunned and after a few seconds said, *"I just do what I am told, sir."* *"Okay, so go on top of that mountain and jump off of it"* I told him pointing at the nearby Arenal volcano in Costa Rica. *"I understand what you're saying"* he replied with a confused look. It was as if I had turned a light switch in the young man's brain. Since I didn't have a mask, I stayed outside and ordered the food to go. The following day when I passed by the same restaurant, I noticed they no longer posted signs enforcing that dumb rule. Apparently, the young man had a nice chat with his supervisors about it and they all put their thinking caps on in agreement. *"Thank you sir, for making us aware of this confusing protocol. You definitely make sense and now the mask is optional!"* he told me with a big smile as he gave me a big thumbs up. I could sense a sense of awakening for this young man, who probably saved himself from being easily recruited into a cult or other mind-controlling situations later in life.

So it always pays to speak your mind and question authority. Always! Maslow's famous theory holds that self-actualized people are not static-minded and robotic — but rather rule breakers and nonconformists. They just don't get on their own boats, they rock them. Being obedient and blindly following rules without having the courage to question authority is antithetical to being empowered and *extra*ordinary. Think about Rosa Parks who did not conform to the segregation rules on the bus; or Steve Jobs of Apple not building a traditional computer; or Gandhi taking on the British Empire. They changed the world by questioning rules, breaking conventional wisdom and defying authority. In my own life, I gave you one great example of being a rule breaker during my Alabama property rights ordeal. If I had conformed to the whims of the authorities to give up my property or had been afraid of retaliating against the intimidating and unethical City Hall, I would have been bankrupt and not had the opportunity to change the property laws for black landowners in that city. In order to avoid being a sheeple, you need to not be afraid of sticking your neck out and face the consequences of being a rebel. You also cannot be intimidated by people whose views are contradictory to yours. When you follow your own instincts and take action to stand up for what you believe in, you'll be surprised how many people will have the courage to join you. You don't have to be ugly or violent in your actions, but rather stay focused and be organized in your thoughts. Avoiding being a sheeple is also about taking the road less traveled and forging your own path and beliefs. Social and political activism begins with the single thought of changing and improving unfair practices or rules for the greater good of others.

BAH BAH FLOCK OF SHEEP

Once you're a fighter of justice and a breaker of unethical rules, you're always thinking, strategizing and acting in accordance with those attributes. Whether you need to speak out at a neighborhood meeting to protect your property value, or go to court to fight your unwarranted traffic ticket, you'll have to practice standing up for yourself. When you confront these random, unethical rules and refuse to swallow them, you won't feel sick to your stomach. Your newfound courage will help you automatically take positive action without any excuses or apprehension. In due time, you'll have a *Bring it on* and *Whatever it takes* fervor instead of a *My opinion or vote won't matter* or even worse, *I can't beat them, so let me join them* self-defeating sheeple position. Being a sheeple is therefore incompatible with The Healium Way. The better way is to embrace nonconformity and stay true to your higher state of being, which generates its power by detaching from fear and avoiding being trapped in a state of comforted loyalty. Unfortunately, based on our experience at The Center, we find the sheeple mindset to be a self-induced cancer in much of our society that metastasizes faster than it diminishes. It is far easier to absolve ourselves from any responsibility by not being in charge of it. It's simpler for a lot of people to be an order-taker than an order-giver. When we add the lack of quality education and a herd mentality to this equation, we find our diagnosis to be even more dire. Prior to the election of Donald Trump, I did a powerful art installation at our Center, where I wrote a poem called, *"Bah bah flock of sheep."* I wanted people to understand the dangers of blindly following a toxic leader. How it came true! It was a show stopper that included a sheep-faced mascot tied up, dangling like a puppet. The event opened the minds of many people who until that day had no idea that they were being attached to and operated from a weakened value system.

Check out the *'Bah bah flock of sheep'* poem & art installation Jim created at Healium Center:

Practice The Healium Way

RULE-BREAKING EXERCISE: *"Get into good trouble,"* said the late civil rights leader, John Lewis. In that philosophy of fighting for a worthy cause and protesting peacefully, you have the power and ability to make a difference. Don't wait until it affects you, or when the NIMBY (Not in My Back Yard) syndrome arises. Take a stand against ANY form of social injustice and participate in it. Be an advocate of peace and human dignity. Do not be intimidated or afraid to voice your views. Go to the streets and join in a peaceful rally in your hometown. Write a letter to your senator or congressman TODAY on something that detrimentally affects your community. Attend a community meeting and speak up for positive legislation on guns, taxes, marijuana, voting rights, etc. Don't be afraid to stick your neck out to help deprived, marginalized people. Be a mover, a shaker and a rule breaker and pay it forward. You don't know when you'll be in a hot seat yourself and require others to join your fight.

Principle #7
Unleashing The Magic of Humor

Humor is a term that derives from the humoral medicine of the ancient Greeks, which taught that the balance of fluids in the human body, known as *humors*, controlled human health and emotion. The Greeks were onto something, as humor is an essential medicine in our lives. It is probably our most authentic uplifting human emotion that we take for granted. Without getting into the psychoanalysis of humor's dark side that can camouflage deeper mental issues, I see it as an essential part and parcel of The Healium Way. It will improve our mood, help open dialogue and deflect uncomfortable and controversial situations such as sex, religion or politics. Yet as adults we don't deploy its magic and power often enough in our heavy and serious lives. It's not so much about carrying a bag of jokes around or acting like a clown in public, as it is understanding humor's simple power in our human condition. A sense of humor can keep the world balanced, even if things feel like they are flying apart at the seams. I can't count how many times in my life humor has gotten me out of trouble or a tight spot. Most valuable for me, it has been the glue to keeping a healthy and honest monogamous relationship with my life's partner.

Over the years, when countless envious admirers have asked my wife what she saw in me (interestingly, these were mostly white men who were jealous of me courting a beautiful exotic woman), she always began h e r answer with: *"Because he makes me laugh"* At first, I found that answer to be disturbing as I thought she'd say, *"Because I love him."* But now I realize how that answer seems so refreshing and authentic. Obviously, she loved me for being me, but she specifically loved a particular personality trait that was unpretentious and real. It was something other than the better-looking hunks did not have — a lively sense of humor. But I wasn't always this way. My strict English boarding school upbringing coupled with my various childhood traumas kept me quite withdrawn, shy and serious as a teenager. It wasn't until I got into more creative and artistic endeavors and began my healing journey that I loosened up. The various childhood creative activities that I enjoyed included photography, painting, jewelry-making and later fashion design — all of which somehow unleashed a certain unbounded freedom and humor within. This is the beautiful side effect of the arts. Still, not all artists embrace humor liberally. In fact, I know many artists with stoic personalities who take their craft too seriously. Often, they're introverted and don't socialize much. I got a taste of all that myself as I was growing up too fast and was missing out on enjoying the lighter side of life. I began to rebel against those conformities and eventually got in better balance. Whether I enrolled in various art classes in school or went to a fashion design academy, I never got too hung up on the grades, technicalities or competitive aspects of it. I just always relished the creative process and had fun on any individual or group project. Soon I discovered an eye-opening phenomenon. The more fun I had, the better I got with the activity at hand. While many of my friends mistook their artistic activities as work or competition and burned out, I continued expanding my inner-creative talent. I simply looked at it as a fun modality rather than therapy. The more fun I had also led to random acts of humor in public settings. By not caring what others thought, I removed all my resistances and went from an introverted to an extroverted personality. My shyness was overcome by random bursts of laughter, followed by some off-the-cuff jokes and comments. I would usually laugh about myself as an icebreaker before I laughed at something else. Soon I realized that my funny personality was contagious and more people liked to hang around me.

In turn, my self-confidence improved and people commented how they loved my open and unbound sense of humor. What's more, it's fascinating to me how humor has helped me cope with and dissipate confrontations. As an entrepreneur, it has played an instrumental part in all of my many projects, businesses and endeavors.

THE WEE WEE GUYS

Humor played a big part in a successful business idea I came up with in the mid-1990s: a pet-accident carpet-business with a funny, catchy name. I discovered this profitable 'niche within a niche' industry that was underserved and just swung for the fences. Today, the pet business is gargantuan, but back then it was in its infancy with little competition. I was definitely a little too ahead of the game and barely understood it's multibillion dollar potential. I called the business idea "Wee Wee Inspector," which included an image of a mascot of a dog dressed in a white lab coat before a pool of bright yellow pee stain. The double-entendre name and the matching logo turned eyes all around Atlanta and brought me a lot of good publicity. My partner brother and I would go into people's homes dressed in a white lab coat armed with a "Wee Wee Gun" (a detection instrument I invented but never commercialized) to detect invisible pet urine in order to better clean and sanitize rugs and carpets.

The invention was not only groundbreaking, but it solved a real problem in people's homes. The human eye can barely see the exact location of a particular cat or dog urine stain especially in carpets and rugs, and hence we could not successfully eliminate the odor. But my portable dual-sensor contraption that I prototyped in my garage solved the problem. It had a powerful UV light bulb on one end, and a uric acid sensor prong on the other. You could say we were the "hired guns" for pet owners. Armed with this instrument, we made a stink with our competitors on the one hand and got our customers' carpets smelling like roses on the other.

Best of all, we guaranteed our service with nontoxic herbal products that I co-formulated. Each of them had catchy names like "Scoopee Doo", "Hocus Pawcus" and so on. Our funny business name caught the attention of the entire community and the press. We got written up in local papers and made a big splash. Although that business didn't make me wealthy, it got realtors, interior designers and pet owners to remove the taboo off the subject matter and come clean with it better! (pun intended).

"The Wee Wee Inspectors: Jim with brother Tony holding a Wee Wee Gun.

YOU DAMN FOREIGNERS!

"You should be a stand-up comic!" one woman exclaimed after I took her rather crude racist comment to me and deflected it with a joke. I had just cleaned her carpets and gave her the bill. She said she was ecstatic at how good they looked, but couldn't understand how I could charge so much money for doing it in such a short period of time. I reminded her that she had agreed to the price before I started, and unless she was dissatisfied with the job, she needed to

pay up. She smiled and handed me a check with an uncanny Southern drawl comment: *"Boy, you damn foreigners sure do know how to rake that mighty dollar, don't ya!"* I was stunned for a couple seconds but quickly fired back, "Y*es, ma'am, and you Americans sure taught us foreigners how to do that well!*"

I must admit in my younger years I was a proud self-made capitalist. And quite unapologetic about it. I loved America and it loved me back in opportunities and financial success. The harder I worked, the luckier I got, and the smarter I became. But it was naive of me to think that making a lot of money would solve all my problems. Money just created new ones. I was so lured into its charm and novelty that I let my ego dictate my relationship with my customers. For instance, I'd often price my products and services based on what car and house people owned. I figured if they could afford a six-figure vehicle and a seven-figure house, they could afford to pay top dollar for my services. And they did without hesitation. I also geared all my marketing towards the ultra-rich and branded myself as the Rolls Royce of the rug-cleaning business. Thankfully, I was raised right and had a conscience and integrity not to screw anyone by delivering on my promises. In fact, I went overboard with pleasing customers and subsequently had a respectable 90 percent referral rate in all my businesses.

I also knew better not to step over anyone while climbing my metaphorical mountain, despite the arduous climb. In the following decades, I'd encounter many similar situations from rich doctors to wealthy wives, who would eventually judge my value and worthiness by the color of my skin — not the quality of my work or my character. As a highly respected and successful *"fiber hygienist'* (a title I coined that sounded better than carpet cleaner) for the wealthy, I marketed and presented myself with a sense of style, professionalism and a polished packaging that Americans would respect and admire — but not expect. It was doing the *extra*ordinary in an ordinary and conventional-minded cleaning profession.

I showed up at their front door dressed in a white shirt and tie and carried a big smile and a great attitude. When I handed the customer a business card, it was a picture of me flying on a rug — it always made them chuckle and ask for more cards to hand out to their friends and neighbors.

In the carpet cleaning business, my image and branding was unconventional and turned a lot of eyes. In order to make many of my Southern customers more comfortable, I'd often have to use humor as a weapon against envy, resentment and racism. In many cases, I'd be quick on the draw to hit them with a joke or a comment that would make them eat their words. Surprisingly, I got more respect for that approach than I expected.

THE ORIGINAL BORAT

During the 1996 Olympics in Atlanta, I wrote an adult comic book with accompanying t-shirts and bumper stickers to expose the many ugly truths of American immigrant dysfunctionality and resentment. I called the character Maurich Inusa (more-rich in-USA, pronounced, *Morich Eenoosa*), whose capitalistic dreams bring him to the motherland of opportunity: America.

Here is where he learns to use his relentless drive and creativity to overcome many obstacles to succeed, akin to myself. The story was based on a broader notion that immigrants make America better, not worse. As a political parody, it was embraced by green card holders and foreign-born citizens who had their own American adventures and successes. I took the persistent derogatory comments from my Southern customers such as *"that damn foreigner"* and turned it into a positive acronym: D.A.M.N (Driven Ambitious Minority with No Excuses) Foreigner. This was my way of thumbing my nose at those who hid their envy or displayed it in ugly and ignorant ways. The project was also great therapy as it helped release and express my own pain of racism with humor. It's also another example of shifting from an ordinary mindset to an *extra*ordinary one.

I wrote this comic book exactly 10 years before Sasha Baron Cohen made "Borat" and made being an immigrant cool — so you can say that my character, Maurich Inusa, was the original Borat. It was also 20 years after America elected a xenophobic president, which upended that notion. How ironic and funny is that!

JIM'S GOT EXTRA BALLS

At Healium Center, I've used humor liberally as an icebreaker, and as a tool to deflect any unpopular or unconventional topics. Interestingly, humor cleverly reveals our hypersensitive and politically correct culture; specifically with those people that easily take offense.

It works great in shining a mirror toward them. Professional comedians are masterful at using their artistic license to convey controversial political and religious views — and get away with it. George Carlin, Don Rickles and Hasan Minhaj are good examples of comics who have successfully used this technique. I am not a political comic genius like Carlin, or a trained comic, but I love to get my political views and cynicism out of my system with art as much as possible. I do it in my sculptures, poetry and even random jokes. It works beautifully, it's contagious and often gets me out of a pickle.

I remember one particular incident that could have actually turned out quite ugly, if I did not deploy the magic of humor. In this particular case, it would have been physical pain. We had a regular female attendee at our Center who would often make derogatory, off-the-cuff comments. Some people said that she was bipolar. To protect her identity, I'll call her Beth. She was a type A, highly opinionated and geeky girl in her mid-20s. One evening she walked in with visible unsettled energy from her long day at work. My son was handling the reception duties and I was standing at the outer edge of the desk. She stood facing me and started complaining about how she was having boyfriend issues. Her face was flushed in anger and I could feel that she needed to release some pent-up frustration. People feel safe and comfortable sharing their life's problems at Healium — and for the most part I don't mind being a sounding board. But on this occasion, the young outspoken woman wanted to vent her dissatisfaction of her sexual relationship by provoking a man to prove that all men were scumbags. As a nonthreatening, happily married older man, I was her perfect bait. She made some assumptions about me that I brushed off with some bursts of laughter. Soon she shared some personal "off and on" sexual desires that her boyfriend had expressed to her. I just smiled and suggested that she bring him to The Center and have him paint out his feelings for her. *"I am asking YOU, Jim, isn't that behavior not manly and weird?"* she asked. I told her that every man was different and that there could be many issues that could be a problem — including her. Apparently, that answer did not sit well and she went into an emotional frenzy. She reached into her bag and flipped open a large Swiss Army knife and yelled, *"What if I cut your balls off right now for saying this. How would you feel about that, Jim?"* I heard my son behind me sighing in a moment of shock as I stood still and didn't hesitate to respond to her while smiling: *"Well, you go ahead and do that if it'll make you feel good. The only problem is you see, I am a very special man. When you cut any one of my balls, I'll have three more that will grow even faster and bigger!"* The woman was paralyzed by my quick-jab reaction. She folded her knife and remarked in frustration, *"Damn it, Jim, what will it take to break you down? Why can't I find a man like you?"* I just smiled, handed her a canvas and told her to go paint.

As she walked away toward the art studio, dumbfounded and probably feeling embarrassed and stupid, my son looked at me and said, *"Thanks for opening a place for crazy people, Dad!"*

Two signs posted at The Center:

Practice The Healium Way

HUMOR EXERCISE: The subjects of religion and politics often get people to clam up. So this will be a fun exercise to break the barriers of discomfort. Pick a religion or political affiliation you're uncomfortable or unfamiliar with. Now attend an event or meeting where this group congregates in an open public setting. Be friendly with everyone and just go along with the ride of the event. When you start engaging with individuals, instead of biting your tongue or disagreeing with them, blunt the subject matter with a dose of humor. For instance, if the church pastor asks you if you like to be saved, just smile and say, *"I'm quite fine, I already saved quite a bit at Walmart yesterday."* Observe what happens. If any person from the political group starts waving flags and comments on your patriotism, smile and say, *"I'm not white enough and don't have the cool accent you have to do that"* or something sarcastic that has a complimentary tone. With enough practice, you will get good at cracking funny lines or jokes. The idea is to stay connected with people you disagree with (and learn something new from them) without being offended or igniting an argument. As long as you are not laughing *at* them but use humor to be a buffer and icebreaker, this exercise can work wonders!

A DAY WITHOUT LAUGHTER IS A DAY WASTED.

Charlie Chaplin

Principle #8
Honoring Your Emotions

"When dealing with people, remember you are not dealing with creatures of logic, but with creatures of emotion."
— Dale Carnegie

Emotion is energy in motion. And as humans, we are natural emotional creatures. Sadly, either through ancestral or societal programming and shaming, we've self-induced a mental timebomb on ourselves by stagnating this energy and disconnecting from our true emotions; our body-driven signals that trigger mind-driven feelings.

In the business of healing, it is important not to repress or suppress these release receptors within us. Yet we do. We somehow mindf*ck ourselves by having different standards of emotional-sensitivity based on our gender roles. As an example, due to the packaging of our physicality, men in general are expected to be tougher in their handling of any emotional pain and to 'suck it up' and 'man up' but not expose their vulnerable side. While women are given a different set of rules and allowed to express and display their emotions freely. This societal double-standard has a boomerang effect on the entire ecosystem of relationships. Men quickly learn to shut off their true feelings and stop honoring their emotions in a holistic way. This in turn discourages them to explore wellness alternatives like Healium to find a healthy release and benefit — preventing an unhealed male to revisit his past emotional wounds to help him get mentally unfu*cked. In many cases, the plugged-up male blows his fuse to get attention and regain his personal power — sometimes losing control by being predatory and resorting to various forms of violence. As a typical response, our society doesn't retrace the causes of the hostility, as much as it confronts its symptoms. We'll shame, ignore, medicate, punish and lock men in cages for their misdeeds, but fall short in showing empathy and unlocking their internal rage with unconditional doses of TLC and holistic emotional-release tools. In this manner, we don't really make progress fixing our imbalances, as much as we become good at shifting blame, numbing people, dividing the sexes and staying in the destructive loop. Perhaps this is a great moneymaking recipe for America, but it is making America sick from the inside out. So we must all work to change this unhealthy gender-role dynamic by honoring ourselves as the naturally sensitive and emotional humans that we ALL are — male, female or other.

Due to gender role expectations, males also learn to find a very different outlet to release pent up-feelings than their female counterparts. For most, it is via competitive sports, outdoor activities (such as hunting, fishing, golfing, etc.) and recently through indoor virtual reality and video games. So I'd consider myself being in the minority of men who prefer to use holistic art as an outlet than these more conventional activities. But that could have turned out quite differently for me if not for my learning environment.

CRYING IS FOR GIRLS

I remember being shamed and punished in a male-only boarding school in England for crying in class when one of my classmates was badly injured playing rugby. *"Crying is for girls!"* exclaimed the teacher who put me in detention. I was mixed in a group of older male students who lectured me on *toughing it out* and *manning up,* as the school enrolled me in more rugged outdoor sports and wrestling that month. Over the course of two years, I injured myself during many games and licked my wounds faster each time. During this tough-love indoctrination, I did receive a softer liberal arts training as a counterbalance. It was quite a juggling act that I didn't understand back then, but today I realize how that balance helped me forge my even-keel approach to life. It resulted in opening my creative receptors to vent and release my emotions in an artistic manner rather than projecting them aggressively. I was growing up equipped with a creative tool box on one hand and an intellectual briefcase in another. It turned out to be a good combination.

I also processed things with more sensitivity and empathy than many of my male counterparts. During my teenage years while many of my friends looked forward to Saturday dance parties, girls, alcohol and weed, I got a lot of my pleasure simply staying at home reading books writing poetry or making art. That was my therapy. One unintended side effect and consequence of this creative outlet was that I was able to surrender to my emotions in a healthy way in front of people. My artistic release gave me the confidence to stop hiding my emotions in public and broke the social stigma I was burdened with since childhood. By the time I was in college and got married, I was not only more mature for my age but had a stronger emotional resilience than my peers. Women loved my sensitivity and my guy friends used me as a mediator between their girlfriends. Often, I helped resolve issues by prescribing creative methods for them. Many didn't know how to engage in artistic activities, so I'd show them by example, including photography, painting and poetry, which are inexpensive and readily available tools to express feelings. I also encouraged the guys to see the girlfriend situation from a more balanced viewpoint. But the majority of them thought I was weird and ridiculed my sensitivity toward girls. I soon discovered that many college men perceived women as simply convenient sexual objects, as a consequence of being socialized at macho fraternity parties, watching sexist TV shows and reading magazines such as Playboy and Hustler. TV fictional characters like Archie Bunker and Al Bundy further solidified the male chauvinistic role models. By the time the '90s arrived, I encountered my own experience with hustlers and playboys, especially during my fiber hygienist career for the rich. Sometimes it was servicing affluent single womanizers and yuppies for their lavish parties and private jets, but often this mentality arose in the company of rich but lonely housewives, which I will discuss in the following section.

THE TRUTH HURTS

As two young, good-looking exotic men with shoulder-length black hair and natural tan, my older brother and I were quite the favorites of middle-aged white women customers. While we cleaned their wool carpets and handwoven oriental rugs, these rich but quite unhappily married women would not just surrender freely to their emotions — but be open books on topics from infidelity to plastic surgery. It was similar to a barber-shop or long cab-drive therapy session for customers — but in their own home. Occasionally, they even enticed us with their bodies, looking for an exciting and exotic afternoon delight. Of course, as married men we had the sense to politely decline their sexual advances and respected our boundaries. But it was quite funny and revealing at the same time. Sometimes it was sad to witness their emotional self-imprisonment manifest and unravel in front of our eyes.

One white client, who I will refer to as Mrs. O, was a petite beautiful 70-something big bosomed widow who'd had as many cosmetic surgeries from face to buttocks as the late Michael Jackson. She looked great, and 20 years younger than her calendar. She lived in the same condominium tower as Elton John and was one of our best customers. This woman was filthy rich but poor in her judgment with men. She also was good at covering up her true emotions and displeasure over a relationship with a conniving gigolo who was half her age. I'm not sure how the two met, but when she was alone, she'd often tell me she knew that she was being used by the hustler and playboy, but didn't have the fortitude to kick him out. Apparently, she'd made the mistake of losing her power by entrusting him with all her bank accounts and private information. She wanted him out of her life, but didn't know how to do it without repercussions. She was too weak and afraid on one hand and too ashamed of telling anyone else on the other. Except for me, it seemed. So on one occasion, after I'd finished cleaning her oriental rugs and silk chairs, she offered me a glass of wine and we sat down for a chat. As she muttered bits and pieces of her disempowering relationship, she confided in me that she suspected the guy of having an affair with another younger girl and that they were both stealing from her. She confessed that she was emotionally drained and felt ill to her stomach just talking about it. I suggested she get her daughter involved to help her cut the cord, but she admitted she didn't have an authentic relationship with her daughter and wouldn't have the courage to address it with her. Then I had a light bulb moment. *"Why don't I sculpt a special piece for you with a waterfall feature, which you can display right here in your den? It will not only be a functioning art piece, but a good catalyst for inspiring you to take action. It could even send a subliminal signal to him and alert your daughter of your distress to help you. You know art is an amazing communicator. It will do the talking for you!"* I told her excitedly.

Mrs. O had a twinkle of hope in her eye, took out her checkbook in joy and asked me how much that would cost: *"I trust you Jim, I like the idea. Let's do it!"* she said. I told her I didn't sell my work, but in this case, I would make an exception. I blurted out a number that I felt comfortable with and she wrote me a check for $4,000 and hurried me out the door before the boyfriend returned. I spent the weekend creating the piece, which I was very proud of. I sculpted a slithery beast with a large penis (the greedy gigolo) being regurgitated out of the mouth of a big-breasted rich woman (painted green to signify money).

I thought it was powerful and provoking enough to do the trick. As a surrealist I was doing my part to interpret Mrs. O's repressed emotions:

"Gigolo"

(Clay, Slate, Rock) Artist: Jim Peera

The following week I was ready and eager to install it for her. But when I got there, she wasn't home and left a note with the building concierge for me to leave it there for her. After repeated calls to her the next day, I didn't hear from her. I knew something was wrong. Finally on the third day, the building manager called me into her office to come collect the work of art I had made for the woman. When I got there, my piece was sitting in a big garbage basket. *"Mrs. O's daughter told me to return this to you. She was furious that you'd even make a disgusting piece like this. I can't believe you'd create such a thing. Do yourself a favor Jim, stick to cleaning carpets!"* exclaimed the distraught condominium manager. I was unhappy, disappointed and confused. I quickly reached into my wallet where her check still sat uncashed and handed it to the manager to give to her. Until that day, no one at that condominium tower had seen my art. And it forever changed the way they saw me — for the worse.

Mrs. O's story demonstrates the disempowering condition that many of us can relate to: an inability to own up to our emotions, our resistance to unclog some truths and our lost opportunity to arrive at a place of reckoning. And without this reckoning, there is no clear path to change. From my viewpoint, art was the necessary catalyst for the mother and daughter to have the opportunity to arrive at that place of reckoning by connecting to their authentic emotions. I figured if they both saw a powerful visual image of what emotions they were repressing, the truth would trigger and motivate them to take the necessary action, i.e, to kick out the manipulative gigolo.

But I never knew if that came to be. At the time I took the rejection as an insult and never called Mrs. O or saw her face again. Was my artwork too raw to unpack the truth? Or was it exactly the medicine that they needed? Were they just too ashamed to show their vulnerability and is that why they returned the piece? It amounted to a missed opportunity from my perspective.

Both Mrs. O's story and my boarding school experiences serve as lessons of inspiration at The Center. The idea is to make it easier for people (artists and the dormant artists) to delve past any superficiality or gender predispositions and honor their emotional receptors with ease. Whether you're a man trying to better relate to women, be more sensitive to their needs and not lose your power or a woman trying to preserve her autonomy in a relationship — the arts are a highly effective truth serum and a bridge to honor our true feelings. Much of it can be through dialoguing with poetry, expressing with creative exercises or being on a deep journey through storytelling and sound healing. All of these modes are intended to unpeel layers of resistances; fear, ego, judgment and pretense and expose vulnerability that shows strength of character — especially in men. As a sensitive man, preserving my personal power is important for maintaining my identity. I don't let any woman seduce, coerce, trap or shame me into relinquishing it.

And many have tried doing that in my adventurous life. By being grounded, strong and staying on a higher path, it helps my energy flow in motion without surrendering to low-vibrational or mal-intentioned forces.

CREATE YOUR EMPOWERMENT SPACE

In order to set the right conditions for you to be grounded, empowered and honor your emotions — you may want to prepare an empowerment space for yourself. I know of many women who do this, and I encourage my fellow men to create one as well to help retain your personal power, joy and inner peace after a hard day's work.

You can implement this healing space very quickly and easily in the privacy of our own home by creating a little sacred area that matches your personality. It can have a small rug with a coffee table and few items on it to get you started. It's your personal healing refuge where you can display inspirational and empowering books, poetry, art, candles, healing crystals, hand drums, photos, Tibetan bowls, gratitude bottle, etc. Typically, it's a closet-sized space and expands as needed — a 'go to' space when you're down and need to reconnect with Spirit and uplift yourself. On certain occasions, you may feel comfortable inviting close friends and relatives to share this sacred space with you. If your circle of friends grows, you may want to expand this idea into a dedicated empowerment room or a larger area. In time, it could evolve into holding the space for private healing/metaphysical gatherings and parties. In this case, for it to be effective, the environment and the host (you) cannot be sterile but authentic, inspiring and all-embracing. Your ego, judgment, pretense and fear must be diminished. In order to have open dialogue and honest engagement, it requires you to sweeten the creative medicine with a homey feel and a fun atmosphere without restrictions. By making people feel comfortable, they'll stay longer. By having them release their feelings without judgment or rules, they'll express more freely. By getting everyone to share their stories, they'll be unafraid to show their softer and vulnerable side. By listening and showing empathy, they'll connect authentically. By providing a light and fun-filled ambience, they'll feel uplifted. By treating them with unconditional love, they'll come back. This is how my wife and I expanded our small empowerment space into an empowerment home and then took the leap of faith towards opening a large public empowerment sanctuary, called Healium Center!

Practice The Healium Way

VULNERABILITY EXERCISE: This exercise is geared toward men as they have a more difficult time showing their vulnerability. If you're a woman who has a man in her life who could use this exercise, this is your chance to share this with them. Instead of going on a hunting, fishing or camping trip with your men friends and "hanging out with the boys" doing manly and macho fun activities such as shooting animals, hooking fish, seeing a ballgame, going to a strip club, talking about women in sexist ways, etc., do something different. Go see an opera or a play in your city, then cap the night off with having a fun discussion about the experience over some adult beverages. You'll be amazed how you have untapped the sensitivity and vulnerability of your macho partner.

A Healium body-art installation: shooting an arrow of love!

Principle #9
Learning To Self-Care

"To err is human. To learn is divine."
— Alexander Pope

In Part 1, I took you through some examples of people (including my family members) who outsourced their responsibility by relinquishing their power to others that resulted in their own loss of personal agency. In this Principle, I demonstrate how self-care and self- reliance becomes critical for regaining our power, as it teaches us to have personal responsibility and matching it up with positive action. Mastering this Principle makes it difficult to blame others and fall for excuses and victimization tactics. This shift will empower you to be an individual who is not needy or attached to anybody or anything — ultimately reducing your stress and anxiety. But how do we become so dependent on others and submit to be led by other people throughout our lives? Not surprisingly, it has its origins in early childhood with our parents, our schools and our environment.

A common condition starts with "parent-helicoptering" that seems quite harmless until it converts into a more permanent condition, where it can suffocate our ability to think for ourselves make decisions and take charge of our destiny. A second catalyst I've observed at The Center is in the form of early childhood domestic abuse — conditioning, silencing and demoralizing you out of fear. If you grow up in an overprotective and/or privileged family, your safety nets and entitlements can also contribute to your weakness.

At school, we get easily 'indoctrinated' as opposed to being 'educated' by our teachers and continue to attach to people, dogmas and systems looking for self-improvement and guidance into adulthood. You can argue that some of this is necessary for our own growth and security. But we become habituated to looking outward and expecting to be protected and 'saved' by others. And it shouldn't be that way. Consider the analogies of training wheels on bikes and floatation rings for swimmers. Once we're capable and confident to do the activities on our own, we remove the safety nets. This teaches us to be independent and learn how not to fall or sink. But as adults, many of us have become so trained not to fail that we're looking to a fallback position to keep us safe, comforted and risk-averse; as when we were kids. These fallback positions come in the form of a particular leader, a dogma, a philosophy — even drugs and technology. We can't seem to function without them.

This overreliance on other people, methods and machines is a disturbing fact that results in many of us being incapable of self-caring or making important decisions without external influences. In order for you to go from ordinary to *extra*ordinary, you must be self-reliant and let go of all your training wheels and ride life's journey on your own terms. Remember, you're not only an adult now, but you are your own healer. In fact, as we've alluded to throughout the book, you're your own self-designated creative and spiritual doctor. Therefore, you must think for yourself, be self-motivated and trust in your own instincts. When you do this, you'll pat yourself on the back for doing well and not absolve yourself of mistakes when you make them.

OUR SELF-CORRECTING ABILITY

Although we've gone overboard with our obsession of looking outward for our self-improvement, we all do have the innate self-correcting ability to realign ourselves by changing our ways and shifting our thoughts. But most of us adults are not going to fix ourselves until we realize how disempowered we are and become aware of some deficiencies within us. This awareness can start when you notice how life's coping rubber-band doesn't stretch as it used to for you. In fact, you realize it snaps a lot faster and you're a lot more fragile and needy as a person. Sometimes you notice how you've become a functional crybaby, preferring to suffer internally instead of voicing your displeasure to society assertively. I can site other examples and symptoms, but at some point though, as an adult you'll have to intentionally make the effort to cut the cords of your unhealthy dependencies, or you will stay miserable and unhappy in your weakened mind and insulated world.

One of the prerequisites to your self-reliance and self-care is to build resiliency. Similar to a muscle that needs to be used to stay strong, a human being needs to flex all areas of the body, mind and soul — to fully harness its full potential and power. When we stretch and test our limits, we become better at dialing up or down and achieving a healthier equilibrium. The Covid-19 experience should be a textbook resilient-builder for us. I see the pandemic crisis as a hard but necessary lesson to test our society's flexibility. What if we view it as a healthy catalyst that exposes the fissures of our unhealthy rigidity and dependency on our comforts, luxuries, machines and set patterns of living? Or will these lessons be forgotten over time? No matter how you see it, we're heading into a direction of human-to-human dis-connectivity like never before. And we will need to bend in our ways and adapt if we plan to take care of ourselves better. The robots are giving us a false sense of comfort and safety. The seduction of AI (artificial intelligence) will induce us into becoming mush-brained and lazy creatures of dependency. We already see an insurgence of virtual and online platforms trying to steal our time and grab our attention 24 hours a day.

But as social creatures we'll need to find a healthy balance and take charge of our own wellness without being glued to computer screens for all our answers. Indeed, holistic self-expression and creativity will be our weapon to beat the programmed robots.

Suppose we spent less time watching other experts tell us what to do and used our own brain to solve our respective problems? Instead of waiting for a professional to guide us, can we educate ourselves on a particular subject matter and trust in leading ourselves? As an example, if you're unhappy at work, instead of asking an online therapist or psychic for guidance, you know what to do: take charge of your own happiness and fire yourself. Alternatively, we need not wait for any leader(s) or experts to come along to improve our economic or social situation. When you start understanding that you have the built-in-ability to self-care, adapt and guide your own life without constant external forces of inspiration or empowerment, it will release you of all dependency on others.

I am not asking you to totally ditch the experts and your high-tech toys, but to take baby steps to reduce your over-reliance on them and rebalance yourself. A self-reliant mindset is a liberating and powerful state of being that transforms us from ordinary to *extra*ordinary individuals. So give it a shot. What have you to lose except your unhealthy interdependence on others? It is empowering to prescribe ourselves a self-care regimen and navigate our lives under any crisis. We better keep practicing this as a lifestyle habit, because there will be many more natural and unnatural disasters to survive.

Is it therefore possible that we could each adapt to our new environment and activate our own therapist, our own guru, our own life coach, our own priest, our own doctor — even our own psychic?

OUR BUILT-IN PSYCHIC GUARDIAN

The simple answer is, yes! — we're complex but highly adaptable creatures wired to accomplish all of those things. We are not only gifted with the Divine medicines to self-correct our imbalances, but we are also endowed with the power of intuition to help us navigate life's unpredictable path. This Divine gift, also called gut feeling, extrasensory perception, sixth sense, hunch, funny feeling, foresight and so forth, is our internal psychic mechanism that cannot be ignored as a powerful self-caring tool. It's our built-in psychic guardian. Instead of outsourcing this task to the many mind readers such as psychics and soothsayers, why not connect with the portal of Divine guidance within ourselves. It is a highly effective tool that's available to us for free. Historically, women have been viewed as more intuitive than men, but there is no scientific evidence to support that theory. Perhaps women trust their gut feelings more than men, and they do tend to readily believe in ghosts, magic, fate, karma and so forth. Men, on the other hand, are more analytical and take longer to be convinced. As an unconventional man, I'm definitely a believer in paranormal phenomena, especially intuition. I've used the intuitive tool to my advantage many times and encourage everyone, regardless of gender, to activate it too. When I've ignored or doubted the power of intuition, I've always paid a heavy price. In contrast, when I am in alignment with my psychic guardian within, I'll avoid catastrophic results, and even reap many benefits for myself. Once I'm in tune with my intuition, I don't hesitate to take immediate action to make the appropriate moves. Some major examples of this include, jumping ship from tech stocks before the dot-com bubble in the late '90s, investing in downtrodden properties prior to Atlanta's economic post-Olympic boom and selling a chunk of my real estate holdings a few months before the sh*t hit the fan during the Great Recession of 2007.

So have faith in the powers of your psychic guardian within, and it will serve you well.

Practice The Healium Way

SELF-CARE EXERCISE: Pick a person (famous personality or a close contact) who you respect and follow regularly. It could be a religious leader, parent, life coach, yoga instructor, etc. Now turn that person off in your life for a week. No physical or virtual contact. Note what happens to you during this period.

Do you go through a grieving process? Do you miss the person's advice/leadership/ presence? What are you doing to fill the void? Note the sensations in yourself to substitute that person. Do you start taking charge of the missing activity or are you lost without it? It's quite interesting to see how dependent you are on that person to provide the service. Can you be self-motivated to activate your own learned skills and self-care without this person? This is your test to become more independent and a more powerful U.

Enjoying an Open Jam session at Healium

Principle #10
Resisting The Art of Replicating

"Imagination is more important than knowledge."
— Albert Einstein

Creativity has been proven to reduce stress, boost energy, heal emotions, increase empathy, stimulate brain connectivity

and induce many other positive health benefits. Yet we are losing the ability to harvest our mind's raw imagination, find inspiration and keep the spark of creativity alive. Our Center has revealed this condition well with the non-participants. With the advent of advanced technology, robots, virtual reality and sophisticated software — machines are now doing that innate activity for us.

It's not necessarily a bad thing living a *Jetsons* lifestyle, moving a mouse to create a work of art, and accomplishing scores of other cool creations in a matter of seconds. The power of new technology enhances our brain functions and intelligence and even makes life more fun and speedier. Global crises from climate change to pandemics are further exacerbating our dependence on technology, as our behaviors and lifestyle habits are becoming more sedentary, introverted and at risk of permanent changes. As noted earlier, this over-reliance on computers is making us lazier, sterile and uninspiring. In the arts arena, the insurgence of online educational art platforms are convenient, but are impeding our imagination and further reducing our deficient social skills. We are showing signs of being afraid to open our mind and explore activities beyond the safe, the predictable and the comfortable. Now more than ever we must not turn into emotionless humanoids — using technology as a crutch to avoid connecting with our Soul and interacting in holistic ways with our fellow humans. A healthier balance is required. But the problem is not limited to online platforms, it is also prevalent in the increasing 'structured' in-person experiences associated with creativity. I scratch my head when I see people going to the various conventional "sip & paint" places where you basically replicate certain preset designs such as ducks or a sunset scene. At best it's a selfie-style moment that's entertaining and an excuse to get out of the house. But at worst it suffocates people's creative receptors and encourages a soul-sucking *paint-by-numbers* habit. Instead of using art to open minds and fill our vacated Souls, our capitalist model shamelessly commoditizes it.

Thankfully, the world is full of inspiration — even in dark times. Therefore, we must resist replicating art whenever possible and instead create from the repository of our own Divine imagination. It's there inside of us, and it just needs to be tapped with a little creative motivation and discipline. Celebrating the creative genius within each of us is to understand that our Divine nature is raw, unbound and limitless — the epitome of freedom. Its beauty lies in its unmanicured state with all its flaws, overgrowth, roughness and uniqueness. By sanitizing and changing this environment to match our man-made domesticated mindset, we f*ck ourselves up. It's no different when taking animals from the jungle to put them in cages for our pleasure. That's because our man-made self is our entrapped state of being, that easily deviates from its original liberated Divine condition. It's part and parcel of our flawed self.

Sadly, we do this with our inner-creative all the time. We'll box ourselves into a programmed mindset and operate on a caged man-made slower frequency — and then normalize the behavior. The Healium Way is about being aware of this unhealthy state of mind and taking steps to undo it. And it's never too late. When we get out of our predisposed safety zones and reopen the brain receptors that have been dormant, we may experience initial discomfort. But as soon as we surrender to the idea of trusting our own creative power, our mind's eye starts to soak in the wondrous possibilities all around us and effortlessly ignites the fire within. You can start reigniting your imagination pathway with simple exercises such as doodling while on the phone, daydreaming, star-gazing, composing a random song in the shower, creating mind images in your head with moving clouds, improvising with items you have lying around the house to fulfill a task, inventing something with makeshift items, creating a delicious dish from leftovers. The list is endless!

INVENTION SESSION WITH DAD

Just ask both my kids how important lighting the imagination fire has been in their own artistic and intellectual growth. While they were both in middle school, I concocted a Sunday morning breakfast playtime activity I called *"Invention Session with Dad."* My goal was to get them to open their imagination by improving on our ubiquitous products and inventing a better mousetrap. Each week I chose a mundane household item laying around the house such as a cereal box, milk bottle, toaster, etc., and gave them an hour to brainstorm and develop a better product. At first, they balked at me, but soon looked forward to the activity. As a part-time inventor myself, I gave them some inspiration but left them to design and innovate freely. It was quite a brain-expanding fun exercise and to this day they appreciate how it helped them flourish creatively and take risks as adults. At Healium Center, we encourage a similar thinking out-of-the-box philosophy in everything we do. The importance of imagination becomes clearer when we understand its role in creating the best you. There's nothing more empowering and rewarding when you take the time to write your own piece of music, paint from your own mind's eye, beat to your own drum, dance your own unique style and embrace the creative genius within yourself. It is beautiful to see the dormant artist become unbound with the unseen worlds that emerge from this practice. Moreover, you don't have to be perfect and can make mistakes without beating yourself up about it.

KEEP JAMMIN'

Take the story of a young man named Miles who came regularly to our *Open Jam*. Each time he got on stage with people, his default position was to initiate a beat from a particular pop song. He was comfortable playing covers of songs but quite nervous just making up something and improvising — as is the norm at a Healium jam session. If Miles wasn't familiar with a song, he'd sit it out. He told me how he'd always played open mics but never freestyled. He enjoyed himself, but hardly let loose and was self-critical. I encouraged him to relax, have an open mind and just have fun. I guess he thought I was trying to change him as he stopped coming to The Center for a couple of months. One evening, though, Miles returned without saying a word to me and darted straight into the basement to jam. He was anxious and ready to find release after a hard day's work. About 90 minutes later, he took a break. He was sweating and emanated a highly energetic aura. This different, smiling person's eyes were full of joy after finally having a fun and satisfying jam session. He apologized to me, saying he had not been coming to Healium because he'd been trying various 'open mic' places around town. He then told me how nothing was more uplifting and therapeutic for him than the freestyle Healium Open Jam. What's more, he had started writing his own music and that the confidence to do so had boosted his self-esteem and even improved his love life. Other jammers came up to Miles, complimented him on his great set, then took him back in to have more fun. Miles is a good example of what happens when you remove the fears, judgment and mind viruses that hold you hostage to a comfortable and conventional way of doing things. He also learned that he had to *find inspiration* and *tap into the flow!*

FINDING INSPIRATION

The world "inspiration" means being "in spirit." Therefore, if you are from Spirit; you must be connected to the unbound sea of inspiration, right? It's logical thinking, but it's not so simple for many people. At our Center we often find inspiration to be a struggle for newcomers. And we know why. We've already uncovered many imbalances and resistances that play a role in that conundrum to include; our environment, thoughts, distractions and addictions. Yet, it's important to mention that we don't find inspiration — it finds us.

How's that, you say? It has to do with being in its path of alignment. It shows up when we're ready to connect, receive and collaborate with something — without resisting its force-field. This is especially true in art. I've witnessed guests at our Center walk pass captivating pieces of art in a gallery and not appreciate any connection with it. But once they get in the present, remove all distractions and look closely — they connect and find value and curiosity in them. Once connected, we let the source of the inspiration talk to their Soul by transporting them into the depths of their consciousness, without any preconceptions, doubt or rules. And pretty soon, magic happens and the flame of inspiration is alight. Miles is a good example of someone who did all that and more that evening at Healium — and transformed himself into an *extra*ordinary healer/musician.

TAPPING INTO THE FLOW

Miles also achieved a sense of *"Flow"*; the mental state of being completely present and fully immersed in a task. In The Healium

Way, flow happens when we surrender and allow ourselves to tap into the universal energy of consciousness that's void of any critical self-judgment, distractions or even awareness. It is about oneness and the lack of mental effort and analytical thinking. In this state we are fully immersed in the moment and have graceful and effortless attention toward a joyful activity. Meditation, music jamming and freestyle dancing are great examples of being in this state of flow. The first step into this state is the hardest; getting out of our head and banish any doubt, fear or judgment from our thoughts. Because once we're in the groove of flow, its powerful momentum boosts the brain's neurochemicals to open our imagination and release limitless creative juices. I've experienced this condition countless times myself as an artist and it is pure medicine for the Soul. In the above examples, the participants willingly participated and entered their respective creative zones in order to experience their respective flow. But not all of us have the ease of surrendering to our inner-creative. In fact, most people are reluctant to enter a creative zone. Here, let me share with you a few do's and don'ts that will prepare your brain to reduce resistance, strengthen its imagination receptors and help you to experience flow.

Without getting bogged down into the complex frequencies and speed of the brain, let's focus instead on the five types of neuro-electrical voltages that oscillate at any given time. These brain waves are *alpha* (during relaxed & passive attention); *beta* (during anxiety or external attention mode); *gamma* (during focus and concentration); *theta* (deeply relaxed and inward focused) and *delta* (sleep). For the purposes of firing our creative receptors and inducing imagination, we need to generate more of the *alpha* and *theta* states. Both of these waves are important and do coexist for the inner-creative to activate without apprehension or resistance. The alpha is often stimulated during playing music, dancing, walking, making art, etc., while the theta activates during meditation, sound healing, praying, etc.

The *DO's* that help me stimulate both of these frequencies are singing in the shower, aerobic exercise, meditating, doing yoga, deep breathing exercises, closing the eyes while practicing visualization, drumming, smiling more frequently, laughing randomly and being in nature as much as possible. The first *DON'T* is making excuses not to try out the *DO's* listed above. The second *DON'T* is refraining from looking at your cellphone or computer at least 20-30 minutes before going to sleep (for a better night's sleep), and after waking up (to set the right mood and attitude for an optimum day). This *DON'T* is a hard habit to break for most of us, as we've chained ourselves to our all-encompassing and ubiquitous smartphones. But it's an essential test of our willpower and for our mental wellbeing and for achieving a healthy balance. With our baby-step formula, you can start with 10 minutes and gradually work up to 20 minutes before you touch any computer-related instrument. Use this short digital purge to do some exercises to help open your flow receptors.

Practice The Healium Way

IMAGINATION EXERCISE: This exercise will take about an hour. Put on your headphones and plug it in your cell phone. Go on YouTube and search for "The Planets by Gustav Holst." Lie down comfortably on a rug, close your eyes (use eye mask, if needed) and play one of seven pieces of the symphonic ensemble. Each piece is about eight minutes. Start with Venus or Mars. As you are immersed in the music, let your imagination run wherever it takes you. You will travel in space and see things with your mind's eye without much effort. When done, take out a piece of paper and unpack everything from this journey while it's fresh. It will be full of vivid imagery and emotion. Now take all this information and see if you can write a poem from it or create a visual piece of art using mix media, paints, charcoal, crayons, etc.

Principle #11
Understanding The Power of Surrealism

"To be a surrealist means barring from your mind all remembrance of what you have seen, and being always on the lookout for what has ever been."
— Rene Magritte

I've always believed that art gives us the power to self-express, but surrealism gives us the power to connect. Indeed, the form of art called *surrealism* is without doubt the most effective, adventurous, easy and fun way I've found to enjoy and express one's creative journey. Not only does this style of artistic expression excel in opening minds and imagination, but it allows for limitless subjectivity and freedom. It also is by far the most effective art style to express dark and repressed emotions. For this latter reason, it is my favorite healing art genre. I find it remarkable that anyone can empty the contents of their heart and mind without any artistic training and create a satisfactory emotional release — for both the artist and the viewer. And neither artist nor viewer has to interpret the art in the same way. It is for these compelling reasons that The Healium Way recommends that you appreciate and use surrealist art forms as much as you can. It is an extremely powerful, highly addictive practice that anyone can excel in. At The Center, we dedicate most of our gallery space to thought-provoking surrealist art and encourage ordinary people to unleash their stories by using their art discipline of choice. As a self-taught surrealist myself, I've been fascinated with this art form since meeting Picasso in the flesh in Paris. I was also exposed to it as a child in Africa when my family curated and cultivated one of the largest ebony wood ateliers for the Makonde people, a small ethnic tribe in East Africa. These artisans used hand tools to meticulously carve and bring to life, ebony; one of the rarest and hardest woods on earth into mesmerizing and beautiful surrealism-style sculptures. Each piece was imbued with such power and induced raw, emotional responses to such a degree that iconic movers and shakers from Indira Gandhi to Robert Kennedy, who visited my family's famous art and gem destination, didn't leave without taking one as a collector's item.

MAMADI'S SHETANIS

My late uncle Mohamed Peera (known as Mamadi by the Africans), who was written up in Newsweek magazine during the 1960's for pioneering the *shetani-styled* (spirit-world) Makonde carvings, explained to me how he inspired the carvers to produce such captivating works: *"I gave them the free hand to unleash on a log of black ebony wood whatever was lurking in their deepest and darkest corner of their heart and mind. I told them not to be afraid to take risks and to just have fun expressing their stories."* This simple yet brilliant laissez-faire style of leadership was the cornerstone of my family's success with this surrealist modern art form that left an indelible mark on 20th century East African art. Coined as the *Picassos of Africa,* the surrealist African carvers and their freestyle *shetani* masterpieces were the inspiration and influence for my own surrealist clay sculpting endeavors. I recall the exact day when this art form entered and changed my life. It manifested in a spontaneous burst of creative combustion without any artistic training or specific plan. As my wife and I were cleaning up after my son's eighth birthday party, my wife asked me what I wanted to do with the unused play dough that was left on the table.

Instead of throwing it in the garbage, I grabbed a big gob and started playing with it. I had no idea what I was doing, but it was therapeutic and fun. I'd never touched this media before, but its soft, gooey texture was relaxing to mold in my hands, especially after a hectic day tending to a dozen little kids. Soon I got attached to messing with the play dough. While drinking a glass of red wine, I found myself immersed in a fantasy world for a couple of hours. Sitting at the dining room table, I formed a spirit-like creature with a large set of testicles hanging from its crotch. It was the most fun I had since I was a child building sand castles.

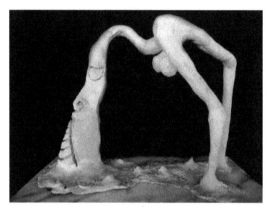

Jim's first surrealism play dough artwork

I showed the art piece to my wife the following morning, who laughed and didn't know what to make of it. Both my children were stunned when they saw it, saying it reminded them of the *shetani* ebony Makonde carvings on the shelf. My adult friends thought I was expressing my male virility in odd and disturbing ways. One person said it was "wild and crazy," while another advised me to see a sex therapist. I guess it disturbed him, or maybe it revealed his own sexual inadequacies. Surrealism art will expose people to images that may make them uncomfortable. The sculpture became a conversation piece for adults and kids who visited us.

All their commentaries were priceless. I was proud to have created something from nothing and was anxious to make more. Soon, I paid a visit to an art supply store and invested in a kiln, a bag of clay and some sculpting tools. So began my serendipitous foray into 3-D surrealism clay sculpting, and I approached this new hobby with passion and purpose. Through trial and error, I developed my own unique mixed media style and to date I've created more than a hundred pieces and dedicated a special gallery at my Center to showcase my wild and crazy creations. This rule-free, non-judgmental approach can turn anyone into an artist. It's also fascinating to observe the audience's reactions and interpretations from a variety of lenses. Since you cannot teach or learn surrealism, it asks nothing of you in return — just that you surrender to your imagination and flow with it. I actually developed a style where I incorporate all my broken pieces and mistakes into one augmented work. In surrealism, noninterference and unbound freedom ignites the flame. Other artistic styles are rooted in more structure and less raw emotional expression.

There's nothing wrong with making a meticulous geometric mandala, drawing cartoons, creating modern abstract art, painting portraits or doing plein d'air landscapes, of course. All of these forms are great in their own ways, and there's not a one-size-fits-all approach to creating. But unless you've got time to take art classes or are a natural-born artist, I suggest expressing your emotions and dialoguing with surrealism as your first choice. Unlike realism where you're bound and judged by duplicating or replicating reality or in abstract painting where paint, patterns and colors are juxtaposed and/or randomly splattered, surrealism offers a depth that fires the Soul and engages the mind simultaneously. Instead of trying to be perfect at drawing the human body or painting a lotus flower, you never need to worry about technical correctness in surrealism. You're simply immersed in the emotional value of your work. It's amazing how it puts you, the creator/artist/healer, into a seat of power. Whether it's with a blank canvas, a sheet of paper or a lump of clay, you get the unfettered freedom and free will to transform your imagination into whatever vision, fantasy or emotion you please. In effect, surrealism celebrates the perfection of our imperfections and validates our message without seeking validation. How f*cking cool is that!

"The magic of art lies in its subjective interpretation."
- Jim Peera

Tribute to Mohamed Peera

Shetani Makonde Carvings

Practice The Healium Way

SURREALISM EXERCISE: Pick an episode in your life as far back as your childhood that is an uncomfortable memory of a traumatic event. It could be a recurring abusive family member (physical or vocal), a bully at school, a serious accident, a drug addiction, etc. Now pick a creative medium (drawing, painting, sculpting, or mixed media) and lock yourself in a quiet room. If you need to loosen your nerves, get a drink (one glass of wine or a bottle of beer is fine). But don't get inebriated or high on any substance. Turn your cellphone on mute and have no distractions. Play some ambient music and get comfortable on a table to start creating.

Replay in your mind's eye one of the specific events and don't be afraid to revisit that troubling moment. Close your eyes and travel back in time to that specific point. It's going to be hard but stick with it. Start jotting some words on paper of your current emotions as you recall the event. Take note of your body, breath, blood pressure etc. Using those words starts releasing your emotions. It's normal to cry out loud or be angry. Now unleash your dark emotions and pain creatively. Just go for it. There's no shame or guilt. Paint a screaming child, draw a stick figure, mold play dough in any form to make your point. Mix and match in any way you see your mind guiding you. Do not get frustrated that your art is not looking good or matching up to your internal lens. Just get it out as best as you can.

Be sure to take your time with it. If it's neat and pretty, you're doing it wrong. Let it be real, messy and raw. You're releasing sh*t, after all. But it's good sh*t that has been marinating and eating you up inside for many years. Once you're satisfied with your piece, give it a name and sign it. If you can, write a couple of sentences of what it's all about. Now congratulate yourself for having created a highly therapeutic surrealism piece that feels liberating.

You just became an artist/healer!

Principle #12
Being An Active Participant of Life

"Yesterday is history, Tomorrow is a mystery and today is a gift.
That's why they call it the present."
— Eleanor Roosevelt

In order to live a full life without regrets, we must be willing to be active participants in it. We must be ready to not only take life by the horns, but ride it with passion and appreciate its beauty all around us. In this Principle, we're about making *new memories,* as opposed to revisiting or relishing old ones. So when someone asks you to participate in a fun activity, such as dancing or drumming, you don't say *"I used to do that when I was younger"* or *"I don't know how"* — but give The Healium Way reply *"Yes, that sounds great,!"* Because we're trying to be *active* participants, rather than being passive and letting life pass us by, thinking of your younger past or being in your head thinking about something else. This philosophy will keep us young at heart and have limitless joy at any age. It helps to have a curiosity and thirst for tasting a little bit of everything on life's menu without excuses, procrastination or reservation.

Our prescription to being in alignment with life is about;

1. **Having the right attitude.**

2. **Embracing the present.**

3. **Loosening our grip.**

Not surprisingly, applying these three traits in everyday life help us reduce loneliness, depression, boredom and monotony, which are common among many seniors and retirees.

HAVING THE RIGHT ATTITUDE

According to a Stanford Research Institute study, the path to success consists of **88** percent attitude and only **12** percent education. This doesn't mean that education is of little importance, but does demonstrate how vital it is to foster the proper attitude in regards to your overall outlook. Having the right attitude makes a huge difference in the way we participate in life. With all the highs and lows of our human condition, we're bound to be on many emotional roller coasters on any given day. However, if we set our attitude dial to *uplift* at the start of each day, as opposed to *Debby downer,* we're better positioned to overcome whatever twists and turns life throws our way. (See *'AM power boost'* toward the end of book). I find keeping a smiley face, greeting people without judgment, making myself and other people laugh, detaching from fear, practicing a daily gratitude mantra and having self-love all help me have a positive and empowering attitude.

The Healium Way is about transitioning from a lowered vibration to an uplifted state by your own volition and intention. At our Center, we've made having a *can-do* attitude part and parcel of our ecosystem. If you come in with a sh*tty attitude, you have a right to it as long as you know you can do better to change it. Because if you're going to stay in that condition for long, it will not serve you well. By holding a space that fosters unlimited personal growth and creativity, each individual is mentally bathed in a ray of light, love and hope —to inspire the transformation.

Since attitude is contagious, it is rare to find a participant at The Center walking out with a worse attitude than they walked in with. The Healium Way's intention toward an uplifted attitude is achieved with a mindset that visualizes the best results out of any situation. We then allow the universe to take care of the rest!

EMBRACING THE PRESENT

In order to experience true joy, we must choose to live more often in the moment. In order to live for the moment, we must learn to disconnect from the busyness in our head and reconnect with the present. We can't change what happened yesterday, nor what will happen tomorrow because that's beyond our control. But the present moment is in our hands — and it is where we must learn to live to the fullest. Living in the moment, (aka mindfulness), is a state of active, open and intentional attention to the present. When we're mindful, we realize that we are not our thoughts but rather an observer of our thoughts. By being our own observer, we stop thinking about doing other things and focus on the activity or situation before us with less distractions. So for instance, a mindful person walking on the beach takes in their breath, heartbeat, sense of smell, sounds and visual imagery — all the beauty around. You will smell the ocean's saltiness, feel the sea breeze, hear sounds of the crashing waves, and will pay attention to the flight of the seagulls, the pelicans diving for fish and the surfers riding their awesome waves. You will experience all the wonders of the moment without having any external distractions, say, a business deal or some personal matter. The voices in your head will become less pronounced and you'll be more in sync with nature and your surroundings. In this moment, you must have the intention to stay present with your environment by clearing your head of all clutter and simply breathing in and out the love and beauty that envelops you. You cannot allow any resistant forces to enter your thoughts. You will stop doing and will start being. Sadly, though, many people don't get this mindfulness memo. On my many trips to the beach, I've often seen how few adults actually embrace the present or participate in the beach or water activities. Most walk with their heads down, or are fixated on their cellphones, and many more simply sit under their umbrellas reading or watching kids have all the fun. So yes, they're at the beach; but they're not with the beach. They *don't participate* in all its awesomeness and wonder. Unfortunately, instead of staying in the now, we allow our wandering minds to drift away and attach to something in the past or the future. A common culprit of not staying connected to the present is our inability to *loosen our grip* on life's many self-induced distractions.

LOOSENING YOUR GRIP

There are three main distractions that hold a tight grip on us and must be loosened to participate freely in life's adventure: our attachment to *old stiff habits, money* and *wireless technology*. I'll discuss them briefly.

Old stiff habits. We're all mired in our old stiff habits that need to be assessed for their usefulness in modern society. These habits emanate from years of sitting in restrictive boxes such as our upbringing, culture and religious beliefs. Most of them we hold on too tightly without much thought, and they get in the way of our full participation with life. It is important that we reassess these conservative habits that inhibit our freedom. I'm not asking you to totally undo them from your life but to begin loosening your grip on them. I experienced an example of this during a guest visit to our Center. The participant, a Jehovah Witness, told me that her religion had forbidden her from freestyle dancing, drinking wine, looking at controversial art and seeing nude bodies being painted. Since we had all these activities going on that evening, she abruptly left and missed out on an amazing night of creativity and upliftment. Yes, it was her prerogative to do so, but had the woman simply loosened her ways, stayed a little longer to observe and appreciate the activities, she might have just opened her mind and would have had a little creative fun!

Money. Besides loosening our grip on stiff habits, money is another unhealthy distraction that gets in the way of participating in life's fun. I've observed quite a bit of this in my real estate world. That's why we cannot use money as a crutch, a weapon or an excuse for inaction. Because having money doesn't define you, it reveals you. The most self-actualized people know to use money only as a tool and not as an end to all means that consumes their life. By not being addicted to money, they stay humble in a healthier balance and are money's best custodian. The way I see it, life is a roulette game in many ways. We're rolling the dice each day hoping to wake up healthy the next day. So why would we leave a lot of our life's chips (money) on the table and have it enjoyed by others or get evaporated by taxes? I know of many people who make their life's "bucket list" as they approach retirement. I've never understood this philosophy. Why not start fulfilling your bucket list with life's pleasures and memories starting today — at a younger age?

There's a well-known African mindset that I grew up with and was advised by my parents to avoid. In Swahili, the term is a *kesho mungu* (pronounced kay-show moo-ngoo) individual, or a "Tomorrow God" person. *Kesho mungu* describes people who are not responsible or smart with money, and leaves their future in the hands of God. Typically, when this type of person receives their wages on Friday, they blow it on the weekend and are broke by Monday. It is the opposite of being an avid saver and a thrifty person. Ironically, neither one of those mindsets offers a healthy balance. The saver personality tends to be a penny pincher and a hoarder by being overprotective of their money — and loses out on enjoying life, while the *kesho mungu* person lives day to day without a plan for tomorrow, his children or his retirement. The Healium Way suggests you split the difference of the two philosophies as your lifestyle habit. It's your better way. Ultimately, we want to have a good balance between having our rainy day and retirement cushion on one hand, and loosening our grip on accumulating a pile of cash on the other — by enjoying life holistically. Therefore, whether you live a short life or a long one, choosing this balanced way is a hedge against not having any regrets. Personally, I want to have used up all the time, energy and most of my hard-earned money before I take my last breath on earth. How about you?

Wireless technology. The cellphone can be one of the most life-sucking devices that distracts us from enjoying life when used incorrectly. If you didn't already know, it is also spying on you when you're surfing the internet, checking your inboxes, looking at your stock portfolio, playing online games, watching porn and so forth. We must loosen our attachment to all types of time-robbing devices that amount to ubiquitous digital distractions. If not, we'll create a behavior pattern that is always in a coulda, shoulda, woulda or anxious state, also known as regret. For instance, when we're at our kid's sports game, instead of relishing in the activity, we'll be talking on the cell about an upcoming sports game on the television. When we're at the gym, instead of concentrating on working on our bodies, we're exercising our fingers on our cellphones. When we're eating a great meal, we're not appreciating and talking about the food in front of us, but about some other sh*t on our handheld computers. Over time we stop paying attention to simple yet wondrous events such as a beautiful sunset or a street musician playing a romantic song. I've seen enough of this in my travels and interactions with people in social settings. I can't count how many times my wife and I have gone to restaurants with live musicians who play their hearts out and hardly anyone appreciates their music. Most people are too busy texting, yakking and gobbling down their food. My wife and I make a point to applaud, cheer, walk up and tip the players. Depending on the ambience, we also take the initiative to dance and enjoy the moment without caring a flip who's watching. It's The Healium Way. Contrast this example to a sports bar where you'll encounter people being vocal, cheering and displaying high energy emotions watching a football, basketball or baseball game on televisions. I find myself wondering how often these same people display the same passion by actually *playing any* sports game. Alas, they don't: This is our sad reality, most adults have turned into spectators, preferring to be entertained by others and being passive observers of life.

PASSIVE OBSERVERS

Because we're not actively engaging in life, we've resigned to becoming a society of passive observers. When we don't practice interacting in any activity (creative, physical or mental), we fall into a habit of not appreciating the beauty and joy around us. Too many of us have also become destination-oriented and forget to enjoy the journey along the way. When we pay attention to the ride and keep our focus on the present, we are less anxious to get somewhere and more satisfied with the joy of experiencing everything along the way. By being involved and engaged in the creative process, we stop being observers of life. By being in alignment with the present, we ignite fun and spontaneity. By embracing the inner child, we play more and stay young at heart. By connecting with our Chi and Soul, we keep the flame burning longer. Is it possible to start looking at life as a fun and creative playground full of possibilities without making excuses about not having the time, the money or being stuck in a pattern of old stiff habits? Let's stop being self-critical and caring what others think of how we dance, sing, drum, throw a Frisbee or kick a ball. How about playing with your kids, dancing and skipping randomly on the sidewalk, drumming on your car's dashboard, singing in the shower, skating in the park, dancing with your partner, and so forth? Instead of texting "LOL" (laughing out loud) and clicking a smiley emoji to someone, how about getting out of the house and actually smiling and laughing out loud in nature or at a stranger without caring about it?

When I go walking in nature, I stay connected to it by partaking in its awe and paying attention to all the trees, animals, water elements and so forth. I'll often combine a cardio-benefiting walk with a creative twist to make it more interesting. Using my cellphone's camera in a positive way, I'll turn an ordinary nature walk into an *extra*ordinary outdoor adventure by taking pictures of things we take for granted such as leaves, insects, birds, butterflies and so forth. You'll be amazed how good of a photographer you are if you do this regularly. Each season offers a different surprise and wondrous element to connect with. In the fall, I'll go out discovering wild mushrooms in the forest and the autumn leaves in the mountains. In the spring, I'll enjoy the birth of the flowers and beauty of all the fauna. In the summer, instead of simply walking on the beach or laying on it reading a book, I'll play with the sand, get dirty and open my creative receptors. The beach offers a blank canvas to make spontaneous visual art with whatever is available: seashells, coconuts, bird feathers, rocks, driftwood, etc. It opens my imagination while being a relaxing, therapeutic and an extremely satisfying fun activity!

Jim being creative at the beach

Wherever you are, get in the habit of using your surroundings as your creative canvas and interacting with it. We often take our own city for granted and forget to participate in the many attractions and beauty it offers. So become a weekend tourist in your own backyard and plan a "staycation." Rent a nice room in a high-quality hotel and pamper yourself to a well-deserved weekend getaway and do things you've not done and visit places you've never seen as a resident. Take the subway, rent a bike, ride a horse and carriage, paddle a kayak, ride on a cable car, go to a day spa and partake in everything else your city offers. When you loosen your grip on your time, money, busyness, old habits and monotony, you'll watch life hand you more joy, beauty and satisfaction than ever.

THE PORSCHE EXPERIMENT

If you want to turbocharge your life's experience, as in dreaming of having a sports car, but you can't afford one or don't want the headaches of owning one — get creative. Rent one temporarily for fun, without being reckless. It will be a memorable adventure!

That's exactly what I did. I had a childhood dream from Africa, to drive a white Porsche sports car (a real version of the toy that I carried with me as a child on the plane from Africa), and I needed to get it out of my system. It was an item on my bucket list. Instead of being reckless and buying a depreciating asset (which I had the money to do), I did it The Healium Way and experienced its thrill by being a temporary owner. When Porsche had a one-month unlimited miles special deal, I jumped on the opportunity. For a couple thousand dollars, my wife and I had a blast of a lifetime touring the Appalachian mountains. As I zipped around the bends and valleys seated in an intoxicating driving-machine, I was simultaneously zipping-up my trauma wounds from Africa and detoxing my brain. Driving the German sports car, at times up to 100-plus mph, was therapy and fun all in one. The icing on the cake was getting a thumbs up by some folks and getting the middle finger from others. I smiled and waved on both occasions. As a bonus, driving the car was one of the most revealing tests in social psychology. I made a conscientious effort not to reveal to anyone — including my family, friends or Center's attendees — that the Porsche was a rental. I wanted to observe human behavior. What transpired was both disturbing and hilarious to witness as the varied reactions were mostly filled with envy. The joke, however, was on those people who turned their heads in insecurity, jealousy, revealing their flawed humanity, and looked like fools when they found out the truth. This is a precious lesson for all of us, and a testament to how being an active participant of life says as much about life's nonparticipants!

BEING A PARTICIPANT IN RETIREMENT

Until you know how to actively participate in life, you will have a hard time participating in your silver or golden years — whatever your definition of retirement is. Because for many people, the transition from a life of hard work, structure and deadlines into the opposite proposition can be a death knell. The excitement and anticipation of liberating yourself from the shackles of conformity quickly withers (usually after several months) as you've been addicted to the grind or have rusted your sparkplugs of free-spirited fun over the years. Lack of passion, inspiration and creativity, conventionality and boredom are often the prevailing conditions. As a retirement-bound CEO or a company employee, you're most likely suffering from *workbox indoctrination*. It's The Healium Way of understanding how your work kept you busy and how your matching environment (co-workers, physicality, corporate culture, boundaries, etc) mind-f*cked and domesticated your busyness. As a result, it will not be easy unplugging many hardwired work habits from your brain and switching from your 'busy-body self' into a 'chill-wave self.' Or going from an 'always doing' to a 'just being' individual. But when you master The Healium Way Principles, you can gradually reverse that situation. I call it the *"Retire with fire"* program. Think of it as a pre-retirement ignition switch where you'll incorporate The Healium Way to prepare you for the best fun and balance in your final stage of your life. The program is available on a personal and group basis. Contact me if you're interested in being a *'retire with fire'* graduate!

Practice The Healium Way

INTERACTION EXERCISE: Each day do something different and fun while being engaged at work, in transit, at home and at the park. Once again do not concern yourself with others around you. Do it "Healium-style." If you're in the car sitting in traffic listening to music, use your dashboard as a drum to tap and lift your mood. At work, laugh more regularly, engage with people with humor and in down times doodle at your desk. During lunch, instead of eating at a deli, take your food out to a park or outdoor area and have a spontaneous picnic.

At home, play your favorite music and dance, sing in the shower, play a board game with your partner or kids, be active in the garden, help prepare a meal in the kitchen. While at the park, take notice of nature and activate your inner photographer. Use your cellphone to capture all the beauty of the trees, birds, flowers, water elements and so on. Try to be in the present at all times and do this exercise for ONE WEEK. Then take note of how much connected and uplifted you feel just by doing these small, interactive things.

Principle #13
Keeping The Inner Child Alive

Do you remember a time when you were a kid playing in the rain, getting intentionally soaked by jumping in a pool of dirt and muddy water? Now as an adult, you're dodging any rain droplets on yourself and are walking so carefully around a puddle of water. This change is due to our societal programming of the adult behavioral protocol: to stay clean, dry and proper. But it's not just us adults who have shifted to being in an uninspiring, boring and rather ordinary state. Today's kids also are getting too serious for their own good. They're growing up with unlimited access to adult toys such as robots and computers that is dimming their creative spark and freestyle child play. Kids are too anxious to grow up — and adults are too serious to lighten up. It's quite sad to see this manifesting in our tech-heavy and overworked society. We can fix it by *Keeping the inner child alive* — reactivating and mining something that's there from birth. I am referring to the inner child within who is playful, fearless, footloose and bursting with creativity. As adults, we've lost our free spirit and become stiff, predictable and mundane. And it is costing us. The idea of being light-hearted and fancy-free is difficult for many of us, but paramount to a life of joy and contentment. A common problem with many people is learning to undo the two most common adult-programmed conditions that get in our way of having fun; structure and analysis. Both of these combine to hold us hostage to our inner child. The problem is further solidified when we transition from being single to getting married and having children. We take on many responsibilities, often spending more time on our kids than on ourselves. If we're financially successful, the rich life of luxuries and higher status often boxes us into a pretentious lifestyle that is too sanitized, manicured, and chokes our playful and creative freedom in the process. If we're struggling financially, we're too busy trying to make ends meet to dedicate some playtime. We need to reverse these unhealthy trends and rekindle our sense of wonderment for a better balance in life. My suggestion? Get out of your head, rest the mind and have judgment-free fun. That's the way to reclaim your inner child.

At Healium Center, my wife and I are often walking around barefoot, randomly dancing, cracking jokes, blowing bubbles and having a lot of light conversations with total strangers. When you do that, it's amazing to see that laughter and freestyle fun are contagious. You can quickly transform the energy of stoic and boring environments into joyful ones. Countless times people enter our premises and breathe a sigh of relief by just being there. But the typical adult who arrives is hostage to judgment, negative societal conditioning and self-imposed restrictive protocols. For the most part, the main culprit for all these conditions is being too self-critical and "overweight" in the brain. The inner critic is our worst enemy when it comes to activating our inner child and our inner-creative. I often tell people that *a busy mind cannot create and a creative mind cannot be busy.* This mantra behooves us to declutter our mind as much as possible whenever possible. Imagine that on a typical day we spend eight hours at work, two hours commuting, one hour eating and another four hours glued to the internet, television or video games. The brain has little time to consciously rest. When we finally do have some quiet time, we spend it on reading or other mind-engaging activity. We then pacify ourselves with alcohol or recreational drugs until we crash. Often the over-wired brain can't fall asleep and then we induce it with more drugs. We don't set aside any time to play or laugh enough.

That's why we're turning into a bunch of grinches and old farts. If you're an adult who never had a fun childhood and was too shy, serious or had an abusive family environment, it's never too late to make up for your lost time by learning to live life Healium style!

HEALIUM-STYLE!

I'm having more fun in many ways today in my 60s, than I did during my adolescence. Obviously, I have the financial freedom to accomplish what I want, but it's more than that. It's also valuing my sense of emotional freedom and brightening the environment around me. I'm always integrating several Healium Way Principles into my daily life, and enjoy lighting up even the darkest Soul in my encounters with people. Whether it's a visit at a dentist's office or a trip to the grocery store, I always make someone's day a little sunnier and funnier. It's my default position in living a life *Healium-style!* — uplifting yourself authentically with spontaneity, humor, creativity and a judgment-free attitude; exactly what carefree kids do! It is not only a liberating philosophy for me, but it has a contagious effect on other people that is priceless. In my travels around the world, I've often made new friends with total strangers by activating my inner child and having unrehearsed combustible fun. To help me turbocharge this light and adventurous mindset, I'll carry my mini djembe (African) drum whenever possible and always bring along my carefree and smiling attitude. Whether it's drumming freely on the streets of Costa Rica, dancing spontaneously on a group tour bus in Italy, making strangers laugh at the airport, or uplifting attendees at our Center — I've had great success shifting myself and others from serious, rundown conditions into happier and younger hearts. Both my wife and I love to dance, make new friends and spread positive and fun vibes wherever we are in the world.

The beauty of doing things Healium-Style is that it's not about showing off, trying to impress anyone, or making posts and selfies on social media. It's quite the opposite. It's about being true to your higher and unfiltered self. When you operate from that higher vibrational energy field, you're no longer starved for validation or approval from anyone. Almost everyone who has come to our Center has been pleasantly imbued with the Healium-Style dancing, jamming, painting, drumming and socializing. This is a mainstay of The Healium Way, and I invite you to try it out and plug it into your life.

Having a blast **Healium-Style!**

MAKING MAGIC

While I was visiting the Angkor Wat Temple in Cambodia, I came upon a group of kids playing on the edge of the river bank. I approached them with a smile and sat across from them while waiting for our tour bus to arrive. One of the kids asked me what language I spoke. I told him I spoke magic. He stared at me in confusion and scratched his head. I smiled back and started doing some hand magic tricks that I had learnt when I was a young boy in Paris. Immediately these kids' eyes lit up, their curiosity stirred. They soon approached closer to sit near me. My daughter who was sitting on the other side saw the excitement in the kids and joined in on the fun, making goofy faces and displaying her own tricks. Within just a couple minutes, the entire energy level had been transformed.

Other local kids arrived, jubilant and excited. They refused to let us go until we showed them our hand tricks. And so we did. We laughed together and interacted without care or judgment. It was quite a beautiful, magical experience with these kids becoming instant friends who were sad to see us leave to the tour bus.

This story is just one of many from my own adult experiences in which I activate the inner child. This practice is essential to triggering the power of being an active participant in life — no matter where you are in the world. The spontaneous and playful act of connecting with strangers in a foreign country may not suit you, but why not try letting loose in sterile social settings at home. For example, try to play fun board games instead of chatting on social media. Or pick up a musical instrument you enjoyed playing in high school and let it rip without excuses or predispositions. Rather than talking on the cell while walking your dog, have fun playing with your pet. Instead of watching the news, try comedy shows or cartoons. Put on an upbeat song and just dance randomly in your home. Rather than just walking in the park, try skipping, skating and dancing — as you did as a kid.

Remember with The Healium Way, you don't care a f*ck who is watching you or what others think of you. You're totally oblivious to being judged and become a 50-year-old kid unchained from life's predisposition and conventionality. Because now, when you let go and rekindle the inner child, it feels quite liberating to jump into a puddle of muddy rainwater again. It's magical because it's the uninhibited and the fun-loving side of you that's been re-activated and re-energized!

*"True strength comes from not caring a f*ck what people think of you."*
— Jim Peera

Practice The Healium Way

INNER CHILD EXERCISE: Go visit a park and walk barefoot and feel the connection with the earth and nature. Get on a swing and enjoy swinging like you did as a kid. If you have a partner or a child, play Frisbee or ball games. Reactivate your skating skills. If that's too hard, ride a bike and a scooter. If your friends' kids are playing some sports games, ask to see if you can join them for a short time. If you're indoors, activate the inner child activities of the arts with your adult friends. When you're invited to a kids' birthday party, interact with the youngsters and immerse yourself in a few of their activities. Notice how renewed and young you feel…especially when you wear a smile and have a positive attitude!

A Pregnant woman being body painted at Healium

Principle #14
Opening The Communication Door

> *"Words are windows, or they're walls.*
> *They sentence us or they set us free."*
> – Marshall Rosenberg

Having an open-door policy to communicating is critical to The Healium Way. Sadly, we're losing the art of dialoguing and not getting our message across safely or effectively these days. And it's costing us. Having lasted almost 40 years in a happy marriage, I understand the value of communication. Therefore, I will spend some extra time on this important Principle.

T.H.R.E.T

Thanks to our ubiquitous digital lifestyles, we're staying more in our heads today than ever. At best, we're also monologuing (a one-way condition), as opposed to dialoguing (a two-way situation). The latter is harder to do as it requires that we face what I call our T.H.R.E.T: *Transparency, Honesty, Respect, Empathy and Trust* with other people. It's my personal metric to glean people's true intentions and have effective communication in any relationship. For many folks however, this five-step process is hard to uphold and becomes a real "threat" to their accustomed modus operandi. People often opt not to communicate their feelings openly and honestly. The cellphone, video games, internet, etc., have all rewired our brains, normalized superficiality, suffocated our emotional receptors, reduced our patience, and caused us to be more robotic and have less empathy for people. What's more, cultural norms, ancestral programming and patriarchy can reduce effective two-way open lines of communication. As I've said elsewhere, men's brains are wired for action, while women's brains are wired for talking. Therefore, T.H.R.E.T. can be easily hijacked if these conditions persist, frustrating open communication. Studying human behavior and different types of people can help us improve our dialoguing skills.

THE ONE-WAY ENERGY VAMPIRES

It's important to understand that having an open, honest and effective engagement with people is a *two-way* reciprocal relationship. Dialoguing is not just about talking at people but attentively listening to them. If we're good listeners, we become better communicators and reciprocators. Unfortunately, there are people who are drains rather than fountains. They'll talk your ears off and not hear a word you say to them. In the process, it's all about them, their problems and drama — and very little about you. One-way people usually lack all the T.H.R.E.T conditions in one convenient box. They're not transparent. They're usually hiding something and they are not being honest. They certainly don't respect you. And you can't trust them. There might be something about you that is setting off their one-way energy. Without a doubt, don't feed their ego and self-serving character or they'll suck your Soul. If you have a one-way energy vampire as a family member that you're stuck with, silence can be the best remedy. That may even provoke them to be curious and open some two-way dialogue.

" *Those who talk do not know. Those who know do not talk.* "
— *Lao Tsu*

HONORING YOUR WORDS

Your word is everything. It can make or break you. In business and in personal life, I've earned my integrity by doing exactly what I say without resorting to drawn-out, long contracts. I've done many million-dollar real estate deals with people, with a handshake and keeping my word. In fact, when a realtor sends me a 10-page agreement, I'll replace it with my two-page one that protects both parties. Once I make a particular decision, such as buying or selling a property, paying an obligation or agreeing to help someone financially, there's no going back on my word — it's the right thing to do and I'll build trust with people. When I made my marriage vows to my wife in 1983, I intended to honor it until death did us part. I'm not interested in wiggling myself out of that deal or any deal (personal or business) unless it's a mutual agreement or parting of ways. Making excuses to undo a promise or to squeeze out more money from someone after you've agreed on the terms, reveals a lot of about your character. It has happened to me at the closing table often in my 20-year real-estate career. It's been said that when one person has a bad experience with you, they're likely to broadcast it to 10 other people. This condition alone can pose a nasty threat to a new business or any relationship. Sadly, in profit-over-people America, folks who stick to their word are becoming extinct.

In many situations, it's as important to pay attention to not just what you say to people but *how* you say it. Our tone, demeanor and body language are more important than the substance. Various studies indicate that up to 60 percent of all communication is nonverbal and 30 percent is about the tone of our delivery. That means only 10 percent communication focuses on what we actually say.

That's quite revealing, isn't it? Therefore, if the substance of what we say is not as critical as how we say it, then we need to further investigate the power of silence and nonverbal clues.

ART COMMUNICATES

From our experience at The Center, we've seen how art is one of the most effective nonverbal tools to open dialogue and connect with ourselves and others. Throughout this book, I give examples of art's ability to not only convey a sensitive message, question or unleash emotions in people, but how art also performs these functions without being a threat to anyone. It is a beautiful and powerful communication tool for bringing relationships together, expressing controversial topics and lifting our moods. This form of communication is not only accomplished via nonverbal means, such as visual art, poetry, miming, and creative writing, but also through music, the various performing arts and similar modes. As an artist, I'm always communicating with my art. I prefer to provoke, disturb and awaken people with my creations, rather than just please the eye with conventionality. When I unleash my creative self-expression without boundaries, I notice an interesting phenomenon; people not only open their own dormant faculties, but they help open it for others' too. By talking about the particular work of art to their circle of friends, they create a beautiful cascading effect that is ever-evolving. That's the communication power of art!

PEOPLE BUY PEOPLE

Demeanor and body language are two important keys that will either open or close the communication door. That's because we make decisions and judgments about people every second, without a word being uttered. Often, we just process it automatically using our predisposed stereotypes about people. The particular judgment could be related to our skin tone, our hairstyle, our attire, or even the type of car we drive and house we live in.

This next story illustrates how perception matters. On a recent visit to a local farmers market, I came into an aisle where two vendors were selling the same item: Korean-style pot-stickers.

They both had free samples of their product. One was a tired-looking, frowning woman busy texting on the phone. On her table was a large plate half-full with cold pot-stickers. The other vendor was an older man who had a bright smiley face and raised his hand out to offer his sample of pot-stickers to anyone who walked by him. Not surprisingly, the guy who had the smile attracted more people, including myself. I took two samples (one for my wife) and smiled back. His sample basket was almost empty. Since people buy people and not things or stereotypes, it is critical that we understand the perception and value of our communication skills, verbal as well as nonverbal such as body language, attitude, emotions and silence. I know in my own life having a frowny face and a matching sad attitude will always get me spiraling into a dispiriting verbal downdraft with people.

So we must learn to fight that sad-seeming tendency. By being aware of my own public demeanor, I am also more effective in communicating my message to others, no matter how controversial or unpleasant the subject.

THE TONGUE IS THE GROOVE

In relationships, nonverbal communication is often not adequate, as the tongue becomes our groove. How we each form and develop this groove is quite fascinating and can make or break relationships. As a natural debater, I encourage others (including my family members) to voice uninhibited views and deep, intellectual dialogue – even in a passionate argument. I invite discussions and questions on controversial and uncomfortable topics – it's my way to keep growing intellectually while maintaining a balanced viewpoint. I prefer to use the tongue as a weapon over a knife or a gun, as long as it's not done forcefully or violently. How about you? I think we all should think in this manner to keep the peace in our society. But for many people it feels unnatural to use words instead of physical force.

In America, that imbalance is exacerbated by our compulsive-impulsive behaviors such as the ease in purchasing guns, even semi-automatic terror machines. From police brutality to domestic violence, guns have become the nation's communication weapon of choice. This penchant for gun-buying has much to do with our profit-over-people model of marketing killing machines instead of valuing our voices. Our empathy skills have regressed to the point that we don't even turn on our listening button anymore — we conveniently use headphones to avoid engaging with people everywhere we go. We're also a lot less patient than we were just a few decades ago. We want instant results for our problems, and dialoguing takes too much time to get there. Psychologists agree that any form of verbal communication is better than no communication at all. In domestic disputes, studies have shown that regular doses of positive communication leads to happier couples. I can definitely agree with that. I would also add that being able to effectively communicate with your partner keeps each other's personal power in a healthy balance. This is especially critical when you're a partner-pleaser personality. In trying to make a relationship work, often one person becomes more subservient and slowly relinquishes their power to the point of having low self-esteem and feeling victimized. In this situation, it's vital to express this feeling of disempowerment early by deploying Principle #8 *Honoring your emotions* and combining it with this Principle, to achieve the desired results. As discussed in Part 1 of The Healium Way, loss of power takes shape in many forms and requires courage and action to rebalance it. Quite often however, our ability to communicate our displeasure is hijacked by our toxic home environment — as it did for my wife.

My wife grew up in a family that was poor at talking through problems. In fact, her family engaged in yelling matches and physical hostility toward each other. Most of her family's behaviors were fear-induced and a function by male patriarchal behavior. Being female, her parents taught her to shut up, which silenced her voice and suppressed her emotions. In contrast, I was raised in a family that taught us to settle our disputes using the mouth instead of the fist. Our choices were to stay silent or speak up. The former style came from my dad, while the latter was from my mom. Not surprisingly, our communicating skills got tested when we tied the knot. In our early stages of marriage, it was quite alarming to witness the dichotomy of the two disparate forces playing out and testing the post-honeymoon period. We were both very young and had no experience dealing with each other's emotions or a fire hose of unhealed childhood trauma. My wife's quiet soft smile and demeanor on the outside camouflaged a boiling temperament on the inside. It festered and boiled without an healthy outlet, until it exploded in fury without warning. I often felt like a punching bag that was yanked around by forces stronger than PMS or her Gemini personality. Somehow, I managed to stay calm, allowing her to freely express herself and not suppress her pent-up emotions. But on deeper investigation, I realized that my wife, unlike myself, had some unresolved issues that were causing her unpredictable verbal and physical eruptions. In due time, she pinpointed the exact source of her violent behavior, and not surprisingly, it emanated from sexual molestation from her father during her adolescence. Her wounds were deep, open and seeping into our relationship to dangerous levels. My wife desperately needed help beyond what I could provide; to grow and transform herself into a beautiful lotus.

Using hypnotherapy, Shamanic healing, past-regression therapy and the medicine of the healing arts, my wife eventually healed her emotional scars through the years. She also took some assertive training classes to boost her confidence and consulted a professional therapist as needed. Happily, she broke the unhealthy passive-aggressive cycle from her programmed mind, and we were able to build a healthy, highly functional relationship. I continued to encourage her to speak her mind without fear at home and in public. Fortunately for us, this story ended well and saved our marriage. We were able to minimize the verbal violence on our kids and for the majority of our married life neither one has resorted to any physical force against the other. Prioritizing honest and open dialogue with my wife and kids has been the glue to our family bond. But it would not have been possible without setting the desired intention to heal our past traumas that were suppressing our communication and individual progress.

Today, our relationship is stronger as a result of speaking our mind, and working diligently to deploy T.H.R.E.T for a healthy discourse. Like any marriage, we're still work in progress, but we've found a groove that evolves with our wisdom, age and strong personalities. Most important, is our awareness and desire to keep a healthy balance of power in our marriage. Your groove could be totally different and unique to your culture, family dynamic and character. It's all good and there's no broad brush to paint it a correct way, as long as it doesn't disempower you. A loud and heated lunch table conversation at an Italian home is totally in contrast to the quiet and reserved one at a conservative English afternoon tea. I've experienced both and enjoyed the Italian experience better for its authenticity, passion and freedom. One allowed people to speak their mind, while the other minded what you spoke around people – definitely not my cup of tea! The important point here is to understand the value of being in the groove of a healthier type of communication; which in The Healium Way is unobstructed and unrestricted. The unhealthy type should be avoided and includes being dismissive, unusually silent and shoving our true or contradictory feelings under the rug. The toxic type using physical force or violent language is even worse and must never be normalized.

I prefer my words be the "window" rather than the "wall", as eloquently described by the late American psychologist and developer of Nonviolent Communication; Marshall Rosenberg. I know my son has been positively impacted by Rosenberg's teachings – especially after his own bout with domestic violence discussed earlier. But there are many more people in relationships who have mastered the art of *not* dialoguing at all, by using various escape shoots and excuses to avoid conflict and face difficult truths. The reasoning here is that eventually time and circumstance will fix the conflict. My dad used this technique often and I don't think it worked that well for him behind closed doors with my mom. My mom felt ignored and counterpunched with unruly behavior and screaming matches to get his attention. So, one could argue that silence provokes violence in many relationships. For this reason, I believe both communication methods are problematic in pursuing a healthy relationship. They each manifest short and long-term damage if we don't act to rebalance their stranglehold on us. Having the fortitude to agree to disagree is essential to make for a sustainable relationship. This skill has a lot to do with not partnering with fear or succumbing to loss of personal power (as discussed in earlier chapters). Furthermore, open and honest communication delivered non-violently forces us to engage our tongues — not guns — and help us stay in the right groove.

WEARING THE PANTS

A prevailing communication problem I find (and a sensitive issue for many) is the idea of a particular spouse *wearing the pants,* or calling all the shots, in a relationship. This subject doesn't come up in many relationships, or worse, is tabooed. The source of this problem can often be traced to the financial breadwinner in the family (as exemplified in my dad's case with our family). In our situation, because my dad wore the entire family's pants, when he died no one knew how to put on their own pants. The healthy approach, in my view, is that the designated captain or pant-wearer sees that decisions made and actions taken address the needs of each family member. By removing the individual egos or patriarchal influences, we can achieve an equitable condition for everyone. This balance is necessary to achieve successful relationships of all types. Using the pants metaphor, why not let each partner wear their own set of pants?

In fact, why not try to figure out what partner is good at cleaning and ironing the particular pants and let them do that job — instead of one person being the big kahuna and having the burden of seeing to it. In my own marriage, this system has been fine-tuned over the years and works well to this day. Both my wife and I deploy our own strengths in making household decisions. For instance, I know how to make money and provide well for my family, so she'll respect my actions on making investments. She's good at taking care of the bills and the nitty gritty details that I don't like, so I trust her doing that. We allow each other to have respective freedoms without infringing on our own personal power. In this manner, we do everything upfront and have the urge to compete or hide anything. Each person's needs are met and satisfied because there's a conundrum of dialogue (enveloped in T.H.R.E.T., transparency, honesty, respect, empathy and trust) in all facets of the relationship. When we disagree on something, we try to find a common ground. Sometimes I get my way, sometimes she gets her way. But the critical point to make is that it's always best to communicate what you feel right away and be straight with your partner if you feel stepped on, disrespected or disempowered. If not, the relationship becomes trapped in a bog of fear and lies. I know of some Healium participants who were raised in either a dysfunctional or abusive family environment, and despite their artistic practices failed to arrest the toxic communication cycle and repeated it in their relationships. In many such imbalanced relationships, the majority of problems arise in individuals who are set in their dominating ways of practicing one-way street (often fear or guilt induced) communication skills.

In this example, the weakened spouse becomes a pushover, loses their voice over time and becomes subservient to the other. I've seen this condition in both males and females. Sometimes the dysfunctional union ends bitterly, but often it just gets normalized and tolerated. In some cases, the weakened spouse elects to stay silent in exchange for financial security and material comforts. In women it is often the case with mail order brides or arranged marriages. In men, it tends to be hidden but pervasive. In both situations, the imbalance eventually manifests in marital problems.

When I try to shine a light on the abusive and manipulative tactics of unhealthy relationships, I find that couples often use a variety of tricks to diffuse the truth, deny their poor communications skills and walk away from this attempt at much-needed healing. This unhealthy cycle will only end when people, who are sitting in their little toxic boxes, abandon their particular fears and communicate — with their partners, friends, family members or even a couples-therapist or financial adviser. In existential domestic abuse situations, professional counseling and intervention is necessary to manage hostility and stop the violence. If this sounds like you, you don't deserve to suffer any longer and need to get the necessary help today.

For the rest of us, however, an open line of communication can begin right now in baby steps. If you're on the giving end of a poor communication relationship, this is your time to *open your ears* and listen attentively to your partner's needs and empathize. If you're on the receiving end, this is your time to *open your mouth* and speak your mind without apprehension. Each person needs to ask *where* the imbalance exists (money, sex, work, duties, children, business, etc.) This is the time to be totally honest and authentic, with no reservations on either side. Soon you'll realize how each of you is holding the same set of keys to a mutually powerful, healthier and happier relationship. You simply forgot to exercise your individual right to communicate freely.

SECRET LOSS

Keeping the communication key in ignition mode is even more invaluable for responsible estate planning. It keeps both partners from slipping into confusion, chaos or paralysis if one spouse croaks. When my dad died, his lack of estate planning and patriarchal habit of keeping secrets from my mom, caused tremendous loss and suffering for the entire family. With no basic 'will' or instructions of accessing his hidden bank accounts and investments, we were in the dark and financially devastated. You don't want to make the same mistake. Trust your loved ones enough to share your responsibilities and secrets with them, so when one passes the other will go on in a healthy way as the lone leader of the family. With this mindset, the surviving family members will have the strength and resilience to keep themselves sheltered, empowered and thriving. That's the power of keeping the doors open to smart, open and effective communication!

LET'S GET PHYSICAL

Being in a monogamous relationship for the majority of my life, I've learned a trick or two about how to say things to my wife that get me the desired effect. And I must say, it's more of an art than a science! As a couple that's getting up there in age, neither of us has the body or physicality we once had (although my wife looks great for her age, and people say I look untypically fit for mine), our aging body is still no excuse not to keep the flames of desire and romance from burning. Or is it? I know many couples who live a miserable life with their significant other due to their inability to be honest with each other about what they dislike about their physical appearance. Although some of us are aging more gracefully than others, or have better genes, there are always some external things about our partner that we may not find attractive, such as weight gain, loss of hair, wrinkles, bad teeth, wrong attire, etc. So if you're in a long relationship, and you prefer to age naturally as we do, but can't communicate face to face what small things bother you about your partner — I have some tips for you. It's time to get physical!

There are three options you have in communicating with your partner that we've discussed in Part 1 of The Healium

Way: doing *nothing,* doing *something* or doing *everything.* Doing nothing is the most typically deployed tool for couples when it comes to discussing their physical concerns. It's the easiest choice, of course. No partner gets offended, there are no arguments and you keep the peace. Or do you? Often by shoving the concern under the rug, a silent war begins brewing within that person and can eventually manifest in infidelity and/or addictions like gambling, drugs, alcohol, eating, prostitution, porn and so on. The cost of doing nothing ends up in either a divorce or even worse, a couple that is miserable and unhappy staying together. The second option is doing something, which can get us on a path to doing everything. In this case, partners open the conversation about the other's physical appearance to test the water. This is where deploying the T.H.R.E.T tenets will help in talking about this prickly issue sensitively. Not surprisingly, taking this risk can really have long-term benefits for a marriage, as it has in my own!

To get the best results, focus on the *delivery* of the message, not the *substance* of what bothers you about the other's physical attributes. I notice that when I use a soft, calm tone as opposed to a harsh one, my message gets heard and digested better by my wife. As a passionate person without reservation, I'm always catching myself violating this rule and paying the price when I get excited or resort to a yelling match. The older I get, though, the easier it has become to stay "soft" instead of "hard-toned" and to practice staying calm and collected to avoid heated arguments. Once the delivery connects, the attention receptors open without any counterpunches and the message is transmitted effectively. This exercise is essential to open honest dialogue in any relationship.

I also recommend that you review and deploy the Principles discussed earlier: *Knowing the Importance of U* (Principle #1), *Unleashing the Magic of Humor* (Principle #7) and *Leading by Example.* (Principle #19).

Here's a practical lesson in how best to talk about physical issues with your partner. If I wish my spouse to lose weight, I'll start by having a calm demeanor. I'll point at myself where I've gained some pounds and ask her if she likes it. Hopefully, she doesn't. Here, I'll make some jokes about myself, perhaps pointing to the belly or love handles onmy body. Then I'll ask her to show me the areas where she thinks her own body is not the same either. If she doesn't feel comfortable, I don't push it. I let her know that I will be going to the gym or jogging to lose weight (without suggesting she take up those activities too). I activate that exercise plan, am consistent with it, and discuss my progress with her regularly. Slowly but surely, my wife will likely join in similar weight-reducing exercises without much resistance or defensiveness.

Practice The Healium Way

DIALOGUE EXERCISE: A positive dialogue begins with having good listening skills and mastering T.H.R.E.T. Here are two good exercises to accomplish this:

1) Our life is literally in our pockets with the advent of the smart cellphone. So do this at least ONE DAY per week and work it up to two days per week. Instead of texting or responding to people by texts, actually use the phone to talk to them in the old-fashioned way. This small shift will help you listen better and help you get deeper and more emotionally connected in conversations. 2) For those of you in a relationship, this exercise is really cool. Use your morning wake-up time to share your respective dreams with each other. Don't interrupt your partner at any point. When both of you are done, you can discuss and interpret the dreams together. This is a great way to become a good listener and share intimate thoughts and subconscious adventures without debates or heavy topics. My wife and I do this habitually each morning at breakfast. Over time you will start discussing heavier subjects without much hostility or resistance.

Principle #15
Activating The Heart of Hugging

The act of intentionally connecting with your fellow human by hugging is one of the most primordial feel-good gifts we can give. That's because hugs are known to release the love hormone, oxytocin, and fill the heart. Despite the fears stemming from the coronavirus pandemic to stop or reduce touching and hugging, we should under safe conditions embrace our instinctive nature to benefit our wellness. Just ask Amma, the Indian hugging Saint who has wrapped her comforting arms around more than a million total strangers from all around the world. Both my wife and I stood in line among a thousand eager attendees at her famous ashram in Kerala, India. It was a once in a lifetime surreal spiritual experience. Most people love to be embraced and hugged when the intention is affectionate and authentic in nature. At Healium Center, hugging is our automatic greeting: We call it the *heart of hugging.* It's an amazing icebreaker that opens dialogue and establishes instant heart-to-heart rapport.

There are different types of hugs, but the most common one is the "bear" hug that is done with two arms wrapped around a person in a frontal position. It is often a tight and reassuring embrace and leaves two people feeling warm and fuzzy like a bear. We also find there are three types of huggers: touchy-feely people who prefer to always hug you hello; occasional huggers who only embrace you if they're comfortable with you; and those who find displays of affection uncomfortable and avoid it. I fit somewhere in the middle of the first two categories — being aware of certain boundaries with total strangers and being a generous hugger with people I know. I almost never hug people in business meetings. I did that once at a real estate closing and the attorney gave me a cold and awkward look. It seems most Westerners are not ready for that level of close touch-connectivity in business. At least not yet.

In my family of origin, neither of my parents were touchy-feely. When I craved a hug, I'd often get it from my grandma or my two uncles who'd offer long warm hugs to fill our hearts, especially after our father's death. When I became a father myself, I'd make sure my kids had all the touchy-feely hugging they desired to feel protected and uplifted. Interestingly enough, recent research by UC Berkeley finds that touchy-feely people may also be happier and healthier than the other categories, due to studies that show a correlation between such close contact and improved mental and physical health. In another study, hugs were proven to have reduced conflict.

Michael Murphy, a post-doctoral research associate at the Laboratory for the Study of Stress, Immunity, and Disease in the Department of Psychology at Carnegie Mellon University, has found that human touch deactivates the part of the brain that responds to threats, which in turn releases fewer hormones to signal a stress response. This results in your cardiovascular system experiencing less stress, lowered blood pressure and a calmer mind, making hugging a proven stress reliever and a peacemaker. But sadly, we're not hugging as much as we need to amid our busy grind, societal stigma, reduced social interaction, fear of strangers, and other negative man-made programming. But The Healium Way is antithetical to the idea of any fear-based conditioning or self-induced imbalance.

Therefore, as a practical matter, it is important you understand the benefits of hugging as necessary to your overall wellness regimen. Best of all, hugs like smiles don't cost anything, so why waste this amazing mutual benefit?

Practice The Healium Way

HUGGING EXERCISE: There's no right or wrong way to hug, except don't fake it or touch people inappropriately (a word of caution to my 'touchy/feely' male friends, #MeToo, a movement against sexual harassment is not your friend, so hug carefully!). Use common sense and do it with respect, authentic intention and without apprehension and it will feel good for both parties. Do it as often as you can with people you love, and take baby steps with people you don't. For example, shake a stranger's hands when you meet them, and if you feel a loving energy from them, give them a quick hug when you say goodbye. With individuals you know, give them a longer hug. Hugs can last from three seconds to a minute. Over time, you will be able to feel people's energies and adjust your level of hugging with them. Happy hugging!

Principle #16
Using The Magic of Spontaneity

One of the most globally recognized iconic slogans is Nike's *"Just do it."* It is probably one of the most powerful and motivating three words that you can put together and have it instantly understood anywhere in the world. To me, it embodies taking action without procrastinating or reservation, which is exactly what is lacking in most adults today, the ability to just go for something without being over analytical or afraid of having a bad experience. Spontaneity is a key important ingredient in The Healium Way. Prior to the internet, if you drove by a restaurant row, you just picked one place that you had a good feeling about and took your chances. Today, you'll use your handheld computer to read online ratings before you make your choice. Although the reviews and stars are helpful aids, this information-overload practice values certainty and comfort over spontaneity and adventure. Our brain gets rewired to this structural and predictable format and has a difficulty taking spontaneous action and *just doing it* without predispositions.

When you layer in the inner critic that lurks in all of us, you can paralyze people from taking action on their own. In the world of the arts, this form of conventionality and structure is counterintuitive to a life of creative freedom and joy. When it comes to exploring our Soul, we need to embrace mystery and the excitement of the unknown. By practicing spontaneity and trusting in the outcome of the moment, no matter what it is, we experience a level of creative alchemy that is magical and priceless. At The Center, our Open Jam freestyle events specifically encourage non musically trained people to go on stage and join in on fun with more advanced players. We remind them that unlike karaoke, they'll need to open their imagination, be unstructured, play from the heart, create their own music and work as a team with others on stage. It's great training for getting along with different people. For many professional musicians, this improvisational method might be annoying to them at first, but soon they relent, become more patient and have a great time. It's quite remarkable to notice how ordinary people who have stage fright will muster some courage to activate their musicality and understand the value of perfecting their imperfections.

CELEBRATING THE PERFECTION OF OUR IMPERFECTIONS

I've witnessed hundreds of shy and introverted people who start off as spectators and soon pick up a drum, sing or strum a guitar and have the best time of their lives by embracing the magic of interactive spontaneity. By celebrating *the perfection of our imperfections* in this way, we liberate ourselves without any excuses. We don't have to be a trained artist, a good dancer or even a talented musician to participate and have fun in social gatherings and enjoy life. By removing this societal pressure to be perfect, we replace competition with collaboration and allow ourselves to willfully interact in a group setting and surrender to the moment. For instance, during the Covid-19 crisis, my wife and I distributed a few sound healing and drumming videos to our community to help them stay calm, uplifted and empowered. Neither of us are professional musicians, but we enjoy playing and experimenting with various instruments and sounds. By doing so, we connect with our intuition and free spirit. My wife has taken some voice lessons and has some training in vibrational sound healing, and Tibetan and crystal bowls. For my part, I have participated in a few drum circles over the years. But that is the extent of our musical expertise. We enjoy doing it freestyle to keep it simple and fun, Healium-style. It has helped us enjoy life to the fullest without predisposed inhibitions wherever we go, whether it's on family trips, in restaurants, at parks, on group tours, at parties or anywhere we interact with people.

MAKING MAGIC WITH E.J.

I know Elton John loved The Healium Way practice of freestyle spontaneity that I revealed to him back in 1996. Elton was one of my coveted clients when I was in the rug-and fabric-cleaning business. One beautiful day, my brother and I were doing some work at his lavish and expansive Atlanta high-rise home. The place has drop-dead views of the Atlanta skyline and is situated in the Beverly Hills type area of Atlanta called Buckhead. Personally, I never met more fake, fragile and f*cked up people per square inch than I did in many parts of that neighborhood. But "E.J.," as everyone called the genius musician, is a shy and a quiet beautiful human being. On that day I was cleaning his favorite Versace silk armchairs and hand-loomed white cotton and wool rug, which apparently cost $100,000. His newly released album *'Made in England,'* was blasting through the speakers and I loved it. A light bulb went on in my head as I heard a beautiful catchy ballad called *"House."* I had this spontaneous idea of doing a parody of the song with our own words and giving it to Elton for Christmas. It was radical and crazy — especially when none of us could sing worth a darn. But I knew it would make him laugh at the very least. Without much thought, I got my brother on board to join me and we created a cassette tape cover with an art cover drawing of Elton hanging down from his condo tower in his Atlanta residence and pointing down, saying, *"This is my house."* On the back cover, there was a drawing of Elton sitting on his piano pointing his finger at me below getting a stain out of his white rug along with the words, *"This is my rug!"* We presented him with the whole package — our version of the song and the drawings. I was told that when he opened it on Christmas morning his close friends said they had never seen Elton laugh so hard. Apparently, he told them that of all the expensive and luxurious gifts he had received in his life, that this thoughtful and comical gift touched and surprised him the most. That news made my day! This cool story reveals both the magic of spontaneity — and the importance of going the extra step to be *extra*ordinary.

A note signed by Elton John on the spontaneous gift Jim and his brother gave him. (Jim is cleaning his white rug under the piano).

Practice The Healium Way

SPONTANEITY EXERCISE: We are a nation of avid consumers with an insatiable habit of buying things for people on special occasions like birthdays, Christmas, Mother's Day and Father's Day, etc. Most of that buying soon goes to waste and will show up before too long at yard sales and in dumpsters. Instead of purchasing a gift, put a little effort in creating something special your recipient will remember. Make a "gratitude bottle" (see instructions toward the end of the book), paint a canvas, write a poem, create a song, bake a pie, make a piece of jewelry, etc. If you have a loved one with illness, paint them a healing gift. Art heals. If you're in a relationship, treat your partner with an unexpected gift for no particular reason. Get out of the norm and be unpredictable once in a while. It will keep your love life fresh and alive.

Going from ordinary to *extra*ordinary!

**A Healium artist paints a gift to
Nicholas Cage at a movie shoot.**

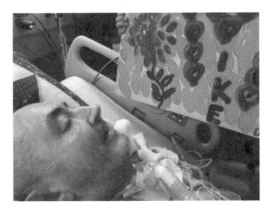

**A Healium participant paints a healing gift for
her stroke-paralyzed dad in the hospital.**
(Note: notice the smile on his face!)

Principle #17
Being An Instrument of Peace

"It's not how much we give, but how much we put into giving."
— Mother Teresa

The village of Assisi in central Italy is one of the most beautiful and captivating places my wife and I have ever visited. A Catholic friar who would become St. Francis of Assisi lived and died here; he gave up his riches and dedicated his life to selfless service. I am not recommending that you give up all your material wealth, become a monk or choose to live in poverty. But St Francis shows us a direct correlation between peace and giving. The more you put into the giving, the more you fill your own Soul and have a positive effect on humanity. Indeed, I believe you can do a lot more for people with money than without it. Around the globe, we see philanthropy improving the lives of people from a diverse set of well-known generous humans such as Bill and Melinda Gates, Warren Buffet, Oprah Winfrey, Karim Aga Khan, Sean Penn and Azim Premji, to name a few. Such human beings understand that they are just custodians of their wealth, fortunate to be able to do God's work. You may not agree with their personal or business practices or ideologies, but you can't argue with their significant contribution to uplift the world's poor.

Unlike many other wealthy celebrities and people, they're not interested in throwing a few crumbs at society with egotistic publicity stunts — but rather having the generosity of their life's work be their legacy. But The Healium Way teaches us that being an instrument of peace is more than being altruistic with your money. In fact, the various components of "peace" on our path of service include *respect, humility, empathy, love, kindness, gratitude* and *generosity.* These are the core values that will create your healed self. Ironically, generosity is a by-product of these attributes that puts a direct spotlight on our profit-over-people and individualistic mindset. Generosity can be expressed in offering your time, money, service and various other resources. But as we've discussed elsewhere in the book, you can't give what you don't have. This paradox compels us to take an inward journey into dismantling the conventionality of the ordinary thinker in order to achieve the *extra*ordinary outcomes of unconventional wisdom. Unless we do the work to respect and love ourselves, see ourselves in others, practice humility and be thankful for what we have, we're not going to be in any position to be generous to others. It is only when we're in a healthy balance that we become genuine givers and ultimately the peacemakers, first within ourselves and then with others.

THE GREATER GOOD

Being an instrument of peace is not just about writing a check to your favorite charity or attending a fundraiser, and feeling good about yourself. That is a myopic lens and a typical Western viewpoint with individualistic and self-aggrandizing traits. It's also the cliche of the bombastic and show-off American — an ordinary person in our definition. We must cast a wider net in society beyond our self-serving motives of getting accolades, publicity, trophies and tax benefits. The authentic giver offers gifts unconditionally and expansively. This type of giver's clear intention is to do good first for others, to promote *the greater good,* rather than being preoccupied on reaping benefits for themselves. Once we get this 'forest from the trees' memo, we can expand our generosity to a larger ecosystem and practice St. Francis' mission of universal serving: *"Lord, make me an instrument of thy peace."* I take that to mean that we should practice peace as a way of life — not simply on certain religious holidays or during charitable events. An instrument of peace is also a warrior of peace, be it to honor and serve your family, community or country. It's your Divine default position. We also have to be willing to stick our neck out and make a difference for others, as we would do for ourselves — growing a spine! For instance, if you're in a family dynamic and see your loved ones in conflict, don't stay silent. Get involved as a mediator to empathize and lend your ear, eyes and voice in the situation. Choose to be a person that unites, rather than one that divides.

How about using our instrument of voice, time, wisdom, status, influence, money, power, etc. to do good in every aspect of life. If you're in a controversial community meeting, respect both sides of the argument and try to find a common ground resolution. At the workplace, always set your ego aside and opt for mutually beneficial negotiations to settle an impasse. In social settings, be kind and loving to strangers without judging and being presumptive. If you're a professional, make available some of your resources and services pro-bono for people in need. If you're retired, donate your time and money to nonprofits that align with peaceful and humanitarian causes. In business transactions, try seeing the greater good beyond your wallet whenever possible.

LEAVING MONEY ON THE TABLE

In the business of real-estate for instance, there's a commonly understood faux pas we're all trained to avoid; *leaving money on the table.* It means selling an asset for less than its full market value and not squeezing every penny from a buyer. As an unconventional thinker, I've found that mindset to be egotistical and shortsighted. In contrast, let's look at The Healium Way's win-win approach. By intentionally leaving some money on the table and giving the buyer a good value, we expand our good karma unto the universe and inspire others to do the same. In the area of land development, I've forgone tens of thousands of dollars in profit when passing down my vision to the most qualified (but not necessarily the highest bidder) builder to execute the best project — for the benefit of a neighborhood. It's being *extra*ordinary for the greater good. Once you think and act in rapport with this more collectivistic mindset, you'll find it to be highly liberating, rewarding, therapeutic and contagious.

GENEROSITY IS CONTAGIOUS

Intentional and random acts of kindness and generosity serve a dual purpose: They put a smile on the receiver and bring joy to the giver. It's a beautiful and contagious experience that I have witnessed many times, in many situations. I'll never forget one particular evening during an arts event at our Center when a new participant with a glowing smile approached me. Vincent, a young handsome man in his 30s, had a certain aura about him as he spread his arms widely and gave me a tight bear hug. As he was talking about his excitement regarding Healium and our various services, I noticed a beautiful labradorite pendant on his chest. I told him labradorite was one of my favorite stones and that it was one of the most beautiful necklaces I'd ever seen. Vincent told me he had made it himself, and then without hesitating, he removed the pendant and put it on me. *"It's yours. I love what you've done with this place, and I am so happy to give it to you, Mr. Jim Healium!"* he said with a captivating smile. I was totally speechless. But Vincent wasn't done. He sought out my wife and daughter and gave them two similar pendants that he had in a bag of jewelry. My wife and daughter also were elated and stunned by this stranger's random acts of kindness. It was the first time that any stranger had spontaneously showered us with such ornate gifts at The Center. Those acts of generosity stirred positive contagious effects during the ensuing weeks at Healium. In my case, I found myself offering more free wine, giving people artworks of my own and keeping our doors open later than usual. Vincent showed during that unforgettable visit that generosity is an unconditional positive action that is divorced from any selfish benefit.

I am always inspired and dedicated to honor the Tao's spiritual words of wisdom on generosity:

"The sage does not hoard, and thereby bestows. The more he lives for others, the greater his life. The more he gives to others, the greater his abundance." — Lao Tsu

YOU'RE DEAD TO ME

As one of my most important core values, generosity also has the power to change laws and affect people's livelihood — as I have been fortunate to do in my own life. My generous contribution to open Healium Center is quite a rare situation. Many people may be hard-pressed to see the benefit of creating an arts wellness center that loses money. Indeed, maybe it isn't a good proposition for a conventional business model. In business, you need cash flow and profitability to keep your doors open. I've been there and done that many times quite successfully. But what if our capitalist society doesn't encourage, support or see value in keeping certain doors open? I found this to be true of the arts.

The banks won't lend you any money to operate an arts center, and there are no hungry investors lining up to invest in you — especially when you tell them the purpose of the mission is to heal people with the arts rather than make them rich with collectible art. They don't get it. Because of the prevailing capitalist mindset, the vast majority of Americans have a limited view of how to spend money. Such role models as Canadian billionaire and TV personality Kevin O'Leary (aka "Mr. Wonderful") don't help the situation.

O'Leary openly reminds America that the only ideas that matter in life are the ones that can be monetized. *"If you're not making me any money, you're dead to me,"* he says proudly. He'll even demean wannabe entrepreneurs on the popular TV show "Shark Tank" by calling them little cockroaches to be stepped on if their idea cannot fill his pockets. Although his words are cleverly devised to be entertaining, the shallow world he champions has real-life consequences for a young gullible American audience. For the millions who religiously watch the show, it can translate into the embrace of economic capital at the expense of human capital — a myopic and dehumanizing philosophy. Unfortunately, O'Leary and others like him inspire entrepreneurs and wealthy people to be cheapskates and hoarders of money. They justify this ultra-competitive mindset by implying that less fortunate members of our society (have-nots) are lazy, ignorant, entitled and burdensome. Perhaps some of that is true, but this sort of profit-over-people attitude runs counter to the idea of places dedicated to the social good. Unconventional propositions like ours are often shunned by investors such as Mr. O'Leary, and get categorized as a charity instead of an investable social enterprise. But why is that?

FIGHTING FOR THE CRUMBS

As a for-profit entity, our Center lost money each year for four consecutive years, no matter how innovative and creative we got or hustled. It hasn't fared that well as a nonprofit either. The problem: being out-of-the-box and not being able to check the many boxes on government grant applications, that are mired in bureaucratic red tape and regulations. The hard reality is there's little pricing power in the wellness-with-the-arts model that is non-conforming, is not clinical and isn't a place to get you high on drugs or alcohol. Our ability to make a difference in society is therefore limited to private donations, which means we rely on the goodwill of people who have disposable income or who are rich. But how large is this segment?

The American economic engine is split twofold. The first one is purely capitalistic and profit-driven, to make you rich: in such potentially lucrative areas as investing in stocks, commodities, cryptocurrencies, real-estate, business expansion, get-rich-quick schemes, etc. The other one is the less exciting: a nonprofit or charitable organization that gives back to society. The latter is a tiny sliver of the pie, consisting of only about 6 percent of America's gross domestic product. This means that 94 percent of American companies are profit-driven, which explains our global slogan of being the world's "land of opportunity."

To make matters more interesting, as I've discovered through our Center, this charitable slice of the pie is tightly controlled by mega-charities and foundations that suck up all the available crumbs people have to dish out each year for their own tax benefit. The competition to attract private donors and government grants is so fierce that a small nonprofit often has to partner with a bigger one just to be eligible to share a tiny piece of that little crumb to survive. The irony is that the public funding arena is shrinking, while the private one is hoarding and mis-prioritizing their contributions. Indeed, everyone is fighting for the crumbs!

With two-thirds of Americans living hand to mouth — it's easy to see how we've come to the point where there are fewer people with a lot of disposable income. What's left are the 94 percenters, or 1 to 10 percent of net worth individuals — in the entire country to tap into. It's this group of Americans that needs to step up to the plate and not throw crumbs, but invest in rebuilding America's crumbling moral infrastructure and contribute to its mental wellness and balance. So where are all these rich people who can save America's Soul?

WE THE CHEAPSKATE PEOPLE

Sadly, if you're fortunate and blessed to be in that top net worth bracket, research shows you're disproportionately deficient and tight-fisted in your altruism. The truth is, you may be rich but you're a cheapskate. It's oxymoronic. Because if you have more money, you should be more generous and not be a tightwad. In many cases at The Center, we've seen not just tight-fisted rich, but rich freeloaders who'll suck up our time and are quick to complain when we charge for our services or refreshments. These are the same people who live in expensive homes and sniff pennies to make more dollars. Sadly, they often don't know how to enjoy life's simple pleasures. Our studies show that most wealthy people are either hoarders or extravagant spenders. The former-types are typically older and less adventurous, while the latter yuppies are more interested in spending money on material things as opposed to creative and spiritual experiences that bring fulfilment and joy.

But you're not doing that much better if you're in the vanishing middle class either. We discovered at The Center that there are way more takers than there are givers. Our observations also reveal that you're more likely to spend money on buying more 'stuff' you don't need, rather than spreading some of it to help your community or the needy. It's the automatic default mindset of our consumerist economy. The statistics are quite jarring. The average American gives a minuscule three percent of their income to charities, according to the IRS. Americans are also stingy with their volunteering. Based on data by nonprofit organizations, the average person spends about 50 hours per year volunteering. In contrast, the average time spent on social media is a whopping 860 hours, according to Digital Information World. What's more, we spend a vast amount of money feeding, saving and domesticating animals in the West. What happened to the idea of saving the homeless and the hungry in our own communities? In my view, it's not because Americans are less caring or generous but rather that they have their priorities upside down. And that makes us sicker from the inside out. The debt-laden consumer economy, coupled with seductive marketing schemes, selfish role models and the lure of the American Dream is eroding our mental, physical and spiritual health to perilous levels. I have met scores of cheapskates during my life's journey. And if this cheapskate is you, don't be insulted — make your shift into your higher and more generous self. I invite you to make your shift from the ordinary to the *extra*ordinary person who you Divinely are by experiencing your better way.

CHARITY STARTS AT HOME

If you're not ready or willing to donate your money to charitable causes, how about looking at yourself in the mirror and investing some quality time and money on *you* where it makes a difference, as in reconnecting your own lost Soul and finding balance. Charity starts at home, and perhaps you are your own charity case. There's absolutely no shame to it either. In fact, your awareness shows strength and courage on your part. Indeed, once you've done that, you'll understand the value of sharing that gift with others. I know how I had to rebalance my own dream by not being a cheapskate and spreading my blessings into helping humankind. By seeing the benefits of multidimensional holistic healing modalities on myself, I began to prioritize my time and money where mattered. Soon, I realized its power and the value for others. By not looking for an immediate financial payoff, it has paid off for me in countless spiritual ways that no bank, investor or capitalist pig would understand. I know I may be a minority among my peers, but I'm happier and in a healthier balance than any of them.

BEING RICH IS A BITCH

Being an instrument of peace means that you are focused on tending your own garden, instead of knocking someone else's. Most people who are quick to bitch about other people's gardens, tend to be the privileged-minded wealthy. They may be financially pretty outside, but they display some ugly characteristics inside that show up externally. I've witnessed this irony many times in my life, for example, during my career as a fiber hygienist for the wealthy, and being a landlord of properties in some of Atlanta's most coveted neighborhoods. I noticed how the wealthy displayed the same or even worse characteristics of the lower classes (i.e., millennials, the poor and black people) that they complained about. They described feeling entitled, victimized, lonely, unfairly treated by the government, discriminated against and so on. It showed how having a lot of money may have insulated them by class, but it exposed their frailties by simply being human. That's because the future of separating people by class may not pan out so well. As a rich person, you won't be immune to feeling f*cked and trapped in some way. You'll be panicked about being taxed more, with more stress and worries about protecting your material riches — and feel disconnected from the lowly 'have nots. But you'll have to interact with your luxury car detailers, your soy latte makers, your dry cleaners, your housekeepers, your pet sitters, your personal chefs, your masseuses and so forth. And as long as you're self-absorbed and a tightwad, they're not going to be happy working their asses off for you, for low wages, lousy tips and unsafe working conditions. Eventually, they're going to strike and demand higher pay, better conditions and more respect. They may also quit and try out being their own bosses ditching serfdom. You may find robots and illegal immigrants to take their place, but that won't buy you joy and contentment. Unless you shift your privileged attitude, you're still going to be a sad, empty and lonely person. Hopefully, enough Americans learn to operate from a higher ground of common sense, and not be consumed by just dollars and cents and the bottom line.

TIME TO SPREAD YOUR SH*T

Interestingly, life is all relative. You can be sitting on a comfortable retirement nest egg with enough money to last until your last breath, and the next day a natural disaster strikes or someone you love suddenly dies — and your life is totally upended.

Therefore, it's all bullsh*t and meaningless, isn't it? Not only should you enjoy your life while you can, but also you should be charitable and generous with your money. In time one realizes like I did many years ago just like the cow dung metaphor by Thornton Wilder: *"Money is like manure. If you let it pile up, it starts to stink. But if you spread it around, then it can do a lot of good."* The truth is, our priorities must change and giving must precede taking. At the rate we're going, if St. Francis were alive today, he'd probably shake his head in frustration and recite three Hail Marys!

Practice The Healium Way

YOUR GIVE-BACK-DAY EXERCISE: Did you know that if you have food in the fridge, clothes on your back, roof over your head, a place to sleep and some spare change that you're among the 10 percent of the world's wealthiest? Armed with this humbling fact, try feeling some gratitude whenever you feel depressed, poor or insignificant. In this next exercise, you will break societal norms and practice compassion while others are busy overindulging. Pick a holiday, say, Thanksgiving, Christmas, Independence Day, Memorial Day, Labor Day, etc., and rename it: *"My Give-Back Day."* On this day while everyone including your friends and family are buying gifts, being self- indulgent and spending a lot of money on material things, you do the opposite. You will be testing personal willpower like never before. For eight hours, refrain from eating any food and only drink water. During the water fast, you will do good deeds for people. Choose a neighbor, a senior citizen, a war veteran, a single parent, an orphan, etc., and offer to spend your time with them. Volunteer to cook, do house chores, clean up, mow their yard and so on. You are not expecting anything in return, not even a "thank you" or validation on social media. By water fasting the entire day, you will train your mind to have discipline, staying power and have better appreciation and empathy for those who are food insecure. At dusk, before you resume to feed yourself, meditate for 10 minutes and thank yourself for a job well done. Over the course of the year, do more of this sort of volunteering and sacrifice a greater part of your life to serving others. You will discover more joy and satisfaction than you've ever experienced!

Principle # 18
Knowing The Value of Adaptability

"The most significant factor in survival is neither intelligence
nor strength, but adaptability."
— Charles Darwin

In early 2009, Satoshi Nakamoto, a pseudonym, wrote a white paper on a peer-to-peer electronic decentralized cash system that was created to change the way society transacted and stored money. It was seen as a disruptive technology that was competing with the banking and monetary system. To geeks, nerds and millennials, the system amounted to the unshackling of the rigged financial central bank way of doing things and level the playing field for them. Encrypted money was seen as the underdogs' financial equalizer. But to the traditional power structure of centralized monetary institutions and governments, the system was an enemy. The digital currency known as *Bitcoin* shook the world and shattered old ways of thinking, spending and investing. It created a new category of an asset class that became a threat to the conventional methods. If you were one of those skeptics who thought it was Monopoly money and a crazy fad, you're kicking yourself in the head today. Those who were quick to adapt to this digitized revolution and believed in the value of cryptocurrencies have become multimillionaires. Many of these crypto investors are the younger generation.

The price of one Bitcoin as of this writing, even with all its wild price volatility has given the initial investor an astronomical 200 percent return on investment per year — eclipsing real estate, stocks, commodities, bonds and all other investment vehicles combined. Today, many of the old skeptics have jumped on board and adapted to *blockchain technology* and futuristic money as a viable and more efficient way of storing, investing, using and protecting money. Blockchain is a decentralized digital ledger of transactions that's duplicated and distributed across the entire network of computer systems. Being totally transparent, blockchain is a trusted method that prevents cheating or altering the system. If you're in the camp that distrusts the government and hates traditional banks, this is your ticket to not being enslaved by the big corporations and greedy power holders. If you're rich, you see the cryptocurrency vehicle as a better and more efficient way to transfer your money to your kids for their future. It sure beats hauling heavy bags of gold or silver coins around from one safe deposit box to another. Based on the cryptocurrencies' basket's short historical performance, it also has shown to be a good hedge against inflation. So now both the *haves* and the *have-nots,* as well as the old and young, agree on using this unconventional but unstoppable revolutionary invention — a win-win partnership for everyone.

The lesson behind this story is not resisting change, but embracing the *value of adaptability.* We humans are a pretty adaptable species overall. Across history there have been many similar situations where those who got on board earlier with new discoveries and adapted to new ways benefited in spades. While those who were rigid in their thinking were left behind to play catch-up. Examples include the wheel, printing press, steam engine, the internet and so forth. This Healium Way Principle tests your level of adaptability by fusing some of the other Principles such as having a flexible and creative mind, not succumbing to fear and not being a sheeple.

As we train ourselves to be more nimble in one situation, we find ourselves inclined to not close doors on the unfamiliar. Eventually, it becomes an automatic reflex, the classic Healium Way of doing things. The value of adaptability is results-oriented and always has a big payoff. Just ask the Bee Gees. The iconic Gibb brothers stayed relevant as musicians/songwriters for five decades because they always adapted to the music in each decade and innovated new material to keep up with the times. They faced the post-disco backlash in the '70s and were ostracized for no reason for many years by record-burning disc jockeys and merciless critics. But the brothers weren't deterred. In the face of adversity and darkness, they stepped up into the light. They took all that sh*t and turned it into more gold records. The Gibbs adapted, got creative and double-downed on what they did best — write hit songs. The trio penned mega-hits for the likes of Diana Ross, Barbra Streisand, Dionne Warwick, Kenny Rogers and Celine Dion — to name a few. Once they gained back their respect, they wrote more albums for themselves and became a stronger and more appreciated band with an astonishing 50-year career. Conversely, many musicians and groups who were rigid in their styles and did not adapt or evolve, simply faded out and had short-lived careers. The Bee Gees' life story is an inspiration for all of us, and one of the reasons I admire and respect them so much!

TRAVEL TO ADAPT

The sad truth is that most Americans are deficient at adapting compared to other cultures. The phrase *the ugly American* was coined in response to our rigid and spoiled ways during trips aboard. Ironically, this condition has a lot to do with our society's lack of exposure to the rest of the world, especially the developing world where adaptability is required in every aspect of life. Whether it's our easy access to neighboring states, our isolated geographic location or simply the lack of affordability for the masses, most Americans don't travel enough overseas. And I'm sorry, but going on a cruise ship and spending a few hours at a touristy port of call doesn't qualify as having an authentic international travel experience. Neither does vacationing in an all-inclusive resort get you the desired exposure. You need to get your hands dirty and experience some level of discomfort and uncertainty outside of your sanitized bubble to have a memorable trip. But most Americans are not prepared for that level of experience. The Healium Way solution; incentivize and subsidize third world travel experience for Americans. If it were up to me, I'd require all American high school seniors to be mandated to spend some quality volunteer time in an impoverished developing country before they're awarded a diploma. It could be subsidized by private & public investment. I guarantee they'd return being more humble, grateful and resilient. In fact, their renewed outlook would help restore America to a healthier balance faster than any other program.

I would also recommend that blacks in America (about 14 percent of the U.S population) be given a dollar for dollar matching government subsidy to visit their motherland of Africa. It's win-win proposition for America and a travel expense that would pay for itself in spades. It would help them resolve their identity crisis, heal their ancestral wounds, enrich and expand knowledge of their true origins and be properly qualified to call themselves "African-Americans!" For America, it would translate into black Americans, especially the younger generation being more adaptable, humble and grateful.

When we compare America to other countries without any predispositions or filters, we clearly see how our nation is overrated in many ways. Indeed, there are more first-rate, smarter and happier people in those countries than in our own. Travel is a great opportunity to take an objective look at ourselves. It also is a terrific training ground to learn about other cultures and strengthen our adaptability muscles. Environments of scarcity make for more adaptable and creative people. I found this characteristic to be true in almost every developing economy I've visited.

In Africa, for instance, I discovered how the Maasai people use mud and straw to construct their homes, and cut up old tires to make ergonomic sandals. In rural Thailand, the impoverished locals resort to using elephant dung to make paper, while in India it is used for fuel.

Since the beginning of time, it is a testament that we humans are the most creative and adaptable when we're faced with the least technological advances, choices and resources. If we can turn sh*t into fuel, we can definitely turn a bad day into a better one, and adapt to any challenge without being engulfed in rage or fury. That is the power intrinsic to travel.

Enjoying a boat trip in Italy   **Adventuring in Thailand**

As an avid international traveler, I prefer to read up on a country's culture, laws and faux pas before I set foot there. When I traveled to Nicaragua a few years ago to visit a cigar plantation, I read up on its impoverished and dictatorial regime and dressed differently than usual and changed my entire demeanor. Instead of sticking out like a rich tourist, I became a chameleon instead. I adapted by brushing up on my broken Spanish, sampling all the typical foods and riding crowded public transportation where possible. This is another key example of how we can make a shift from being ordinary to an *extra*ordinary American. Let's all get out of our bubbles and comfort zones and taste different foods, meet diverse people and go off-the-beaten path. There are 195 unique countries in the world, and each will open your horizon and teach you different ways of thinking and a lot about yourself. To truly immerse in diverse worlds, you must be willing to take risks, adapt and have an open mind for adventure. If you're unable to travel overseas or have a limited budget, don't make excuses to be stagnant and turn into a hermit by staying at home or working just to keep busy. Go hiking, boating, kayaking, fishing, camping, etc., and enjoy the beautiful outdoors in your own country.

Obviously, the earlier you start and the younger you are the more you'll partake in life's adventures. But it's never too late — especially when you have the right attitude, are free of distractions or resistances and understand the value of adapting and engaging in life. Planting the seeds of traveling has a positive effect on our kids and their future as well. We may not all be alive to travel to space, but our children will, and we must set a good example as parents to encourage and inspire them to be adventurous-minded and unafraid to explore above and beyond this box called earth.

Practice The Healium Way

YOUR ADAPTABILITY EXERCISE: Next time you travel abroad to an exotic place, take note of how you carry yourself around with your attitude and set ways of doing things. Do you detect a resistance to adapting to new and unfamiliar ways of getting around or accomplishing what you want? When you're in countries that take a two-hour siesta in the afternoons, do you freak out or do you relax and experience the benefits of resting? If you're making a permanent move to a foreign country, observe how you act and behave with locals. Do you respect their culture, laws and limitations — or do you complain and are quick to judge and impose your predisposed and rigid ways? Do you feel the need to be territorial in your mannerisms and actions? How flexible are you with adapting to *their* way of life — instead of being stuck in yours?

Principle # 19
Leading By Example

"You don't lead by lip service. You lead by example."
— Jim Leyland

Jaipur was an intelligent and curious person who was new to the Atlanta area and had heard about our Center through Meetup, an online social network platform. Like many IT people, he was more an observer and a thinker who dipped his toe in the water slowly before he jumped in any activity. But he was always inquisitive and as a result each time he came he grew more comfortable with socializing and participating in the creative events. He'd pick up a canvas and join painters in the Open Studio group; I was pleased to see his creative receptors opening up as he became part of the Healium family.

Often during the end of an evening, my daughter or I would start a spontaneous freestyle drum jam session as people completed their paintings. Anyone could join in the fun. I'd always see Jaipur standing with a smile, observing us or taking pictures and videos on his cellphone. Each time, he'd have a bigger smile watching us all have a ball dancing and drumming. While playing the djembe, I'd occasionally smile back and invite him with my eyes to join in. But he always blushed and didn't have the courage to play. *"You sound great, but it's not for me. I've never drummed in my life"* would be his usual excuse. I'd never force him to play, and as a way of encouraging him I let him know that I had not been professionally trained to play, but just do it *Healium style* to have fun.

After a couple of months, as Jaipur watched many novice people jam and interact with other musicians, he did begin using the hand drums. One evening as I was about to start making some noise, he picked up a rattle and a doumbek (a Middle Eastern hand drum). He rolled up his sleeves, and said, *"Do you mind if I join, Jim?"* I was elated, and asked him to start a beat for me to follow. He and I began a simple beat and pretty soon we had more people join in. It was another amazing immersive drum jam, as I watched Jaipur just let go and have authentic fun. We lost track of time, and at the end of the session, he looked at me and said; *"That was amazing, Jim. That was great! You know that's the beauty of this place, is that you don't impose. You just lead and inspire by example."* For an East Indian, I know what he meant by that comment — because in our culture almost everything is led by aggression or force, until you choke.

It's an Eastern method of doing things, even if the messenger or leader is well-intentioned. Often, we are unaware of this habit because it is an automatic response to get people to engage in some activity. In the Western culture, this behavior is often seen as being rude and a big turnoff. Jaipur's experience, therefore, exemplified not just the value of having a non-interfering learning environment but his respect and appreciation for it.

This Healium Way Principle is quite hard for many people to learn because it stresses allowing and inspiring, rather than imposing, which many adults tend to do with family members and friends. Once we learn to deploy this practice, we see its benefit almost immediately. We notice how it is more effective than the stricter or authoritarian method, as it gives the observer an opportunity to think for themselves, remove any underlying fear, be more self-empowered and thus better appreciate its value.

By not imposing, shaming or nagging, but rather being an instrument of inspiration, we're almost always able to get the desired outcomes from people. Whether it's our kids, friends, lovers, parents, employees, etc., it is more effective to persuade someone than to force them to do a new thing. The trick is to have faith and patience. And to know that if you persist in your urgings — most people will only resist you more. Often it requires that the close-minded or the unadventurous be in the presence of more enlightened and balanced people. By observing open-minded, peaceful and joyous people, observers realize how 'boxed in' and rigid they are. It is only with this self-realization that many will start seeing other possibilities beyond our limited realm. I've witnessed this happen many times at our Center with people who've been operating robotically or stuck under a rock for long periods of time (or their whole lives) getting pleasantly or unpleasantly awakened.

Our experience shows that there are usually four prevailing outcomes with our attendees on any interactive activity: a) *They will look away and walk away; b) They will roll their eyes and criticize; c) They will appreciate and join in; or 4) They will just observe.* I've seen people who walk away from seeing a nude body painting art installation for the first time come back the second time and enjoy it. Some of these people even ask to be models as a way to remove their phobias and feel more connected with their bodies.

So as long as we keep the portal of curiosity and awareness within others open, we've found they will eventually participate. It's best to stop convincing, lecturing or pontificating, and simply walk the talk, if we want better engagement from people. The counterpoint to not leading by example is preaching without practicing the sermon — a condition known as hypocrisy that exists almost everywhere in America today. A good prescription doled out in these places often belittles people with doses of guilt, shame and fear. It is typified in environments of worship centers, motivational seminars and autocratic governments. The example has occurred at the church above our Center. Each time I walked up as an observer during worship hours, I heard the pastors yell out to the crowd how messed up, weak and misled they were and how Jesus was the magic solution to their misery. The declaration was not just a demoralizing untruth, but also a hypocrisy as it sets up the notion that the pastors and the religious elders were somehow perfect or knew the ultimate path to salvation. In contrast, The Healium Way invokes a self-empowering and a self-autonomous way of doing things.

As a result, we've found our retention rate is better and our effectiveness more mindful of our participants than any other dogmatic method of self-improvement. The Healium Way is not about doing something because you have to, or are afraid of being punished for not conforming to a set of commands — but because you want to, as you value yourself and you can think for yourself.

"I cannot teach anybody anything, I can only make them think."
—Socrates

Practice The Healium Way

LEADING BY EXAMPLE EXERCISE: Pick a person you know who's difficult at doing something you want them to do for their own good. It could be your partner, kids, a friend, etc. You want this person to share an experience or product, but you know that the more you persist, the more they seem to resist it. You've tried repeatedly, but it goes nowhere. Using this Principle, try a reverse psychology of not imposing but rather just allowing. Make absolutely no effort in asking them — but rather be the example of experiencing it yourself. Be sure to show and share your sense of excitement and pleasure for this thing or activity without seeming like you're eager to influence them — no matter how tempting that may be for you. You will notice how this person is no longer resisting or making excuses and starts engaging and partaking by their own volition.

Principle # 20
Practicing Soul, Body and Mind Balance

"It's far better to be a late bloomer,
than walk around like a wilted flower."
— Jim Peera

So far throughout the book I've shown by example how by simply being aware of our imbalances, we can readjust to a healthier equilibrium. In this Principle, we take a deeper dive into the three most important underpinnings that make up this balance: *body, mind and soul* — or as I'd like to say, *soul, body and mind.*

In the ancient East Indian medicinal science known as Ayurveda, all diseases in the human body are caused by our imbalances. The Ayurvedic doctors are trained to understand the *cause and effect* of the human body; their knowledge of bodily karma. They're so in tune with the body's nuances that they can diagnose an out-of-whack vessel simply by taking our pulse and looking into our eyes. When any aspect of the soul, body and mind are out of alignment, we suffer. Like the Ayurvedic medicine man, we all need to be our own medicine man, constantly self-diagnosing and nursing each of these three components. Being in balance is the cornerstone of The Healium Way for obvious reasons. It not only guides us to a more sustainable path of living, but it also helps us experience the fullness of life while being on that healthier path.

The result is a person who develops lifestyle habits that experiences all the beauty of the world, reduces toxic influences and attachments, and wakes up each morning in gratitude of simply being alive. This type of person shifts into a *roots*-type individual who goes into *extra*ordinary mode every day, and lives a life without regrets. On the flip side, when a life of balance is not practiced intentionally, the outcomes can have detrimental, cascading effects. The price of imbalance is a heavy one because of the natural interconnectedness of the soul, body and mind. For instance, if you're neglecting your body with a poor diet and are overweight, you raise the likelihood that you will be imbalanced in your work, and produce more negative effects like stress and sleeping issues that can lead to abuse of drugs and alcohol. This domino effect can be avoided by rebalancing just *one* aspect of your life. And it's never too late to take that first step. You may never achieve an ideal state of balance, but that's no excuse for not pursuing it. The danger of not doing anything will normalize your state of unhappiness, and you'll never discover your full potential and higher self. In The Healium Way, health is our wealth, with mental, physical and spiritual components always being prioritized over the material ones. Sadly, this balance practice is foreign to the Western or other workaholic cultures. It's not even taught in our schools.

According to the International Labor Organization, Americans work 137 more hours per year than the Japanese, 260 more hours per year than British workers, and 499 more hours per year than French workers. We may be more productive, but we're not happier than people in these countries. This litmus test shows that we are out of balance. In fact, we've gone from a culture of "work hard and play hard" to *work hard and hardly play.* The profit-over-people corporations are demanding more from their employees, and the result is a generation that shows more signs of *burnout* and work-life imbalance. But don't wait for your boss to help you get better. Take charge of your own health. If you're your own boss and you're experiencing burnout, you've simply allowed your work to boss you around — a situation that only *you* have the power to reverse. As a parent, mastering balance is even more critical. A very common sign of an imbalanced couple shows up *after* the kids are gone during the 'empty nester' stage. American parents dedicate about 18 years of their lives to raise their offspring. In this period many fail to practice balance (work, home and play) and lose their zest for life and adventure. The erosion takes place slowly and by the time they realize what's happened to them individually and as a couple, it's often a coulda, shoulda, woulda proposition that becomes hard to reverse. It is the main reason why I created a Center that is a playground for adults — to keep the flame alive at *all* times.

Now, let's go back to why we say *soul, body and mind* instead of body, mind and soul. By putting the Soul first, we actually manage and prioritize it in that order. In the business of healing, the busy and heated mind needs to get out of the way for the Soul to ignite. As a result, I like the Chinese terminology of the *water up, fire down,* mantra — keeping the mind cool and activating the Soul and the Chi. This orientation has helped me stay sane and in balance during many difficulties in the course of my life. Of course, being in balance isn't easy and obvious, otherwise we'd all be a lot less f*cked up as a people.

EVERYTHING IN MODERATION

Balance is about understanding the importance of moderation and avoiding being yanked around into any one end of a spectrum. Moderation is achieved by knowing how to realign ourselves when any one component (soul, body, mind) is out of whack and not allowing the damage to seep into the other areas. I see it as a rebalancing act of having *self-awareness, willpower and discipline.*

Let's use the mind as an example to demonstrate how this works. We know for instance that when we're having a bad day from a confrontation with someone that we are typically stressed and anxious. We know from past experience that it's a low-vibrational state of being that will have negative cascading effects to the body as well as the Soul. This information from our memory bank is our *self-awareness.*

If we fail to process this information to nip that problem, dark and violent thoughts can manifest into a restless brain and cause silent damage in the gut, heart, lungs and other vital organs. This is because all thoughts (negative or positive) are programmed in our body on a cellular level. These cells are highly sensitive and can quickly trigger an imbalance. In order to avoid this trigger and cascading collateral damage, we need to reverse the brain's trajectory by removing our attachment to the source of the stressor, which could be negative thoughts about that person. At this stage we're usually prescribing holistic/creative medicines to cool off the brain by boosting its positive and happy-making chemicals (serotonin, dopamine and endorphins). This is our *willpower.*

We then need to be diligent in taking these meds and not revisiting the source of our stressor for the rest of the day. This is our *discipline.* I've used this rebalancing act often to great success. Not surprisingly, a person who makes an effort to deploy self-awareness, willpower and discipline will learn the value of detaching or dialing down from the unhealthy elements and dialing up the value of the healthier ones. That's how we practice the art of moderation, which is essential for us to achieve good balance.

During the stage of establishing willpower, my favorite counteractants always include a combination of the creative and healing arts. I'll start with deep breathing exercises (aka breathwork) to get my oxygen levels up in the brain and my blood pressure down. Sunlight also increases oxygen and produces helpful neurochemicals, so if practical, I'll use it as my antidepressant with a jog or a walk outdoors. If I'm stuck indoors, I'll do some laughter medication, drumming and meditate for a few minutes. Body-tapping and reflexology from head to toe will also release any pent-up tension and improve immune response in the gut. Hands-on energy healing like Reiki can be combined to get a more targeted healing and has fast-acting results. All of these activities help the brain shift into a more positive place. Now, without fail, notice the domino effect: The mind settles, the body feels relaxed, and the Soul and Spirit are automatically uplifted. This self-care habit that I've painstakingly learned over the years helps me stay in a healthier balance throughout my day no matter who tries to unravel it. It is accomplished without any drugs, alcohol or other crutches. Try practicing it yourself in any stress-inducing situation and start getting proactive.

Moderation is therefore an important aspect of The Healium Way that must be mastered by all of us as a lifestyle habit.

A LIFE'S LESSON

My first lesson in moderation came when I was 11 years old in Paris. My parents often poured themselves a small glass of red wine as we sat to eat dinner together. One day my mom was busy in the kitchen while my dad was in the bathroom. I took a chance and took a small sip of Mom's glass of wine; I must say it tasted delicious, but I got caught! My dad saw me and I thought I'd be punished and be sent to my room. But to my surprise, he just gave me one of the most important pieces of advice of my life: Consume everything in moderation. He looked at me with his dilated brown eyes, pointed a finger emphatically at me and reiterated how alcohol, drugs and smoking were bad for our health and sternly said to me in our Indian Kutchi dialect: *"I know you're going to try all those things, my son, but when you're an adult remember to never get addicted to any of those substances. See your mom and I only drink wine in small quantities, almost always with food and never drink to get drunk."* Luckily for me, those prophetic words were permanently etched in my brain and have ruled my life for the better. I call it the 'Don't be a dumbass' common-sense lecture. Dad was teaching me the value of not being attached to anything to extremes. They were invaluable words of wisdom that have helped me not resort to anything as a crutch or an excuse to cope in my life. I've passed this philosophy on to my own kids, hopefully they'll do the same to their offspring.

"In Control of the Bottle"

(Clay, Mixed Media) Artist: Jim Peera

Alcoholics and addicts always face the choice between balancing the emotions of pain and pleasure (as depicted by the two faces — one happy and one sad, dangling on the corkscrew).

FRIENDS DON'T LET FRIENDS DRIVE DRUNK

Not everyone is lucky enough to get the moderation lecture that I did. I'm reminded of one particular close friend of my daughter, Michael, who was a talented lead guitarist band member by night and an intelligent practicing lawyer by day. The two of them made some powerful music together and he had his whole life ahead of him. Sadly, Michael succumbed to the excesses of a rock 'n' roll lifestyle and drowned his darkness and unhealed pain with alcohol and harmful drugs that eventually killed him. Michael accidently overdosed himself and died in his sleep at the tender age of 27. His story is an important lesson for all of us.

THE ADDICT WITHIN

I never learned the source of Michael's deep unhealed pain but I know his drug and drinking didn't originate with him. As with many societal labeled 'addicts,' their coping mechanism and crutches are often programmed during childhood, passed down the family and get justified and normalized. I know one of Michael's family members battled with a similar addiction and he allowed the unhealthy karma to pass onto him. I once confronted him with his alcoholism at our Center, only to have him deny, lie and get defensive about it, the classic tactics of many addicts. *"Don't patronize me, Jim, you're not my Dad,"* he abruptly replied. At one point, I mentioned his unhealthy condition to his friends, but they didn't act to help him, and I realized he was surrounded by enablers who were either too weak to confront him, were afraid of losing him as a friend, got intimidated by him or didn't care enough about themselves to care for him. My daughter often told us how Michael was a great manipulator and was too smart for his own good. Whatever the justifications, his death by drug overdose put him in the same league of human tragedies as Elvis Presley, Michael Jackson, John Belushi, Kurt Cobain and Amy Winehouse — to name a few.

But how different is Michael's story from ours? Labeling someone as an 'addict' absolves us from our own responsibilities to change and rebalance our many unhealthy attachments. How about we look at ourselves as the 'unlabeled addicts' — *the addict within*? An addict doesn't manifest their stigmatized label overnight, but over time. Afterall, isn't an addict someone who simply lacks self-awareness, willpower and discipline to self-correct their unhealthy attachments? Armed with this simple raw truth, aren't we all guilty of being attached and addicted to some bad sh*t, because we can't effectively cope with our stress, anxiety, traumas, loneliness, boredom, and the many pressures of life? Isn't it also true that an extreme version of a good thing can lead to a bad thing? Over-exercising and overeating are good examples. In fact, a seemingly healthy habit can slowly turn unhealthy, and if left uncontrolled, can begin to rule our lives and morph into a self-destructive addiction. Typical examples of our common addictions include; social media, work, junk food, cellphone, alcohol, caffeine, porn, video games, drugs, power and money. Since we're *all* guilty of being seduced by one or more of these things, what if we figure out how not to become a statistic like Michael. Can we start by admitting our condition?

Most of us will never admit to any addiction. It makes us feel weak, sick and stigmatized. This reality puts the onus on society or the circle of people around us to get involved. Fortunately, a place like Healium is an idyllic non-threatening Truth Lab to start the process. Once a loved-one or an advocate brings the labeled 'addict' to The Center for help, we inform them that it typically takes a few sessions to break through their defenses and see some improvement. Although we've never offered a specific prevention or recovery program at our Center, we've always seen addiction as a symptom and a disease of the mind — that necessitates out-of-the-box, creative solutions as a first line of treatment. We have seen workaholics, alcoholics and drug addicts find benefit using this approach. Let me share some insights.

Our primary goal is to diminish their barriers of resistance and match their intention to a realistic path of self-transformation. This is done using a non-clinical back-door approach. First, we deploy Principle # 19, *Leading by Example*, in a group setting. We make the person feel at home and have them mix in with the other unlabeled addicts, to observe and just enjoy the particular activity. They're not treated any differently or given special attention. There are no conditions and never any shaming or judging at any time. This inspires them to engage on their own terms. Often, they'll quench their curiosity by dipping their toes and try out our varied offerings such as sound vibration healing, yoga, creative release exercises such as; poetry writing, drumming, painting, etc. The premise is to use these holistic modes to slowly and patiently unearth the source of the emotional pain and imbalance residing subconsciously in their brain. It is this embedded trauma that's often causing the addict to enter the box of temporary pleasure, trapping them into a spiraling habit-forming hellhole that they can't get out of. Next, we deploy Principle #14, *Opening the Communication Door*. In this stage, we use the T.H.R.E.T tenets (discussed earlier) as a one-on-one (often private) dialoguing to further loosen up the resistances and excuses from the addict. We'll listen and allow them to share the information they're comfortable with. Usually, this is where the 'addicts' show readiness to get   some help, as they've interacted with Soul-filling activities and know   that someone cares for their wellbeing. Once we're able to get the person into the intention mode; to *want* to help themselves, we begin referring them to healing professionals specializing in Reiki, Reflexology, past-life regression, hypnotherapy and even psychedelic medicines. All are helpful to unplug the addicts' hidden trauma and get them on a path of recovery and healthier balance. If none of these methods work, and they're too smart and manipulative for their own good, the next step is the 'intervention' stage where you must enroll them in the various (highly costly) addiction rehabilitation centers across the country.

Looking at the glass half full, perhaps tragedies like Michael's don't go in vain and serve as a lesson to the unhealed to arrest their crutches and be awakened before it's too late. Until they're ready to be fixed and have the true intention and commitment, most addicts (labeled or unlabeled) will continue down the path of self-destruction, and one day like Michael — not wake up.

At his memorial ceremony that was held at our Center, I could not help noticing how many of his (mostly millennial) friends who paid respect to him, elected to drown themselves in a sea of alcohol to cope with his loss. How oxymoronic is that, I thought to myself! In many ways it revealed the fragility of this generation not having the societal support and lacking the resiliency and natural coping mechanisms to deal with pain and reality. I saw a certain guilt in their eyes, and began to doubt that these young people would view his death as a painful wake up call, a lesson to self-correct their own imbalances. I hope and pray that it was both. I was particularly concerned and afraid for my own kids. After all, they were raised in the liberalized Western culture of sex, drugs and rock 'n' roll that could easily take them down this dark, self-destructive path. As we burnt a memorial bonfire for Michael and lit candles in a ceremonious prayer beneath starry skies; we all joined hands and prayed for the ascension of the young man's Soul. It was a reminder of our own fragile destiny — some of which is in our control but mostly in God's hands. I attentively watched my daughter that night mourn her friend's loss by not getting inebriated and staying in control of her emotions. She took a more spiritual approach to healing her pain and by using the many tools of The Healium Way she'd learned working at The Center. I was relieved and thanked the brightly lit stars above for that. I'm sure Michael did too.

STUCK IN THE MIDDLE WITH YOU

In the next example, I'll demonstrate how it's possible to shift someone from a predisposed and extreme behavior to a moderate one — by being courageous and creative. The story is about a 50-year old rather rigid and self-admitted racist white man who worked for me as a handyman. His name was Mike. Mike was poor in wallet but rich in heart. He was a highly talented, kind, generous and honest man. He had blue eyes and a likable personality. Sadly, he was operating his life stuck in many unhealthy boxes battling methamphetamine addiction and racism — the latter of which got him in trouble and the former eventually killed him. Mike's racist views were not mired in hatred but rather ignorance and ancestral programming. Like a lot of white people in the segregated deep South, he was raised in a home where colored people were viewed as second-class citizens. When I heard Mike use the 'N' word on several occasions, I confronted him about his racism, and he told me he didn't feel comfortable taking lunch breaks with blacks or even sitting in the car with them. He was stubborn and unwavering in his views. So instead of appeasing him, I tried applying a combination of a few of The Healium Way Principles as a rebalancing act, including authenticity, creativity, non-judgment, detachment and removal of fear. Each time I gave him a ride to a job site, I squeezed him in the front passenger side of my van with a black man named Doug.

Doug was a street hustler and an alcoholic. But when he worked, he was a hard worker, self-motivated and saved me a lot of money. He was also was colorblind and friendly to everyone. Often, they were sitting elbow to elbow for almost an hour, and Mike appeared very uncomfortable. On a couple of occasions, he refused to come to work if Doug was in the vehicle. So I picked him up first. Mike even demanded I put Doug in the rear cargo area filled with supplies. I simply laughed and told him he was being a racist ass. About two weeks into the project, Mike threw an ugly temper tantrum, accusing Doug of contaminating his fries by touching them. He called him the 'N' word and then quickly turned his back on him and walked away. Doug, who was a lot stronger than Mike, could have inflamed the situation and started a fight but he refrained. Instead, he took his packet of fries and handed it to Mike, saying *"Don't worry about it, man, you can have all of my fries that I haven't touched."* Mike was speechless and stunned at Doug's response, and a few minutes later apologized to him. It was a wake-up call for Mike, who told me that he felt stupid by judging Doug unfairly. *"I see what you were trying to do by having me ride next to him, Jim. Hell, I thought he'd kill me when I called him a ['N' word]!"* exclaimed Mike in a distraught voice. I patted Mike on the shoulder and told him in simple lingo how he had deviated from his higher self as a human being and this experience was his life's lesson. From that day onwards, Mike and Doug became good friends who joked, shared their lunch and even bought each other beer at the end of the work day. They worked for me as a team for several years and I never heard Mike utter racist remarks against Doug or black people again. It was a beautiful transformation that erased a white man's ugly racist views. All it took was a little courage and creativity on my end to put Mike in a "too close for comfort" situation to get to know Doug on a personal level. Indeed, this act of awareness and kindness undid Mike's hurtful stereotyping from years of bias and racial programming.

As I've said before, The Healium Way is not about trying to get you to shift from any predisposition or belief system, rather it's in simply making you aware of them in the context of your personal growth and balance. The above example took a conscious decision by Mike and Doug to shift to a more balanced condition.

"Restore The Balance"

(Clay, Chrysocolla, Petrified Rock, Stones) Artist: Jim Peera

Balance is also about thinking from a centrist position on politics, policies, ideologies and social values. And much of this correct mindset can be achieved by understanding the importance of our daily influences. I always tell my kids that they are a product of their environment. If they're going to hang around with 9 fragile people, chances are they will soon be the 10th fragile person. It is for this reason that being around a good mix of people who are diverse in their economic status, ethnicity, education level, spirituality, philosophy and upbringing is the key to staying even-keeled and striving for a more sustainable balanced outlook.

THE MIRROR OF TRUTH

Knowing oneself is the prerequisite to fixing your imbalances. As a doctor in charge of your own wellness, you must first know *who* you are (your character) before you can know *what* you need to alter to achieve that healthy balance. When I look at the attainment of balance in my own life, I use a multidimensional lens of our human condition and character assessment. I want to know where I stand in relation to others in my beliefs and uniqueness in areas such as material vs. Spiritual values, Eastern vs. Western cultures, liberal vs. conservative politics, and so forth. After all, I don't live on some remote island so I have to get along with different types of people. When we take inventory of our character in this way, it helps us readjust our areas of deficiency and enables us to get to a healthier personal equilibrium. This unbiased self-recognition not only gives me a more accurate reading of who I am, but paints a more accurate picture of how others see me as well.

In order to achieve a successful shift, I find it a lot easier to get to a state of balance by making a simple checklist of what I can control: *my soul, my body and my mind.* Before we delve into further detail, I've prepared a neat little *mirror of truth* exercise that will help you assess your own *character.* By taking a few minutes to identify our personality traits, we can help ourselves get back on a healthier path to restoring our balance. It's a two-sided magical mirror. One side of the mirror shows me who I am, as the other side shows how others may see me. Since perception is reality, I need to know how other people view me in order to fix my particular imbalances. This mirror helps to reduce the ego, lessens our rigidity to change and makes us have more empathy toward others. It also reveals if we are operating authentically and unfiltered with people or putting up a facade and being pretentious. How we each fit into these various categories will indicate our particular state of being and purpose. For starters, I always have an internal dialogue and ask myself where I stand at that moment. Then I educate myself on the components that I feel missing or am deficient in. This allows me to then extract the positive aspects of the missing parts and infuse them into mine. As an immigrant, the Eastern/Western upbringing scale is instructive. Although, I've spent 50 years in the West, I grew up in a Muslim/East Indian culture and family upbringing. Looking at this chart, I'll put a mark that is two-thirds heavy on the Eastern side of the scale. It reminds me that I need to adjust to a healthier 50 percent balance. I'll have to make more effort in learning about the Western culture from my wife and kids. Interestingly, I now also see the opposite relationship on their scale. In order to have a healthier balance, we agree to help each other get to a better understanding with some detailed lessons in Eastern and Western ways. I make a conscientious effort to teach my wife and children the best aspects of Eastern culture, and they in turn teach me what I don't know about the traditions and nuances of the Western culture.

For instance, I'll show my kids the etiquette of being a good host when guests visit them in their home. In Eastern culture, any guest who enters the house is first offered a welcoming drink, something that isn't common in America, which bothers the heck out of me. My kids will in turn instruct me in the Western way of not forcing people to eat or drink something that's foreign to them, a common practice in the East which bothers my kids. We mix and match the teachings and beliefs of both cultures as necessary and extract the better attributes to emulate. This brings me to a healthier balance while also staying even keel and consistent. This method has protected me from falling prey to the emotional extremes of hot/cold, high/low and happy/sad bi-polar conditions. As a person who preaches moderation to everyone, I also avoid people with radical views. Interestingly, similar to our healing journey from dark to light, we'll often test aspects of a particular extreme in order to appreciate the benefits of adjusting to a healthier moderate level.

I've met a good share of unhealed and fragile people at The Center who are easily attached to extremist mindsets. Whether it's their vulnerability, gullibility or resignation of their self-worth, they're attracted to a controlling philosophy, preferring to be told what to do, when to do it and how to do it. Not surprisingly, these folks tend to find The Healium Way to be too unstructured and unconventional for their purposes. In some cases, their shift into the deep end of the extremist mindset is temporary, but in many situations; it is permanent, giving rise to the sheeple condition. Being in balance is tricky because it can take a lot of work to erase old patterns, to re-examine societal pressures, and to have self-awareness and admit that you're on the wrong track. In a world where workaholism, drug addictions, fanaticism, greed, compulsive behaviors are rampant, failing in the rebalancing act holds harsh consequences. It may often swing us too far, to a point of no return.

THE MIRROR OF TRUTH EXERCISE reveals your character and how you can tweak and improve on shifting into a healthier balance for each item.

Mark your character position that suits you best on this scale:

Material---Spiritual Values

Eastern---Western Cultures

Liberal-----------------------------------Conservative Politics

Profit---------------------------------------Charitable Motive

Active ---------------------------------------Passive Activities

Educated--Uneducated

Introverted-- Extroverted

Rich---Poor status

Worldly---------------------------------------Unsophisticated

Religious-- Atheist Beliefs

Diverse---Closed Mindset

Unbiased---Biased Views

Generous--Frugal

Conservative---Risk Taker

White--Non-White Race

Straight---LGBTQ

Healthy---Unhealthy Soul

Healthy---Unhealthy Body

Healthy---Unhealthy Mind

In this exercise, be honest about yourself. There are no right or wrong answers, shame or comparison to others. If you're a tightwad, mark the far-right scale of "Uncharitable." If you're overweight, mark the far right of "Unhealthy." Being transparent about your flaws will show you where you need to adjust yourself. For instance, if you're on the closer end of the "Material" side, it indicates your need to improve on simplifying your life. If you're closer on the "Poor" side, it means you must make an effort to stop thinking from a place of scarcity and hang out with more upwardly mobile people. If you're closer to a "Liberal" side, it asks that you get small doses of conservative news into your life. If you are a white person, you need to educate yourself more on colored people. If you're on the less "Educated" spectrum, hang around smarter people. The idea here is to get out of the preset boxes you're in and expand your knowledge beyond your comfort and predisposed levels. Being multifaceted is highly liberating. But this expansion is not easy as it requires you to detach from your beliefs and/or state of mind and accept a different reality. Before you can change the world, you need to first change yourself. And the Mirror of Truth is a great starting point to help you do that!

"Not everything that is faced can be changed, but nothing can be changed if it is not faced."
– James Baldwin

Feeding the Soul

"The soul does not love. It is love itself. It does not exist. It is existence alone. It does not know. It is knowledge itself."
— Patanjali (Yoga Sutra)

In many religious, philosophical, and mythological traditions, the Soul is the incorporeal essence of a living being. It has no scientific explanation, but is the essential glue within each of us that binds us to our Creator and that never dies. For this reason, in the pursuit of living a well-balanced life, being *extra*ordinary and having no regrets, we must put the Soul before the body or the mind. But just because the Soul never dies, it doesn't mean that it is healthy and alive in every one of us while we are in human form. Quite the contrary. If you live in a materialistic way, the Soul takes a back seat to superficial and egotistic forces. Since all of a person's moral values, character and abilities emanate from the Soul, it is the one essence within us that is controlled by our own actions and deeds.

For the purposes of The Healium Way, the power of the Soul rests in the following categories: *passion, purpose, creativity, intuition, compassion, empathy, emotion, pleasure, service to others, and our connection with the Divine.* If you've been deficient in any of these areas, you're probably experiencing an erosion of your Soul and operating at a lower-vibration and frequency. This imbalance is further exacerbated by our rapid attachment to the machines, robots and digital economy, as they further suck the soul.

So reducing our attachment and participation in life's many soul-sucking entrapments is critical. *"If you've lost your Soul, you've played a role"* is what I say to people who complain about feeling empty inside. What's even more disparaging for some people is that you can't push a button on your app or swallow a pill to recover it. You have to do the work. And here's the good news — if you can lose it, you can win it back.

With this in mind, it becomes easier to prescribe a conscious three-part regimen to keep the Soul healthy and alive by;

1. Connecting to your Divinity.

2. Practicing the art of forgiveness.

3. Living life.

Not surprisingly, all three of these elements play a critical role in reducing our *coulda, shoulda, woulda* condition of being trapped in a box of life filled with regrets.

1.   **Connecting to your Divinity** is paramount to feeding the Soul. Whether you consider yourself to be religious, agnostic or an atheist, remember you are still a Divine being. You did not magically appear here and your existence is not a coincidence. Each one of us seven billion humans on this planet are here for some reason. Unfortunately, the harder challenge is to decipher that reason and purpose. And in so doing, we'll need to stay connected with and be guided by our maker. We'll resist, question, doubt and sometimes fear this mysterious Source. But in the end, we must agree to respect and befriend this all-loving, all-encompassing Creator. You don't need to change your outlook on your personal belief system, but rather see yourself as part and parcel of the miracle of creation itself. In this context, you are love, light and compassion. So be it, own it and share those attributes with everyone you encounter as much as you can. It will help you live a life without regrets. Each time you interact with another human being, of any type and in any situation,

see them as a part of the same system of creation and Divinity as yourself. When we stop seeing people as white, colored, rich, poor, party-affiliated and all other man-made labels but simply as Divine beings, we transform from ordinary to *extra*ordinary. When we retrain our mind and eyes to think and see like our Creator, we liberate ourselves from judgment and become more effective observers of people. By treating people with love and compassion, our Soul permeates everyone it touches. From just one act of kindness, it is possible to spread our source of energy into a powerful field of collective consciousness. I've seen it often at Healium. I notice how differently people are treated with this interconnective lens. Do you become more compassionate and loving toward them? Do you reduce all thoughts of hostility and dishonesty? Do you take less and give more? Are you more forgiving? Do you become more charitable? Do you have more empathy? What's fascinating is how our generosity quotient increases while the greed factor decreases. It's quite remarkable how we become better human beings by changing the way we look at things. This is because we realize that whatever we do to others — we do to ourselves.

We are linked in the cosmic realm of one Divinity and higher consciousness. In this realm there is no separation. When we step over others, we're stepping over our own self. Each good deed toward another human being will manifest in good things for you, while any bad action has a boomerang effect of harming yourself. Each time you steal from someone, you're stealing from one of God's children. In Christianity, it's confirmed by the *"Do unto others, what you'd want done unto you"* principle. Interestingly, the Soul doesn't care whether you worship a particular book, man or theology. It's formless, label-less and judgment-free. Since we're all part and parcel of this mysterious Divinity, each of us has a vested interest in every action that we take with our fellow human beings. In the end, your deeds will determine the health of your Soul and supersedes your words or your belief system. The Soul is your eternal connection to your maker. It is holding you accountable at all times — alive or dead.

2.   **Practicing the art of forgiveness** is about liberation of the self — releasing oneself from misery. It frees our psyche and our Soul from the pain of attachment, and it eases the burden of others who may have been consciously or unconsciously involved in our pain. It is also about giving up your right to condemn others and handing that job over to your Creator to judge. Unfortunately, many of us don't get this memo, and we suffer internally. Too many people get stuck in a pattern of wanting to punish the wrongdoing by not releasing the person from their actions. Often, we come to our senses too late and die with regrets. For this reason, I'll spend some extra time on this very important subject. You'll know when you have forgiven someone unconditionally because you cannot mistake the feeling of emotional freedom and detachment from a predisposed outcome. When I forgive anyone for something, it feels like an albatross has been lifted from my chest and it's an amazing feeling. What's even more powerful is how forgiveness can be accomplished by meditating and sitting in isolation for our own peace of mind. But what if we don't know how to do that?

LOVE THY ENEMY

Many people just don't know how to let go of their attachment to achieve a certain outcome. Ego, pride, bitterness and obstinate forces take over and become the overriding voices in our head that hold our peace hostage. In Christianity, Christ underscores our Divine interrelationship with one another when he advises us to *"love thy enemy."* I've asked dozens of people to tell me what his words mean, and every person has pointed to conventional wisdom about "not hating others who do us harm." But The Healium Way sees it differently. Christ's message becomes way more powerful when we put on an unconventional hat. We've established that our complex brain is responsible for all our thoughts and actions and that we're flawed beings. By using our brain as a weapon to harm ourselves and others. we can also decipher that when we call someone our enemy—we're talking about ourselves. Since the enemy is our mind, the enemy is actually YOU, not the person or group of people you despise. This revelation is critical to understand. Indeed, Christ's words guide us to fix *our own* hostile mind, to replace the self-sabotaging, the blame game, the pride and the ego — with self-responsibility and self-love. By loving the enemy within, we create a condition that will reduce our enmity for others. By loving ourselves (and I don't mean being a narcissist or self-absorbed person), we love others.

Now our need for ill-will, wars and destruction toward humanity dissipates. By thinking in this way, we've just created a better and a more *extra*ordinary version of ourselves! The idea of self-love as the antidote for healing the mind and the unhealed and troubled Soul is of course an old prescription for mankind. But "man" is not kind to himself because of his reptilian brain and human nature's penchant for attaching to low-vibrational forces like ego, greed, power, jealousy, self-righteousness and fear. What's worse is that, due to his bullheaded mind, he fails to forgive himself for his fu*k-ups and forge a better path — but rather indulges in self-loathing and can't forgive others. Alas, he creates a nasty feedback loop. A lot of the resistance results from our inability to get to a vulnerable state and rewire the social and patriarchal programming within. As you've come to know, The Healium Way Principles will work to loosen up that condition and get you on a better path to your *extra*ordinary self. Once you've applied the many ideas successfully and have removed thoughts of hostility from the mind, you may be ready to forgive a person.

If you're having a hard time doing that, you may want to initiate the next step to prepare for a face-to-face encounter. This is an optional step, but it is highly effective for closure of any wound.

I've used this technique successfully many times and am sharing it with you for your use. I call it *facing forgiveness:*

FACING FORGIVENESS

Consider this neat little three-stage visual exercise that you can initiate with a person you care about and seek to forgive.

a.   **Visualization.** Reconstruct a mental picture of the person in happier times with you. Before you meet this person, fill in your mind with moving images of those moments. Take a few minutes to bask in the various scenes of this past memory. Feel the emotions and your body language. Then re-imagine it in the present, feeling all the emotions from head to toe. Note the change in emotions and heartbeat between the past memory and the present. Each time you feel angry or hurt, go back to the older happier memories. Keep doing this until the emotional gap between the older memory and the newer version is lessened. This stage may take some time, but slowly your boxing gloves and offensive mental weapons will come off.

b.   **Partner with an advocate.** Find a trusted relative or friend to help arrange a short face-to-face meeting with this person. This way you'll reduce any stress on yourself by not having any expectation of a positive outcome. Once you lower your bar, your intention is no longer about "demanding" a meeting, rather it is an "ask." In this instance, your path to forgiveness is not conditional for this meeting to take place. You make a conscientious decision before you get to this stage that no matter what the other person's actions or inaction are, you're on the path to forgive them. That is your clear intention. The face-to-face meeting itself is simply icing on the cake, so to speak. Once you get the meeting arranged, make sure you're not judging, pontificating, venting, finger-pointing or justifying your position. Instead, you're practicing a mindfulness technique of listening and sending love their way. Look at yourself from the other person's eyes and be a good observer. Take mental notes of all the emotions and body language from the person sitting across from you. Store those emotions in your memory bank — you'll revisit them later. When you get a chance to talk, you'll need to acknowledge to this person that you understand their pain by saying; *"I hear you,"* or *"I get it."* The more you say this (even if you don't mean it) the better. This simple act is a powerful mental signal to both parties. For you, it sends a subliminal message to your brain to move you closer to breaking down your defenses. As for the other party, there's a sense of being heard, respected and feeling valued. At this meeting, some people will bury the hatchet, hug, cry, forgive and begin to jumpstart their relationship. But for many others, a third stage is necessary to get the desired results.

c.   **ARTiculate the meeting.** In this final stage, you'll be converting the notes from the meeting into a self-expressive art form at home. You can write a poem, draw stick figures, paint, etc. These hands-on creative tools are highly effective to unearth and heal emotional scars harboring within us. This is your visual journal of forgiveness. Don't hold back and be as accurate in recreating the person's feelings from your memory bank. What you're doing here is turning someone else's pain into your own piece of art. This expressive empathy exercise is quite revealing and effective as a tool for letting go of grudges and moving towards forgiveness. After you've completed the piece, look at it closely. Did you translate the person's emotions accurately or did you dilute and contaminate it with your own personal biased feelings? If you did the latter, you're not alone, many of us do that. Feel the healthy release. The more you sit with yourself and unleash your emotions with uninhibited self-expression, the less you'll judge yourself and exaggerate the story. Once you've completed your creative-expressive exercise, place it in an area surrounded by two or more candles. Each night for an hour or so, light the candles and allow the art piece to soak into your thoughts without any judgment or predispositions. In a few days, observe what happens to your viewpoint of the other person. How has the story of the original incident changed? Does it even matter? In a typical scenario, you will be a lot closer to forgiving the person unconditionally. During this period, a regular dose of mindfulness meditation, prayers and spiritual upliftment can also speed the process.

Note: At this stage, you can choose to phone, email or even meet the person face to face to apologize in your own words: *"I am sorry for any pain, anger or bad blood between us. And I forgive you."* Be as sincere as you can. And mean it. For you, it's a gesture of your willpower and intention to move forward — and for them, it's a reason to talk freely. But you must not harbor expectations. You want to keep it as personal and authentic as you can. Sometimes we have the urge to not let the person off the hook for their actions and for us to speak our mind about the grievance. Avoid that at all cost. Instead, forgive the person entirely and unconditionally. You do not want to cut another wound in a person when you just spent a lot of time stitching the first one up!

MANAGING THE MULE-BRAINED

If we are absolutely unwilling to forgive anyone for their transgressions, are stubbornly grudgeful and not willing to communicate with them in any manner, it is often a reflection of our own deep unhealed wounds that we must work to uncover and heal. In most cases, these are not first-time offenses, but a pattern of unforgiving behavior. Our resistance is simply a convenient cover made from a cloth of self-righteousness with pride and ego woven into the fabric. We smother it on anyone we have disagreements with. Often people in this category thrive on adversity and spend their low-vibrational energies on justifying their resentments and sucking you into their unfulfilled world.

Misery loves company, and if you're this type of person just look back at your history with people you've blasted out of your life with angst and still suffer from the recoil. It's especially concerning when the other person has taken the initiative to ask for forgiveness or apologized for their f*ckups, and you don't accept the apology. This is your concrete tomb that you need to ditch for an aquarium. It is self-sabotage and masochistic behavior that is exposing your imbalances. It doesn't go away until you look into the Mirror of Truth and self-prescribe the medicine of forgiveness to repair it. Sometimes a good mediator can be the bridge to troubled waters and knock some sense into us and get us to a place of reckoning. Sadly, many people never get professional help and suffer without ever knowing the liberation of the Soul while being alive. They simply die with regrets.

For those of us who take the corrective action to forgive, the reward is priceless as it leads to our awakening. From my own experience, the more I practice forgiving people, the easier it gets. The hardest part is that first step into the frigid water.

> *"The journey of a thousand miles begins with the first step."*
> — Lao Tsu

Once we've healed our own past unattended wounds, our Soul strengthens and we stop making excuses to justify our victim and entitlement conditions. We no longer marinate in the cesspool of unhealthy crutches or seek validation for our unhappiness. We begin to realize that we are more resilient and powerful when we're emotionally stable. The question I ask myself when my rigid, egotistic and immature self suffocates my logic is, *"Do I want to be right, or do I want to be at peace?"* Once we are healed, the answer is clear and becomes automatic in any confrontation or domestic dispute. We also know in our heart and mind that our emotional stability is dependent on our Soul being detached from all pain and suffering. Since a hate-driven mind created the problem in the first place, we'll need to use a different approach to fix it. Otherwise, the same mind will only breed the same low-vibrational results.

Therefore, our default position is always to choose the higher-self tools and deploy love versus hate and peace over torment.

In one of the Beatles songs, *"All You Need Is Love,'* the Lennon and McCartney penned lyrics remind us that *"There's nothing you can do that can't be done. There's no one you can save that can't be saved.* Turbocharged in The Healium Way it means, *"There's nothing so f*cked that it can't be unf*cked. It's easy. All you need is love."* The message of love is once again the lifeline to our sinking ship (our Soul). It's our answer to liberate ourselves from a place of loneliness, misery and darkness into light — and use the key of forgiveness to uncage ourselves from our self-imposed boxes of agony and self-defeat. It is only then that we understand that forgiveness is a win-win outcome, and stop waging war against our enemy; our own mind.

3. **Living life** is to be truly alive and not be trapped by inertia. Nothing tarnishes the Soul more than being stuck in restrictive boxes and being imprisoned from unbound joy and pleasure. The sooner you get on board to create a healed life for yourself, the better you will enjoy and live life without any excuses or distractions. It may sound trivial to some of you that I am suggesting to 'live life' with passion, but what is happening in America is quite the opposite. The American mindf*ck indoctrinates people to work hard, save for retirement and enjoy life when *in* retirement — an ordinary and conventional proposition.

Although those goals have some merit, they're not in balance and are flawed. The *extra*ordinary person is not waiting until retirement to enjoy life's fullness and adventure, as it is counterproductive to living life without much regret. For one, it programs us to accept the notion that we need a lot of money to enjoy life. We've already debunked this untruth throughout this book. Secondly, it ignores the fact that you may either not live past retirement age, or may be unfit to enjoy your saved money. The latter issue is a common situation with Americans who are living longer but are physically unhealthy and mentally imprisoned. Although you may be financially healthy in your 60s, you're living in a worn and torn body that's not going to enjoy your money the way you did when you were younger and healthier. I've met a lot of people who are diagnosed with a terminal illness or the elderly who reflect on a life lived half-full and blame it on being over-consumed by money, materialism, competitiveness and busyness. "*I never took the necessary time off from work, and accumulated over two years of paid vacation working for the city, how crazy is that!*" a retired government worker who attended our Center lamented to me. He said he was dying of prostate cancer and had never traveled outside of America.

Not surprisingly, for many Americans, this man's coulda, shoulda, woulda story sounds too familiar. The work grind and *doing* gets in the way of *being* — and the imbalance is not corrected until something tragic or a terminal event happens to us or to the people we love. But why do we have to be confronted with an illness or come close to dying to start living? Sadly, the Soul has been held hostage by the forces of ego, greed, monotony and other excuses or convenient man-made distractions. The most obvious excuse we've found at The Center is, once again, the obsession with making money. Isn't it interesting how those that don't live life to the fullest, find excuses to wallow in self-pity until they accumulate more money? While similarly those that have accumulated enough money don't find true joy and satisfaction either? Ironically, what's often common in both these camps is the obsession to fill the void in their Soul by going shopping and finding temporary happiness that way — a short-lived fix. That's because our Soul cannot be bought. In fact, the Soul is weakened by the ego which destroys its ability to connect to our Divinity. Without activating the Divine light within, the Soul dies. In order for it to flourish, it needs to be in the present, stay authentic and have no attachments such as money or a particular status label. The Healium Way of "living life" is more to do with finding inner contentment and uninhibited joy with less expensive toys and material things — rather than with accumulating more. It follows the "less is more" philosophy. To live life is to savor all of life's delights and beauty by fully engaging in it. It is not about owning big mansions, yachts, gold watches and such. It's also not dictated by what the stock market does on any given day. That's a man-made trap, an excuse not to look deeper into ourselves. The truth is, life doesn't suck. It's your definition of life that sucks — by choosing to suck the joy out of life, or for that matter to think that life will suck unless you keep accumulating money to flaunt your lifestyle and be validated as "successful."

As a successful person myself, I can tell you that to live life is to be able to rearrange how you think about success — and it's not conventional wisdom. For one, I've learned to not take life for granted and live every day in the healthiest balance I can. That is something I do for myself and for others, everything possible in my capacity and power; spiritual and material. Some days will be better than others, but I never look back. The second point is to understand the difference between what *feels* good and what *is* good. One is about the temporary dopamine high of feeling like a winner, validating one's ego and boosting self-esteem (profiting in investments, stock market, casino, lottery etc) — like a drug or a substance that feels good for a while — until we keep building resistance and keep increasing our dosage of the drug and get addicted. The other is about spreading some of that money into the hands of the less fortunate (outside of our own bubbles) where it makes a difference. Interestingly, this too feels good. But it's a different type of good. It's deeper, richer and more sustainable. And unlike the first addictive kind, it has positive and longer-lasting side effects. Therefore, both conditions can coexist beautifully, if we know how to discipline our mind and have a working hybrid model that fits our lifestyle.

In this manner, The Healium Way of living life is also about getting high on life holistically — without being high on addictive substances or attachment to unhealthy habits and vices.

TRYING TO MAKE IT

Our hyper-consumerist economic model ignites the fire, and clever marketing feeds the flame. It's an engineered self-fulfilling prophecy of the profit-over-people American system. Even our governments are in on the fix. The legalization of casino gambling and lottery tickets is a good example of convoluted legislation that is doing a disservice to most Americans. Why would any government encourage gambling on its soil when so many of its people are money addicts and suffer mental health problems? Gambling exacerbates our imbalances and addictions, negatively affects the poor and results in depression and anxiety. Sure, it's a great source of revenue for states that brings jobs and investment. And for some folks, it's legitimate entertainment that feeds the ego and boosts dopamine levels in the brain. But is it worth the trade-off? This temporary high is quite counterintuitive to our mental wellness because gambling is only fun when you win. Since the odds are always against the player, the avid gambler is practicing an exercise in futility, which results in more anxiety, depression and discontentment. So, is the shortlist of positives for gambling worth people's obsession with it? If we can ban smoking in public places and have mandatory seat belt regulations to protect our health, why is gambling not banned or at least restricted to provide the same benefit? Sounds like hypocrisy to me. Perhaps it's our societal pressure for trying to "make it," (i.e. in get-rich-quick schemes). But what does that mean anyway? If it's a measurement of financial success or achieving the oversold American Dream, then it's a flawed metric. The fact is, that if we're educated, successful and have a comfortable lifestyle, we'll still keep working harder to make more money, have more toys and buy more things that we don't need. That's human nature testing our limits. The chase never stops. If we're millionaires, we're not satisfied with all our vacation homes, private jets, yachts, cars etc., and take on more egotistical projects to build more wealth in pursuit of becoming even wealthier. If we're multi-millionaires or billionaires, we're bored with money and set our sights on attaining more power, creating monopolies, ruling the world and taking expensive joy rides into space. Instead of being good custodians of our egg baskets by spreading the eggs to make a difference; we get more stressed making, accumulating and protecting our overbearing loot.

It's all not without a heavy cost however, as we end up paying a hefty price with our family, health, marriage, work, relationships, etc., to name a few common casualties. In the end, the trade-off to "make it" is a lose-lose situation. I've witnessed much of this imbalance with my association with wealthy people and prefer the simpler lifestyle. And you can, too. You'll see as I have how this profit-over-people mindset is calamitous, and how the high-risk and low-reward paradigm leads to a downward trajectory — that only you have the power to reverse. It entails that you pay attention to the signs of the unhealthy imbalances within you. It is about decreasing the man-made trappings such as having a gambling habit or addiction and increasing your higher-self attributes. It means that you need to stop complicating your life by not resisting change to a simpler life, especially if you're financially loaded.

KING OF FOOLS

If you're that person who's already "made it" and has stowed away ample amounts of money, this humorous fish-penis analogy may help you understand a better and balanced path forward; "It's not how deep you fish — but how you wiggle the worm." This message has important applications to The Healium Way. It means you can still have a lot of fun in life without hoarding all the big toys or surrender to your egotistical beast. You just have to get creative. And the arts are the most affordable ways to have fun. But we Americans generally aren't satisfied with that way of thinking. Indeed, we follow the rubric of "bigger is better." Examples include; big butts, big penises, big boobs, big mansions, big cars, big egos, Big Macs, bigwigs — and even big idiots and big bigots. Our obsession with having more, more and more of something throws us into an excess of not appreciating anything unless we have everything. In this way, we correlate our wallet and bank size with our happiness. We deduce that a person living in a big mansion, driving a big SUV, smoking a big cigar and talking big must be happy as sh*t. How wrong. This false narrative is our downfall. Many wealthy folks I've met in my life are actually quite a bunch of sad f*cks. They're so fixated on accumulating and hoarding their pile of gold that their eyes have become blinded to its luster and beauty. I call them *King of Fools,* a self-inflicted (bourgeois) caste system. We've practiced this form of class separation throughout history. But it's not getting us anywhere. Often it manifests in stereotyping people outside the caste based on their attire, skin color, attitude, status symbols, etc. It happens to my wife and me often in our travels as we appear to the King of Fools as "happy, care-free hippies" joking and enjoying ourselves in expensive hotel lobbies and restaurants. In this programmed egotistic mode, the King sitting on his throne of riches carries a serious demeanor and fails to see the fun and excitement in giving, sharing and interacting with anyone who is beneath him (working class or simply different). Many of us often fall prey to this condition in our climb up the mountain, and don't realize how our unnatural privileged behaviors negatively affect our own happiness.

I've encountered dozens of wealthy bachelors and couples perched comfortably on their illusive mountaintops with all their man-made material riches at their disposal, yet devoid of real joy or contentment in their hearts. It's not just an American thing; it's a global human defect. The gold of these Kings tarnishes their Soul, and it's by their own doing. So often the tarnishing begins its subconscious viral attack from a place of a poor upbringing in childhood. The person grows up determined to overcome the parents' economic hardship by having bigger ambitions and proving his/her worthiness to society. When these types of individuals become financially successful, they succumb to the ego, greed, fear, insecurity and temptation of accumulating, hoarding and protecting the only security blanket that they know; their material wealth. They flaunt their wealth and thumb their nose to those beneath them. But as these individuals sit counting up their riches on their respective metaphoric mountains, they find a hole in their Soul and often can't pinpoint their source of emptiness or loneliness. If this is you, here is The Healium Way solution: Understand that when you're looking down from on high, it doesn't reflect your superiority to those below you; rather feel gratitude for how far you've come. This is your test. Perhaps you need to reassess your contribution to society with a more objective and a humble lens. Furthermore, you must remind yourself that you're simply a temporary custodian of your maker's property, not its permanent owner. To do otherwise, is to be small-minded and foolish. In a society that's increasing its income gap disparity and loading its citizens with guns, isn't it smarter for the "haves" to be less shiny and carry a low profile and reduce the propensity to be singled out and be attacked? It is only with some common sense, gratitude and humility, that you eventually discover that true joy and contentment doesn't manifest externally, but internally in the Soul.

EVERYTHING IS TEMPORARY

I'd rather live a full-lived short life than a half-lived long life. Since life is short, having a mindset of living life to the fullest every day while we still can makes a whole lot of sense to me. If you're sick, notwithstanding a debilitating illness, you'll typically have two outcomes: you either get better or you'll die. With this philosophy, you tend to look at your life and all calamities with a specific outcome rather than a protracted set of circumstances. By seeing everything as temporary, not only will you live a more fulfilling life each day, but you'll embrace gratitude over disappointment. When you realize you have no control over time, you'll spend it more wisely. Sadly, many people don't get this memo, and continue burying themselves under work until they burn out and die unhappy or a life of regrets. Perhaps it means that you have to start the process of *allowing*.

THE ALLOWING

When you give yourself permission to have pure adulterated fun and enable your Spirit to be liberated from all the deadweights; the resistances, inhibitions and distractions — you arrive to a place of *allowing*. By surrendering to an 'open to receive' condition, our definition of "living life" now takes on a more multidimensional and broader meaning. We're not making excuses of not having enough money, or being bored with too much money — and avoiding interacting with others outside our socioeconomic sphere. Our egos and pretenses are diminished enough to where they don't interfere with our upward trajectory to our higher self. We don't have to judge others because we're not insecure. We don't fear being ourselves because we are well-grounded as individuals. We don't need to be validated by anyone as we don't care a f*ck what others say, think or gossip about us. We're allowing our higher vibrational energy to flow freely out of us and not operate in fear, doubt or shame. And it feels good! By adding the creative and healing arts into this mix, it fills us with joy and radiates the Soul without much expense. We just have to let these medicines work their magical power, everywhere and anywhere we go.

You can start by taking some small steps into life's abundant offerings available in your hometown. Make a date with yourself once a month to do at least one of the following: going to see a play or an opera or a musical show; enjoying dancing to a live band; visiting an art show or museum; doing an interactive art or healing activity; experiencing a Tibetan or crystal bowl sound bath; taking a nature hike; enjoying the beach; joining a yoga class; going to a social gathering; hosting a jam session or a drumming circle in your home; attending a party and so on. Be the first to initiate creative fun at a party. You'll be amazed how many people start clapping and join in. When you're at a house party, break away from the conventionality of mingling and drinking by getting socially creative. Start telling jokes, laughing, dancing and getting people to engage differently. You'll be surprised how everyone in the room will come alive, too. During your vacation, make an effort to befriend newfound Souls and be open to experience adventure with fun excursions and different foods. Whenever possible, leave your cell phone (aka jail phone) on mute and do not concern yourself with selfies and phone-documenting every detail of your outing. Stay focused in appreciating the very essence of the moment for *your* own pleasure, rather than trying to validate it for others. This is the power of allowing.

THE BUMSETTERS

I never heard of dress codes at restaurants and social functions until I came to America. Although I'm a pretty sharp dresser, I hate anything that infringes on my personal liberties. But I can understand why dress codes are mandated in certain places. The simple answer is because Americans have had a lot of influence initiating them, by lowering their fashion standards and looking like bums to most of the world — especially in this generation.

We Americans are the proud *bumsetters* of the fashion world, so let's make 'the worst dressed' award for us! When I lived in Europe, everyone dressed well in public — especially when they were socializing. And until the late 1980s, most Americans took pride in looking good and making an effort to dress attractively. Then all hell broke loose as the casual look wave swept in with designers like

Alexander McQueen's bumster trousers, the 90s grunge-ripped jeans look and similar street-inspired loose and baggy attire trends. Some of it was in response to the fattening of America. Sadly, though, that trend hasn't waned. We went from ironing our clothes, shining our shoes, and coiffing our hair, to slipping on wrinkled cotton T-shirts, putting on sneakers and tossing our hairbrushes out. We've normalized wearing pajamas in public and looking like we just woke up. This dressed-down, lazy *American bum* look has resulted in places and cruise ships mandating that people dress "appropriately" or they're not allowed in. In many cases, we're asked to dress up like penguins and Ken and Barbie dolls. How absurd is it for anyone to be forced to do this? By not having the common sense to not embarrass ourselves in public, we gave rise to a counterpoint regulative condition that infringes on our individual freedoms. How's that for self-sabotaging our own liberties? It's f*cked up and oxymoronic. I would love to see the next generation reverse this condition and bring us to a better fashion balance. I don't want to be told how to dress going out anywhere, do you? Let's all help ourselves fix this issue. How about being tactful and looking in the mirror to see if you are presentable enough to leave the house? Remember, when you're looking at the world, the world's looking at you, too. Next time you're invited to a party, refrain from throwing a favorite old T-shirt and jeans, but put some effort into wearing a cool outfit and dress well. You don't have to be fancy, just tasteful to set a positive mood for yourself. Honor yourself by treating yourself. When you look good, you'll feel good. So let's stay young at heart and inspire others to do the same. That's the kind of trendsetters Americans need to be!

PARADISE IS WHERE I AM

As I continue writing this book, I've lost yet another family member, my beloved mother in-law. A second family member has succumbed to Covid-19 since I began this writing adventure. Aida was 80 years young and a happy go lucky Soul.

Resembling a smiling Buddha, my wife's mother was an embodiment of a lotus flower that blooms in a bog of mud while it reaches for the sun. Despite her long and unhappy marriage, she chose to be a fountain — not a drain on anyone. My father-in-law never made any effort to heal his PTSD scars from the Vietnam war for more than 50 years, which manifested in self-inflicted mental illness. Sadly, the entire family, including my wife, suffered the blowback.

You can call him a classic coulda, shoulda, woulda example of a man hanging his head down in self-pity and regret. As a postwar narcissist and a walking wounded turned walking dead, he tried to pull her into his victim and hurtful world. Instead of leaving him and being happier, she chose to stay loyal and honor her wedding vows. In hindsight, it was ultimately a bad decision as she lived under fear and pretense until she died. Aida's regrettable choice to stay in the marriage is not that uncommon in dysfunctional or problematic relationships where cultural, financial, and religious undercurrents prevail. It's a classic disempowering condition that is antithetical to The Healium Way of doing things. But to her credit, she went on living her life the best she could by finding a ray of sunshine under her dark clouds. Her therapy was simple: keep smiling, laughing and mustering some sense of peace for herself. My mother-in-law may have died poor, but she had a rich heart, dressed well and lived life for herself in spite of her challenged environment. She reminds us all that our self-imposed boxes are not concrete tombs of eternal hell and confinement, but more like glass cages or aquariums that will allow the light to shine upon us. Some of us can even muster the strength and courage to crack the walls and eventually break out. I'm not holding my breath for my father-in-law to have an awakening after his wife's death — an overdue healing from his manic depression. Alas, he has to take the first step, to be sick of being sick and be ready to take action toward embracing his higher self. It's important to understand, no matter how unique or difficult the circumstances, the possibilities for each of us are always available by simply allowing the light to enter and heal our wounds. By breaking free of our shackles of conventionality mired in our own self-induced reality, we can begin smelling the roses of life while we still can.

The grass is always green on our side when we spend time watering it. The flip side is that if we neglect it, it turns into weeds that people start hating and want to remove. Voltaire said it well, *"Paradise is where I am."* That means we've got everything we need to make us happy wherever we are. We can't use temporary escape chutes or run away from our reality to find lasting contentment. Our issues and habits will simply follow us wherever we go. So, our perception of our reality must change. It starts by immersing all of yourself in the beauty and joy of the now, wherever you are and to live a life without regrets. Rich or poor, big or small, you're a success when you know how to let go and activate life's beauty and abundance. More important, don't waste any precious moment by having a wandering mind stuck in the past or anxious in the future — you may not have a tomorrow to look forward to.

R.I.P Aida Short (1940-2020)

Live life! Music, dancing, party, body art and creative nights at Healium Center

Activating The Body

"Exercise is to have fun and be healthy, not just to lose weight."
— Jim Peera

Our body is our temple that defines and reveals a lot about us. Most important, it is a vessel that transports and houses all the complex components that keep us alive. So why do many people neglect it? According to Bloomberg Healthiest Country Index, America ranks 35th out of 169 countries in this category, behind all developed countries including third world Cuba. With 4 out of 5 Americans diagnosed as overweight or obese and many addicted to prescription drugs, the average American is willfully trashing and self-destructing their temple. The reasons stated are quite disturbing but obvious: absence of universal health care, poor quality diet, lack of exercise, lax opioid regulations and a high level of economic inequality. Often high anxiety and depression trigger bad and excessive eating habits as people tend to eat their feelings. Covid-19 tested Americans' health quite well. It not only revealed its soul and mind imbalance, but a weak immune system that was a contributing factor to such disproportionately high casualties in relation to other countries. This imbalance and neglect of the body has a domino effect on our entire wellbeing. It's all interconnected: *garbage in, garbage out.* The genetic engineering, preservatives, pesticides, steroids, dyes, additives, antibiotics, diet sweeteners and various chemicals the FDA allows corporations to enhance our food and beverages spells our man-made downfall. It toxifies not just the body but the brain too. We're killing ourselves by our own choices. In order to get into a healthy balance, we have to take baby steps to swing the pendulum in the right direction. For one, it's never too late to start this transformation. No matter how fat or f*cked up you feel, it just takes a personal commitment and a clear intention to get yourself into high gear. Once you throw out the guilt, shame, victimhood and all other excuses, it's a lot easier to make progress. Don't beat yourself up for what you did yesterday and haven't done but rather what you can do going forward. The practice of moderation discussed earlier, combined with a baby steps methodology can pave the way to your rebalancing.

For example, if you're drinking sugary sodas every day, don't go cold turkey and expect to replace the habit with water. You won't last. Also, don't replace those beverages with diet sodas. They're worse for you. Instead, try carbonated fruit-infused drinks. Work to substitute those drinks with non-carbonated ones. Eventually start reducing your intake of the fruit drinks and begin drinking unsweetened teas. Slowly but surely, you will then enjoy drinking water! The Healium Way puts the power in your hands and starting today you are in charge of rebuilding your temple, a baby step at a time. So let's get started.

1. **Energy must be activated.** Nothing is more toxic to your physical body than keeping it in a state of stagnation. All your organs including your muscles and blood function at a higher frequency when activated and operated in the kinetic field of motion. Health experts at the Mayo Clinic suggest 150 minutes of moderate aerobic activity or 75 minutes of vigorous exercise spread out during a course of a week will do the trick. Personally, I like to use a round figure of 30 minutes per day of some form of energy activation routine to detoxify and strengthen my organs and body. The Healium Way body balance recommends not just toning and stretching (yoga, tai-chi, martial arts, etc.) and cardiovascular exercises (jogging, walking, biking, sports, swimming, boxing, hiking, etc.), but also qigong, dancing, laughter yoga, sound bath, reflexology, massage, etc. A typical weekly regimen consists of a

combination of these indoor and outdoor activities for our health. The trick is not being stuck doing one type of exercise but getting out of your comfort zone and sampling other methods and activities by mixing these modalities.

In our sedentary lifestyles of sitting and being glued to our computer screens all day, getting motivated to activate our body is more critical than ever. The entire body (feet, legs, butt, back, shoulders, neck, arms, hands, fingers) are screaming for you to do that! So, the first task at hand is to not see the exercise as a burden, but as a necessity for our balance. The second task is to think unconventionally by *not* being goal-oriented. That's counterintuitive to a typical workout belief system, but it works great to get you started and keep you motivated. Especially, when you're not in a regular habit of activating your body. By applying a paradoxical way of nonattachment to a workout plan, you will find that you'll stick to the regimen and eventually make it a conscious lifestyle change. Let's rename the word 'exercise' to *playtime* and make it feel less daunting. This shift will rewire your brain to think of body exercise as a fun activity as opposed to a chore or work. Instead of dreading to do stretches or pushups, now you can't wait to get up and have some fun playtime before or after work. When you're in this play mode, you're excited and find you do the activity with a big smile. You're also not struggling or intense but relaxed. Rather than having a specific goal of losing weight or increasing muscle mass, your intention is to just have fun — just as you did as a child.

Whether you're in a group setting or by yourself, I recommend you deploy a *Healium-style* playtime attitude in your workout routine by singing, dancing and having spontaneous fun. My wife does this all the time in her spin and aerobics class and has a contagious effect on her surroundings. The more fun you have, the more you will look forward to regular workouts without resistance and become your own coach. Within a month of using this technique, you will notice your body looks better and feels healthier.

Once you've taken these baby steps at your own pace and trained yourself to activate your body for at least 30 minutes daily, you will be able to then expand your knowledge and enroll in more advanced classes in your preferred workout modalities. Staying fit and having a body that's flexible, energized and healthy is addictive and sustaining.

Both my wife and I have been keeping our bodies activated and energetic since we were in high school — and that was over 40 years ago! We've tried all sorts of exercises from aerobics to zumba and keep exploring new ones to this day. Our top favorite is freestyle dancing that we routinely do around the house and during our travels. Often, we'll combine Eastern and Western styles into one routine that is fun and easy to do. What's more, I've created an exclusive morning exercise video for you to check out in upcoming chapters. This short routine will help you get started with energy activation in a fun way that you can practice every day wherever you are.

2. **The Flexitarian Diet** is a smarter diet for those of us who like to eat healthy but not miss out on fish and meat delicacies. If we are what we eat, then do yourself a favor and be moderate in your diet; it is the best way to avoid illnesses and stay healthy. Since 70 percent of our immune system is located in the gut and it is our second brain, we must keep it clean, free of processed foods and chemicals and in a healthy condition. As one of the most unhealthy and overweight people in the world, Americans are binge eaters and drinkers who leave this earth to an early grave by glorifying gluttony. In fact, during Covid-19, people added an average of 15 pounds on their already oversized bodies, according to one study. Instead of taking the opportunity to learn to cook at home, get more exercise and be healthier, the average quarantined American doubled down on comfort foods such as pizzas, processed fried chicken sandwiches, donuts and washed it all down with caffeine, sodas and alcohol — creating a perfect storm in the gut for any disease. But if we get smart and not eat our feelings, we can

reverse this trend. We know a healthy body yields a healthy mind and optimum joy. It's not rocket science; it's just common sense. When we look healthy, we feel better about ourselves and hence enjoy life to its fullest. Therefore, if we can have a dietary lifestyle that gives us the benefit of eating mostly plant-based foods and allowing animal products in moderate quantities, what would that look like? You would be a *flexitarian,* a flexible vegetarian. It is deliciously a good balance option and a practice of intentional moderation. Since food is medicine, I take it very seriously and have been eating healthy my whole life. Although we didn't label it flexitarian, my wife and I have been big on plant-based foods and fish over the course of our lives.   In our case, we eat fresh home-cooked meals that consist of roughly 50 percent plant-based ingredients, 30 percent seafood and the rest in organic farm-fed meats. That's right, vegans and vegetarians, we're equal opportunity eaters! For this reason, wherever we are in the world, we never go hungry. We adapt easily to any type of food and are open to trying anything. And I mean anything. Just recently I tried fried worms and locusts in Thailand and drank snake- bottled whisky in Laos. If you're not that daring, I highly recommend making a switch to a flexitarian diet. This option is a baby step approach that allows you to slowly and gradually decrease unhealthy factory processed meats (beef, pork, chicken) from your life.

Today 99 percent of all meat sold in America come from factory farms. As my wife always says, *"Factory food makes for factory-brained people,"* which underscores the cliche, you are what you eat. A lot of meat including poultry contains antibiotics, preservatives and steroids that are ingested in our guts and cause damage to our digestive tract and other organs, including our brain. When you wash it down with a chemical-based diet/caffeinated sodas and sugary drinks, you are tempting a self-inflicted health disaster: cancers of the colon, skin, lung and prostate, diabetes, obesity, heart disease — and even depression and mental illness. America's health crisis is in large part caused by lack of education and clever marketing relating to the toxic ingredients in food. Convenience, relative low cost and allure of tasty fast food are also factors. But it's not too late to customize the plant-based percentage of your diet and make healthier, affordable meat-less choices. The more plant-based, the better, though. Secondly, a flexitarian is an easier model to adapt to than being a vegan. Third, it helps our planet. From an environmental perspective, eating less meat reduces 1.5 tons of greenhouse gas per person per year by decreasing methane gas produced by cows.

Indeed, the benefits of reducing meat consumption are truly life-changing from all perspectives. Eating healthy doesn't have to be expensive, difficult or bad tasting, either. It's quite the contrary, if you care enough about your body and learn to cook. Unfortunately, according to a Harvard Business Review study, 90 percent of Americans don't like to cook, and it is costing them dearly in the wallet and in the gut. The American consumer spends an atrocious amount of money buying prepared foods and eating out — an average of $232 per month in 2020. So, if you're not preparing and cooking your own food, you have no idea what you're putting in your stomach. If you have time to surf the internet and text throughout the day, you can surely make the necessary sacrifice to prioritize and prepare a healthy meal for your one and only temple, can't you?

Once you learn how to cook and prepare your own delicious food at home, you will not only save money but get healthier. The critical thing is to avoid fast foods and only eat prepared meals outside as an occasional treat. Be vigilant about what you eat, too. Rather than eat factory-produced chicken, I prefer Cornish hens, rabbits and quails. Instead of eating conventionally raised red meat, my wife and I prefer goat, lamb, elk or venison. Equally important is to practice a moderate alcohol consumption, as discussed earlier. Why not try out CBD and THC-infused beverages instead? (if they are legal where you live). You'll get the buzz and take off the edge in a much healthier manner than drinking hard liquor.

Also, unless you want to be a walking mummy, eliminate your intake of diet drinks with all those additives and chemicals that toxify your gut. In addition to healthy eating/ drinking habits, I also use supplements, probiotics and enzymes regularly to keep my colon, liver, lungs, brain, prostate and heart in optimal shape. This entails detoxing and fortifying the organs with herbs, teas, juicing and taking vitamins and tonics. Visit a health food store online or in person to get you started.

My wife is an amazing cook who self-taught herself many years ago to prepare delicious gluten-free meals for my celiac son. In 30 minutes or less, she can whip up mouthwatering healthy meals with natural probiotics, antioxidants, enzymes, etc., that are tasty, low in fat, salt and sugar.

In the video link below she has prepared a fast, fresh and fabulous recipe for you to get started. Bon appétit!

Minding The Mind

"Have a mind that's open to everything and attached to nothing."
— Dr Wayne Dyer

According to medical science, one-third of our brain's intelligence and memory is predetermined by our genetics and biology, meaning two-thirds are in our control. While we're only using 3 percent of it, we seldom take the time to understand this ingenious electrochemical organ, as we're too busy being busy with it. Without getting too complicated, we know that in a paradoxical way, our brain is man's best friend and also his worst enemy. Its cognitive and emotional intelligence is wired in such a complex myriad of neurological synapses, that even Albert Einstein threw his hands up in awe of it. For the purposes of The Healium Way, I've uncomplicated it and summarized these three important factors that will help us keep our mind in a healthier balance:

1. Opening it 2. Pleasuring it 3. Quieting it

Before we expand on these points, it is worth noting that *minding the mind* starts by detoxing the low energy clutter and disempowering the inner critical voice that tries to sabotage it, i.e, *"I'm not good enough, not pretty enough, not smart enough, not capable enough"* etc. These are the typical narratives the mind tricks us into believing about ourselves. As I've said earlier, many of our mind viruses begin their incubation during our childhood and slowly grow into parasites, engulfing us by the time we're adults. In my own example at the beginning of this book, my version of the story surrounding my mom's nervous breakdown could have been totally different for me had I not been properly healed from that incident. What started as perhaps a nonthreatening or hasty remark by your parents can transform from harmless perception into a full-blown untrue reality about yourself. In the process, if the mind is not disciplined to decipher fact from fiction, it takes you into a tailspin of depression, loneliness, lack of self-esteem — even thoughts of suicide. For me, the antidote to these low-vibrational conditions was not to prescribe the addictive man-made temporary solutions that Western medicine dishes out, but to turn to the Divine Source that gave you this brain that's malfunctioning in the first place.

We must turn to our Creator for answers. I am not necessarily talking about going through a divisive and conditional middleman such as organized religion to get there — but a direct connection to our Divinity. This open line is accessible to us wherever we are and whenever we want it. You can call it prayer or silent knowing. As we close our eyes and enter this silent realm, we become the observer of this imbalanced brain of ours rather than its victim. The quieted mind soon reveals its separation from Source and realizes that it is weakened in that state. In order to reverse course, it must undo the muck of man-made lies, ego and self-inflicted toxicity. This re-alignment starts by administering a powerful medicine to heal its unhealthy burdens. That medicine is what we call *gratitude.*

GRATITUDE IS THE MAGIC POTION

At our Center, when people come to me complaining about being depressed — the first medicine I prescribe to them is gratitude. Gratitude is the magic elixir that when activated liberally and consistently into our brain has shown to rewire it positively. Copious research has shown how it has the ability to unshackle us from toxic emotions and induce many uplifting mental benefits. It is critical for unhealed people to practice gratitude daily to help advance their healing process. Once we understand its power and are capable of telling our brain that 'We *have everything we need, are thankful for what we have, were born winners and are fortunate to be alive'* — everything starts to look different. If we wake up to a rainy day and are expecting sunshine, we're grateful for the beauty of the rain. We convert our mood by adjusting our thoughts and enjoy the weather we're given. We're not finger-pointing or complaining as much because we're connected with our own internal power source: our Divinity. We go from a place of scarcity to a state of abundance that converts our thoughts of "Oh no God!" to "Thank you God!"

When we count our blessings, somehow everything about us adds up positively. If we lose our job, it's not the end of the world, it's a fresh beginning. Rather than stick a middle finger at your boss — you shake his hand and thank him for opening new opportunities for you. It's The Healium Way of dealing with temporary setbacks.

This is because the unconventional mindset sees such life-altering situations as blessings, instead of curses. If our stock portfolio drops, we stay disciplined and don't take it to heart or lose our mind. If we don't get a good crowd at our Healium events, we're grateful to those who are in attendance. *"Everyone who is supposed to be here, is here"* is the gratitude-based mindset. In business or personal situations, we stop feeling small and insignificant because we don't let the dark voices in our head rule our more secure and grounded higher-self. This state of being is our *root*-type modus operandi; the foundation of our growth and higher consciousness. It can never be shaken by anyone or anything. The payoff for being in a constant state of gratitude is undisputed. For one, all the positive and happy neurochemicals are activated within the brain and reduce feelings of depression, increase self-esteem, induce better sleep and remove self-doubt. This in turn reduces stress and increases our state of joy. All this happens without any interference from anyone or any induced substance, because it is a beneficial elixir generated by you — to re-connect with Source; your connection to oneness and peace. If you're not sure how to activate the state of gratitude, try some simple exercises that start and end your day by feeding the brain with a prayer of gratitude (that I've done for you at the end of this book). It is about self-love and unlimited personal growth. It is about appreciating nature, the arts and the beauty within and all around us. It is being thankful for our loved ones that we take for granted. It is about doing something *extra* nice for someone and being generous with your time and money. It is about carrying an uplifted attitude and practicing laughter on a regular basis to counteract the worldly burdens. It is making an effort to send a gratitude note to yourself by using your personal *Gratitude Bottle* (see instructions at the end of the book) every day. It's doing short mindful meditations during your work day and remembering to say a 'thank you' prayer whenever you eat. It is not being anxious about what you need more of — but being grateful for *what you already have*. Just by consciously making time to practice and be consistent with practicing these exercises, we're able to reap gratitude's countless benefits and make it part of our mental-wellness regime. So be sure to master the art of gratitude for inner peace and a healthy mind!

1. **Opening the mind** is about keep it expanded by *feeding it* and *flexing it.* When I was growing up, reading newspapers and books was a daily activity to obtain current news and knowledge. I've still kept this brain-feeding habit alive by the internet, radio and cable news to the mix. But unlike mine, today's young generation is *readically* different, and does not like to read. Their average attention span (in 2021) is a mindboggling eight seconds, making it one second shorter than a goldfish. So, today's kids are either not reading enough or they're mentally incapable of focusing for long periods of time. I believe it's both, and once again technology is the accelerator. Expecting a millennial or Gen Z to read an entire magazine or a book, cover to cover is a lost cause. Most would rather watch a YouTube video or listen to an audio book instead. Does that make them stupid? Not really, as they're quite intelligent

in many ways. But what do we do? The answer is to be objective about our definition of *feeding* our brain. It would be hypocritical to say that less reading means having fewer smart people. But it is troublesome. And in the context of The Healium Way of keeping a healthy balance, we must not replace reading with video and audio learning or we'll soon even stop writing. These two methods also don't get processed in the brain in the same way as good old-fashioned reading. Reading is more interactive, helps us focus, is a lot easier to reference and makes us better spellers and writers. Reading this book is pretty cool, right? Why eliminate it and make it your dinosaur? If you're a millennial or Gen Z and you've gotten this far with The Healium Way; you're atypical. Pat yourself on the back for your commitment and focus! The secret is to make reading a fun activity and think of it as necessary food for your brain — not just to gain knowledge but to keep you sharp, current and always interesting in your interactions with different people.

STREET SMART

History shows us that education is the best prescription against poverty. It is only by constantly *feeding* our minds with a plethora of diverse resources that we expand our knowledge and become smarter, wiser and don't strangle our common sense. The secret is to never stop learning, whether it's in the classroom or the school of hardknocks called life. This unconventional wisdom is knowing the importance of being *street smart*. Most Eastern cultures often prioritize a conventional mindset of academic excellence to secure their children's future. The parents will sacrifice everything to save money to ensure their kids go to the best schools. My dad was no exception. Although he was bankrupt after our family's African expulsion, that man somehow mustered enough money to send me to a top elementary school in France and a highly rated private Catholic boarding school in England. I know it was hard on him financially because I was sent back home from that school on several occasions for his failure to pay the school fees on time. It was a humiliating experience for me and for him, but he never gave up on me. Looking back, it was one of the best investments my family made for me. In sharp contrast, many Western parents, specifically Americans, have a low bar of education for their offspring. That's evidenced by their lack of sacrifice and inadequate savings, as well as a laissez-faire attitude on high quality education. Most Americans expect their kids to get scholarships or borrow the money and get into debt. And this mindset has the kids making their own choice for their future and often taking the easy road.

The result is the dumbing down of our society that is showing up in our present reality. The raw truth is hard to digest: Americans are not the smartest or sharpest minds in the world. According to an OECD (Organization for Economic Cooperation and Development) study, we rank 28th out of 76 countries in math and science. If we use the IQ measurement as a metric, we are not in the top 10. As a nation that has fallen behind the developed (and even many undeveloped) countries in quality of education, we see America's detrimental effects manifest in a variety of ways. Examples include an increased blue collar and part time workforce, reduced wages, expanding income inequality, lack of common sense and a heightened level of stupidity ignorance and silliness as measured in its lifestyle choices and actions. Many employees are enslaved by the powerful corporations, while the small mom and pop entrepreneurs are squeezed out of business or engulfed by them. If you're someone trying to make a living out of your creative talent — it's even tougher. At our Center we've noticed how many highly talented artists and musicians are deficient in their marketing/selling skills and struggle monetizing their craft. I often tell these artists and wannabe entrepreneurs that a good entrepreneur knows what he's good at, but a great entrepreneur admits what he's *not* good at — and partners with or delegates the task to others.

Mastering the latter point is an Achilles' heel for most Americans who see any personal deficiency as vulnerability and weakness.

All this equates to an imbalanced and inequitable playing field that is showing up in dire statistics. To have a wealthy nation in which 69 percent of its population does not have $1,000 in emergency savings and worse yet, 45 percent have zero savings (source: GOBankingRates-2020), proves my point. We're selling ourselves short at all levels of economic mobility and that is why it's critical to not only educate ourselves and be book smart — but to learn how to better sell, market, hustle and be creative in monetizing our talents. We must therefore get more *street smart*. It's a prescription that trains us to have better people skills, good ethics and to work without excuses. Being street smart involves being passionate, disciplined, persistent and most of all staying creative.

Creativity once again becomes the key that unlocks the power of education and elevates us to our full potential. We can start swinging the pendulum the other way one person at a time, with each of us having the intention to grow and expand our mind by using our persuasion skills, charm, critical thinking, character and unique abilities in addition to our knowledge and talent. The combination of these skill sets has helped me advance despite all the pitfalls and downturns in my own life. When we are proficient at being both book smart and street smart, we succeed where others don't and can adapt in all economic climates. One of the key components in being street smart is salesmanship. Salesmanship is part of our DNA. We just don't realize that we're all selling ourselves, our goods and our services every day at any given time. From accountants to politicians to doctors, everyone is a sales person. As you travel around the world like I have, you'll notice how the world's economy revolves around more street-smart people than book smart people. The camel rider in Egypt and the cigar maker in the Dominican Republic had to hustle as hard to get my business as the travel agent that booked our trips. Those who connected with me in an authentic manner, had a good demeanor, got creative and had a quality product or service, got my business.

Having two degrees under my belt before I reached the age of 23 was helpful to get my foot in the door of any company, but being street smart and knowing how to hustle was the key to my life's success. Especially, when I had no job security and was enslaved by low wages by many fashion houses. I remember being laid off or fired each time I asked for a raise. So if I didn't sell, I starved. My street-smart entrepreneurial training was the ticket to ditching serfdom. It gave me financial freedom on my own terms. Cold calling and door-to-door selling my fashion accessories and cleaning products in the 1980s and 1990s was the best street-smart education I ever got. It taught me how to take rejection, be persistent and always put people first. If you're not a natural-born salesman or entrepreneur like myself, sharpen your selling skills by cold calling or taking a job that involves commissions. You'll try harder and learn quickly how to make your own money and get a taste of financial security. Eventually, you'll have the confidence and courage to start a business and you'll never take orders from anyone again. When you're selling anything, make sure you know your product well and believe in it. If you're not sold on it yourself, don't try to peddle it to others or fake it just to sell it. Even worse, never promise what you cannot deliver, make exaggerated claims or cannot guarantee satisfaction. You won't last.

THE FLEXIBLE MIND

Once we become proficient at feeding the mind, it's important we never stop *flexing* it. This entails not stagnating it with procrastination, passivity, laziness or fear. The brain is just a big complex muscle that expands and contracts with each conscious or unconscious choice we make — programming new behaviors and shrinking unused receptors. Since it has the capability to transcend all limitations, why do we allow it to be held hostage by own constricting behaviors? Let's discuss and fix this dichotomy. For one, being that we are creatures of habit, we limit ourselves to *easier* choices. We won't question installing an automated voice controlled robotic spyware device in our homes to take over a multitude of tasks. We like it because it's faster, smarter, frees our time to do more sh*t and it's a cool gadget. But the trade-off is that it's doing all our thinking for us. Over time, our mind is habituated to that pattern of thought and self-adjusts to reduce cognitive activity, which in turn shrinks our brain receptors.

In another scenario, we'll program the brain to make low-risk choices and gravitate toward what we know as opposed to what we don't know. It's our *fear of the unknown* that trains the mind to shrink to a level of our predispositions. For instance, if you're on a cruise ship, you'll elect to stay on the boat while some of your more adventurous friends go on an excursion and swim with the domesticated stingrays. If you're going out for dinner, you'll stick with a true and tried restaurant instead of walking into a newly opened business. At our Center, we've experienced a similar mindset. People who attend our nude figure drawing class will be hard-pressed to sign up for a sound healing or drumming workshop: But for those who do take the leap of faith, the payoff is great. They typically report a high satisfaction rate and become more adventurous in their choices. In fact, our studies show that those who take a chance to cross over into a new activity and have a good experience, tend to take more risks and participate in other workshops. Once we become risk-averse about trying a novel or foreign idea, the mind will keep us from exploring any other new things, even if our heart thinks otherwise. Eventually, the boxed-mind wins and there's a nasty contagion spreading across our life. We become an unadventurous person missing out on experiencing the joy and beauty of living life to the fullest. Living life in this fashion also makes us close-minded and myopic in our views about different people and the world. This in turn makes us gravitate towards groups with rigid and homogenous views and we become tribalistic. Tribalism leads to an inflexible mindset that leads to prejudices, biases and ultimately we separate from our Divinity. So being inflexible has an upsetting domino effect. I've met many racist people in my life and beneath the skin lies a person who is rigid close-minded and often fearful — all self-imposed traits. It's not to imply that all risk-averse people are racist, but when you refuse to have an open and flexible mind, you not only tend to be more fearful and cautious, but you're also more judgmental and less tolerant of diversity as a whole. The key is to remember that it is best to practice flexing and expand the brain by not staying imprisoned in your thoughts and liberating yourself by taking some action. Even if it's a small step toward the unknown. That's The Healium Way of doing *something* as opposed to doing nothing.

UNCOMFORTING THE MIND

Being uncomfortable bends and stretches the mind in amazing ways. In the Mirror of Truth exercise, your character showed the level of risk you're willing to take to try out something different. Using this scale to assess yourself in a social setting and in your decision making, put this test into practice and get *deliberately uncomfortable* to re-balance. Break the barriers of your confined mind and don't resist any discomfort. Slowly, you will notice how new knowledge and hands-on experience on the foreign subject now makes you *more* comfortable. For example, read a book on a subject matter that makes you uneasy, try a new hobby that you despise, watch a play that's controversial, do a creative activity that you've always avoided because it was difficult, talk to people who don't align with your core values, visit a different religious house of prayer. Do it all without any expectation. As a Muslim-born person, I've prayed inside many Catholic churches and Hindu and Buddhist temples. What an amazing experience it was! You remove all the ancestral and programmed predispositions from your brain, throw the fear and judgment out the door and just enjoy the moment. Once you get into the habit of opening and flexing your mind, you will hunger for more and your brain will expand — full of unbound possibilities in other areas of your life. You will be more experimental and curious about learning new things and grow the mind, as it is simply too precious and beautiful to cage, stagnate and allow to shrink.

In the 76th verse of the Tao, we are reminded by the ancient teachings that having a flexible and gentle way that bends is stronger, while the stiff and unyielding will break. It's a great metaphor for not being rigid in our thinking.

76TH VERSE OF TAO

A MAN IS BORN GENTLE AND WEAK;
AT HIS DEATH HE IS HARD AND STIFF.
ALL THINGS. INCLUDING THE GRASS AND TREES,
ARE SOFT AND PLIABLE IN LIFE;
DRY AND BRITTLE IN DEATH.

STIFFNESS IS THUS A COMPANION OF DEATH;
FLEXIBILITY. A COMPANION OF LIFE.

AN ARMY THAT CANNOT YIELD
WILL BE DEFEATED.
A TREE THAT CANNOT BEND
WILL CRACK IN THE WIND.

THE HARD AND STIFF WILL BE BROKEN;
THE SOFT AND SUPPLE WILL PREVAIL.

2. **Pleasuring the mind** is all about an uplifted attitude. When I had the honor of seeing the Dalai Lama over a decade ago, I was quite impressed by his wild sense of humor and candidness. I expected to see a slow-moving aged man who'd preach mindfulness and inner peace in monotonous and orderly fashion. What we got was quite the opposite. He was high-spirited, a glowing ball of light that resembled a young kid rather than an old man. The secret to his youthful presence and playful demeanor was as he put it, *"To have a smiling face and remember that the universal purpose of our existence is to be happy."* How simple yet brilliant advice! It was refreshing to see a revered

religious leader not have a chip on his shoulder and just be so real and down to earth. He was spontaneous, funny and spiritual at the same time. I took note of his words of wisdom seriously and plugged it into my life immediately. I began smiling more, randomly laughed during my day and lightened up on taking life too seriously. By plugging in those simple habits, my outlook on stress, people and work became more positive and manageable. I even used the Buddhist spiritual leader's inspiration to design a smiley face on the Healium logo. Now you know!

After all, there is clear scientific evidence on how our positive outlook, smiling and pleasurable activities affect our mental state. Basically, there are four primary chemicals that can drive the positive emotions you feel throughout the day: dopamine, oxytocin, serotonin, and endorphins. Without getting bogged down in the technicalities, we just need to remember to have a healthy balance of all these happy neurochemicals activated. Intentionally engaging the mind through art and music does wonders to elevate many of these brain chemicals without much effort. Research has shown that activating them can better regulate heart rate, lower blood pressure, decrease cortisol (stress hormone) levels and increase serotonin and endorphin levels in the blood.

"Sexual healing is good for me" – Marvin Gaye

Besides keeping a positive mental outlook, having a smiley face and using the activities of the creative and healing arts regularly to fill your soul, you need a healthy prescription of sexual healing for a healthy mind balance. Sex is one of the most important medicines responsible for many health benefits in the mind and body. It releases our brain's endorphins and keeps us young. Oddly, not everyone views the benefits of sex in our busy grinds. According to a recent study by the University of Chicago, people across the globe are less sexually active than they were at the turn of the century. Indeed, the U.S. comes in second as the *least* sexually active culture in the world, with Japan the leader in this category. The alarming depression rates in our country, as well as porn addiction (related to sexual apathy), are some of the reasons cited. Not surprisingly, there is a correlation between happiness and the frequency of sexual activity — and a lot of Americans are obviously not getting this memo. Although there is less taboo with sex today, we seem to be prioritizing work over sex in many situations. According to the General Social Survey at University of Chicago, *"The stress and busyness of the modern world leaves less time for sex."* Pleasuring the mind holistically with real people and real experiences should be part and parcel of our daily regimen and not be exclusive or separate from other activities.

At our Center, we're not shy about celebrating our sexuality in a tasteful manner. We showcase many erotic artworks and create specific events to inspire attendees to light their fire and keep the passion alive at all times. No, we're not all walking around naked, but we're exposing people to the beauty of their sensuality with creativity, humor and respect. We notice how people smile and laugh more, stay engaged in the arts and set aside the time to make romance with their partner(s). Sexual healing is my default answer to solving our many mental-related issues such as depression, anger, bitterness, lack of self-esteem, and so on. When people appear to be bitchy, dissatisfied and unhappy in their lives, it's often due to their lack of regular sexual activity. I've seen it firsthand with my family members, friends and even attendees at our Center. Why resort to a VR goggle, online porn sites or an avatar to keep your flame alive? Those may be fine as temporary inspiration tools, but they're not healthy in the long term. If you're single, make an effort to socialize in the outside world with real people covered in real skin and find a suitable companion to light your fire. If you already have a companion, spend less time sitting on your sorry ass and become a bad ass instead. Shake it, break it and do your groove thing with this person as much as you can.

Let's remind ourselves that we were born naked. We must live celebrating and honoring our raw and natural beautiful state — free of shame, intimidation or other excuses.

MASTERBATOR

Masturbation is a natural expression of self-love that releases endorphins and is beneficial to our health. But what happens when you're addicted to it and it detrimentally affects your life? Meet a Healium guest we'll call M (to hide his identity) who walked into my 'forbidden' art gallery and confessed to me that he was an incessant masturbator unable to control himself; a *master*bator. The handsome early 20s male who was new to our Center proceeded to confide in me without any reservation of his unusual condition that was causing him much emotional pain and suffering. He openly revealed to me that he couldn't perform well with girls and it was affecting his mental health and self-esteem. M had also spent a lot of time and money on therapy and medications without much success — until he walked into my gallery! He complimented me on my work and then pointed to a piece called "Kiss of Life" that showed a man wrapped around a cauldron of fire with a snake kissing his penis. He told me that he had engaged with the artwork on his prior visit and it helped reduce his addiction. I was floored! In all my years of candid and interesting encounters with my audience, I had never heard such a mind-blowing story (no pun intended), and I was curious to know more. He continued to tell me how the piece spoke to him, had triggered a surge of embedded and emotion and was his much needed therapy. *"That's an amazing story, and I am so stoked that my art has helped you. I bet your left hand will be happy too now!"* I joked. We both laughed as he hugged to thank me, and left my gallery carrying a big smile and feeling much lighter. The young man had just witnessed the healing and medicinal power of art without judgment or shame!

Check out Jim's clay sculptures to inspire you to light YOUR own fire:

" Man on Fire"   "Kiss of life"

(Clay/Amethyst)   (Clay/ Copper)

3. **Quieting the mind** is paramount in our busy lives. It is said that the memory of God lies in the quietness and stillness of the mind. But since the human-controlled mind is always restless, trying to attain peace of mind is therefore an oxymoron in many ways. Therefore, it becomes necessary to unplug ourselves and not feel guilty about doing nothing — a difficult task for a majority of Americans. It involves resting the mind while being awake. But how do we get to consciously quiet the busy mind? From a practical day to day point of view, besides reducing eye and mind activation from our ubiquitous computer/cellphone screens and getting a good night's sleep, the secret to calming our brain is to understand the importance of doing nothing in a conscious state.

At any given time, our mind is in a constant seesaw between wanting to keep busy and not being bored stiff. Trying to maintain a delicate balance between these two opposing conditions is much harder than it appears, especially in our multi-tasking technological society. In fact, many of us are led to believe that keeping busy prevents us from going insane and helps us fight depression, anxiety, loneliness, sadness, etc. — by not having the free time to dwell on the bad or negative. Although this might be true for some, it is much better to strike the right balance of self-induced brain activity. Because the issue is not so much that a busy mind is bad for us, but rather what kind of busyness it is and how much of it we are being exposed to everyday. Since our brain releases the pleasure hormone dopamine after completion of a task, we get drawn to the activities and become hooked to this pleasurable feeling. This addiction then satisfies our cravings and we go into an unhealthy loop. Much of this self-induced addiction avoids difficult issues in our life and dealing with our emotional response. Often, it's societal pressure to be a high achiever coupled with guilt or shame for not being productive. As a self-admitted high achiever, I'll catch myself starting multiple projects and having the pressure to complete them in a set time. So, I must readjust. In The Healium Way, since we're all about balance, it means not overloading our brain. By being in tune with our bodies, we can dial up or dial down as needed. With enough practice, it's possible to pace ourselves and put the mind on pause during the day to repel the notorious drug of busyness. The price of overthinking or constantly being in our head is not cheap. The overheated or highly analytic brain can send invisible stress signals to the entire body and organs and manifest or accelerate underlying health conditions like back problems, nerve pain, headaches, high blood pressure, sleep apnea, etc. It's all correlated with our central nervous system.

In addition to listening to music and chanting, my three favorite ways for calming the mind are *meditation, drumming* and *vibrational sound healing.* I've included *breathwork* in this chapter as it has shown to provide a deeper therapeutic release and benefit for many people. All of these modalities have been studied and facilitated at Healium Center and proven valuable for the mind.

MEDITATION IS THE MEDICATION

Wolfgang Amadeus Mozart once said that the music is not in the notes, but in the silence between. It is only when a musical note is interrupted with a break of silence, that the monotony of noise converts to the sound of music. Quite a brilliant and logical observation! In the same way, The Healium Way encourages you to interrupt the noisy mind and serenade it with conscious-based silence —to make it sound and blissful. This condition is also known as meditation. The importance of meditation for healing the mind has been proven to calm the busy brain, reduce stress and anxiety, promote better sleep, generate kindness, promote emotional health and many other benefits. It is also about activating the theta brain waves that reduce depression and help open our creative receptors. The Buddhist monks swear by it as a necessary mind medicine to not only do all that, but to get connected to our higher consciousness and the self. It's about decluttering man- made thoughts and surrendering to our spiritual and higher frequency ones. Stillness of the mind is the secret to mental wellness. Therefore, we should all be meditators. But a lot of us can't sit still and do nothing — for various reasons. Some of us, like myself, have to work hard at being still due to our high energy personalities.

Jim meditating in a Thailand temple

Billionaire entrepreneur and life adventurer Sir Richard Branson clearly admits to being unable to meditate and relax — and that man has an entire island all to himself to Zen out. So money doesn't buy peace of mind. What's more, many people have never even tried being consciously still, to experience the health benefits of doing nothing and being still with their minds. Others battle past trauma or unhealed wounds that make them feel uneasy in their awakened state of stillness. Although there are many different techniques, my favorite and the easiest to implement is *mindfulness meditation*, the mother of all meditations. My eldest brother has been an avid meditator of this type for more than 40 years, and it has helped him cope with stress and recharge better than any drugs or medication. I am not as automatic as my brother is in his practice, but my goal is to eventually make mindfulness meditation as habitual as eating.

Mindfulness meditation is the psychological process of purposely bringing one's attention to experiences occurring in the present moment without judgment. The concept of this type of mind quieting focuses on the *breath* as its anchor. When thoughts come up in your mind, you don't ignore or suppress them, you simply note them, remain calm, and use your breathing as an anchor. After a month of being regular, you'll notice the difference in your mental state. You will be pleasantly surprised how much more focused and calm your mind is. You'll also sleep better, have a sense of clarity and feel less stressed. American folk singer/songwriter Bob Sima who performed with his wife at our Center wrote a beautiful song called 'Meditation is the medication'. The song's chorus says it all about this powerful practice:

"Meditation is the medication, to cure the illusion of separation. We are one when we are all together. We are one when we are all alone."

MOTHER'S HEARTBEAT

If you have a chronic restless mind and cannot meditate for even 10 minutes — drumming will be your ticket to mind calming. Drumming may sound like an oxymoronic activity to quiet the mind but it actually promotes the release of the neurochemicals in our brain that act as a relaxer and stress reliever. The Shamans use drumming to call the Spirits during their rituals and healing ceremonies.

The rhythm and vibration beat of drums is a sacred sound that resonates within us while we're listening to our mother's heartbeat in her womb. So drumming is automatically ingrained in our DNA at birth. And it's an amazing brain-calming and uplifting medicine. We encourage participants at our Center to play drums spontaneously as needed, and offer it during group drum circles. It has shown to benefit the mind by enhancing inner focus and reducing stress. I find it to be not only beneficial for the brain, but also to lift the Soul. Like meditation, it provides immediate positive results — and if you do it long enough in a session, it's even a terrific sweat detoxifier for the upper body.

Drumming is such an easy instrument to learn that everyone with two functioning hands can play it. And once you try it, you'll never stop — fact that's been proven at our Center countless times. There is no right or wrong way to drum for fun. The secret to drumming as with any creative activity, is to get out of your head and just do it *Healium style* as opposed to trying to be technically good at it or be competitive. The most user-friendly drum is the African djembe, and I strongly suggest investing in one and making it a part of your healing regimen. I carry a mini djembe with me in a suitcase whenever I travel and it has made me more friends than I can count. I've randomly jammed with violinists, flutists, guitarists and other musicians on streets, beaches, restaurants, etc., all around the world. When drumming a hand percussion instrument such as the djembe, conga, doumbek, hang drum, etc., you need to simply get a crash course on the basic techniques and let loose. Lucky for you, I've made a quick djembe video tutorial for you to watch from your smartphone!

VIBRATIONAL SOUND HEALING

I was introduced to vibrational sound healing in my late 40s and regret that I hadn't known about it earlier. Once I tried it and surrendered to the experience, I was hooked and I guarantee you will be too. Sound healing is a proven modality for mind-quieting and improved mental wellness. It does wonders for both the sound therapist and the participant(s) due to its powerful vibrational energy field that resonates without barriers. I've witnessed people report intense energy radiating through their entire body during sessions.

Crystal Bowl Sound Healing at Healium

There is a direct correlation between vibrational sound therapy and many health benefits such as reduced stress/anxiety, improved sleep, lowered blood pressure, bliss, clarity and much more. It is an incomparable tool for relaxing the mind and a turbocharged alternative to meditation. There is a lot of anecdotal and scientific evidence that validates the positive effect that the sounds of vibrational therapy has on training the mind to access the *flow* state discussed earlier.

The two most popular instruments used during sound healing are Tibetan bowls, (made from a bronze alloy of either copper, tin, zinc, iron, silver, gold, or nickel) and quartz crystal bowls made from silica. They're also known as *singing bowls.* Alpha-theta brain waves are activated while playing these singing bowls to connect the unconscious and subconscious mind. The physics of sound vibration as a mind-relaxing and healing medicine is thousands of years old. The vibrations and resonance are created by striking and gently swirling the bowls with a mallet. The size, shape and weight of the singing bowl can affect what tones are produced — activating specific vibrational frequencies found within the human body.

In this energy-radiating temple of ours, we have seven main chakras (Sanskrit for energy centers) and each chakra is designated to specific physical parts of the body such as organs, glands and adrenals, as well as emotional parts, mental patterns and spiritual awareness.

Each chakra has its own related resonance, color, intention and note, and can act as a map for our own inner harmonic or disharmonic resonance. (See diagram).

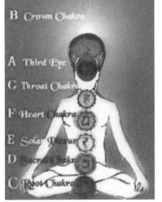

For example, the crown chakra has a purple color with a B note. Thus, when the sound moves from this bowl through the atmosphere and touches us, it causes our cells in this energy area to move in different directions at a variety of speed in rhythm with the sound wave.

Singing bowl chakra map

Although the benefits are different for each person — the wealth of evidence indicates that singing bowl tones have positive physical, mental, and emotional effects on those who experience them. I've witnessed many incredible effects on hundreds of people at our Center using a combination of both types of bowls in varying sizes and combined with other complimentary instruments such as rainsticks, gongs, flutes, chimes, drums and shakers. Therefore, unlike meditation, you will need to invest some money to enjoy its benefits. If you want to self-administer a sound healing session yourself at home, you'll need at the minimum an investment in Tibetan and/or crystal bowls and some basic training on their use. For those who lack discipline, I suggest attending "sound bath" sessions in your community. At Healium Center, we call it *Sound Immersion,* and it is one of our more popular offerings that we integrate as part of our healing arts programs. We provide it in a more intimate and spiritual setting for deeper healing — as opposed to a musical performance. Also use the internet to check out virtual sound baths, which give you a different feeling than in-person group sessions. Or just access our exclusive *Sound Immersion* sample video in the next chapter.

BREATHWORK

Most of us don't breathe correctly. Our breaths are often too shallow and don't supply us with adequate oxygen to help us stay calm, especially when we're stressed. When we combine vibrational sound healing with a breathing practice called *breathwork,* the results can be quite powerful. Breathwork is a New Age word for a method of conscious breath control that is meant to give rise to altered states of consciousness, and to have a positive effect on physical and mental wellbeing. By breathing from the abdomen and intentionally changing and manipulating the breath for an extended period of time, deep breathing increases the supply of oxygen to your brain and stimulates the parasympathetic nervous system, which promotes calmness in the mind. It has a therapeutic effect on a person's mental, emotional and physical state. We've hosted many breathwork sessions that combine New Age music and/or sound healing sessions and have noted quite a difference in people before and after. I've seen people cry, dance, laugh, get in trance and even scream in a healthy release of pent-up emotion. As with sound healing, every facilitator will vary in style and methodology, resulting in varied results. If you want to practice a self-care breathwork exercise on your own, you can start by checking out YouTube and online videos. As a fun alternative, you can also get an amazing deep breath workout with a didgeridoo. This aboriginal wind instrument produces intoxicating sounds while increasing oxygen supply in the lungs and brain for powerful therapy. Check it out!

MIND MEDICINE

Our discussion on mind-wellness wouldn't be complete without mentioning the various metaphysical and medicinal plants that have been scientifically proven to help us heal. The important point to stress here is that we caution against abusing these medicines in habit-forming psychedelic escapism. Using The Healium Way Principles, let's discuss the proper use of plant medicines. Shamans and indigenous tribes have used these natural elixirs and compounds for thousands of years as therapy to connect with Spirits and as a mind-enhancing medicine to reach different dimensions. Today, psychedelics and natural plant medicines are gaining mass appeal and respect from the scientific and pharmaceutical industry throughout Western countries from Switzerland to Canada. Indeed, consumers are discovering the benefits of these alternatives to improve mental wellness and replace more addictive and toxic compounds. Biotechnology is also enhancing these natural plants at a faster speed than any time in history.

Besides the widely popular cannabinoids such as found in the hemp or marijuana plants for treating pain, sleep apnea, anxiety and other ailments, an Amazonian psychoactive centuries-old brew called ayahuasca is gaining popularity in treating PTSD, drug addictions and depression. Childhood traumas and open wounds have been known to have been healed in professionally guided ayahuasca ceremonies, although it's not known if it has lasting effects. Psilocybin, the psychoactive ingredient in 'magic' mushrooms that previously got a bad rap in the '60s along with LSD, is now being given serious attention to combat opioid addiction and help reduce anxiety, depression and even increase creativity. Some studies are indicating it can be used to help repair brain injury and restore memory function. The American visionary artist, Alex Grey, explained to me how his works were created by tripping on magic mushrooms. He described to me how the brain receptors and synapses are rewired and can often have lasting therapeutic effects after the psychedelic journey. What's more, microdosing using certain plant medicines is being seen as the future of mind wellness and maintenance. Microdosing involves regularly consuming a small amount of psychedelic drugs to improve mental wellbeing and productivity. The amygdala (the brain area that mediates emotion and memory) is altered to reduce fear, increase positive moods and memory and help us cope better with stress. I advocate using these out-of-the-box pathways (without breaking any state laws) to reduce anxiety, expand our brain capacity and empower our state of mind. We use caffeine (a stimulant drug) to boost our mood and stay awake, so why not try other ancient and sacred faculties to better condition our brain? It definitely beats becoming pill-zombies or alcoholics. This practice is especially important today as we shrink our brain receptors by using computers and robots to do the thinking and creative tasks for us; we need to replenish our imagination and enhance our third eye. In some severe anxiety and PTSD cases, the psychoactive drug MDMA has also been proven to be useful and more effective than other pharmaceutical drugs with bad side effects. But when using any plant medicine, be sure to have the right facilitators and professionals to guide you and the highest quality naturally sourced compounds available. There are many cheap but dangerous imitations that can kill you, so do your homework before you dish out any money to anyone — especially if they are not willing to reveal to you their origins.

I'll go out on a limb to recommend taking a magic mushroom trip — before you die. It should be on everyone's bucket list. I have to say that it has been one of the best gifts I've given myself; I've never experienced so much peace and enlightenment at one time. It was also a cathartic and healing-mind journey that released years of pent-up crap lodged in my subconscious mind that I didn't know existed. Other creative medicines didn't work in the same way. My brain was rewired for about six hours, inducing my third eye into an adventure of pure nirvana. Alas, the downside was that afterward I had to come back to earth and face our man-made reality again.

Principle # 21
Staying Consistent

"It's not what we do once in a while that shapes our lives, but
what we do consistently."
— Tony Robbins

In the summer of 1981, while I was studying at the University of Arizona, I was fortunate to enroll in a Kung Fu class taught by

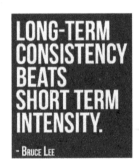

LONG-TERM
CONSISTENCY
BEATS
SHORT TERM
INTENSITY.
- BRUCE LEE

an apprentice of Bruce Lee. I endured 3 months of grueling self-defense martial arts workouts that tested my willpower, discipline and mental agility like never before. During each session the instructor would remind us of the importance of practicing the exercises on a "consistent" level. *"My master always said the secret of a good fighter is to practice long term consistency"* he told the class. In this final Principle, we come full circle to understand the importance of mastering consistency for attaining the best results on our transformational path. Consistency is about being disciplined in our thoughts and actions. It's critical for achieving sustained joy and contentment rather than short-lived happiness. It requires both focus and willpower to help us forge a healthy and balanced routine. What we've noticed at The Center is that consistency in the healing arts is essential not only to become better versions of ourselves in soul, body and mind, but also to stay even-keeled and grounded. Doing an *extra*ordinary deed or going the extra step to be nice to someone is not a one-time occurrence that you can rest your laurels on.

You've got to show passion, commitment and drive every day as part of your life.

As previously stated, the majority of Americans don't have a lot of *'stick-to-it-ness'* in their DNA. We are conditioned to be akin to flighty *leaves* and fragile *branches* rather than sturdy and grounded *roots*. The advent of hyper-technology combined with a plethora of choices has also reduced our attention span and made people impulsive, unreliable and inconsistent. Western society trains its people at a young age to want quick fixes, magic pills and easy buttons to push. When they can't get those desired results, they're easily discouraged and grab on to the next fad or fix. Then the cycle repeats itself.

It's also hard to focus on what matters while we're in the throes of financial woes, relationship issues, job stress, ill health and so on. These problems stack up on a perfectly normal mind and destabilize it. It doesn't take much to push people over the edge these days. Our coping rubber band snaps easily today more than ever and our reactionary behaviors can manifest in unhealthy actions that harm ourselves and others. We see this phenomenon play out tragically in the unprecedented levels of mass shootings in America today. The solution, as we're stressed in The Healium Way, is to consistently nurse our mind with creative therapies and practice the exercises in this book to fortify our rubber band. It's important to do each exercise in the book to the best of your ability without any expectations as opposed to measuring your strength or competing with people. Activating yourself in this manner will set you apart from those who are not using this book as intended. Fortunately, this book is in a format where you can access it anytime and there is no set entry or exit timeline. Your mission is not impossible and Tom Cruise is not giving you 60 seconds before this book self-destructs. You've got as much time as you need to plug the Principles into your lifestyle in a healthy and consistent way.

THE EARLIER, THE EASIER

Habits can make you or break you. Ideally, we want to reduce the consistency of the bad type and increase the use of the better type. For example, if you develop a habit of eating healthy, exercising and saving early in life, you'll likely continue that good regimen during adulthood. Conversely, if you're a tightwad and self-absorbed as a poor struggling teen, you're not likely to be generous and grateful as a rich and successful adult. The hardest part of achieving a healthy balance involves being disciplined in the beginning, when you're usually at your weakest, poorest and hungriest stage. Since the age of 10, I've worked hard to making sure that I not only learn good habits but don't get addicted to bad ones, which are easier to attach to and harder to lose. Discipline comes from getting to know yourself from the inside out. That means being in touch with your body enough to know when you're overeating, under-hydrating, feeling lonely, starving your Soul, not smiling or laughing enough, etc. If you're not in proper balance, then self-correct. As the self-designated doctor-in-charge, you must be passionate about prescribing creative and spiritual medicines as needed.

The beauty of The Healium Way is that it inspires you to be self-motivated to get into a better equilibrium by not being reactive, but proactive. Yes, it's more work at the onset, but it pays off huge in the long run. And the earlier you get started, the easier it is to make it a lifestyle habit.

PLUGGING INTO YOUR ROUTINE

Long-term consistency becomes automatic when we insert the particular task into our daily routine. Most of us already operate in a life of routines. We brush our teeth in the morning, dress ourselves to go out, take our supplements, turn on our computers, eat at a certain time and so on. We're already doing many things that require consistency, so why not add The Healium Way-inspired activities that provide proven healthy benefits to that routine? Some of us tend to go overboard with a structured way of living, becoming rigid and predictable in our ways. Here's the paradox: On the one hand I'm asking you to adopt good consistent habits, and on the other hand I'm warning you of the dangers of turning into a robot or a drill sergeant. Once again, the lesson is about self-awareness and the onus is on you to dial up or down to your level of comfort and challenge. There's no right or wrong answer. What's important is to understand the value of having a healthy and balanced lifestyle — and stick to it.

YES, EVERYTHING ON THE MENU IS GOOD!

In the following pages, I've made it easier for you to implement a consistent soul, body and mind regimen at your own pace. It's designed to be a balance routine, that is an *all-encompassing* way of seeing and doing things, as opposed to cherry-picking the ones you understand or like. The Healium Way works best when we incorporate ALL the offerings available to us on the plate of life — especially those that make us uncomfortable. That's how we get to experience the fullness of life. I suggest you try everything out on the menu below, like the server in a Chinese restaurant who says, "*Yes, everything on the menu is good!*"

The frequency I'm prescribing is realistic and you can adjust it to your lifestyle. As I said at the onset of our literary journey, you must start somewhere and just do *something* to experience everything that your maker has in store for you. By now, you know that The Healium Way is about reducing our resistance to change and increasing our thirst and curiosity for the unconventional. That translates into tasting life's bountiful offerings no matter how foreign, weird or difficult anything seems. Having lived in the American South for most of my life, I've seen my share of unsophisticated and closed-minded folks. It's an uphill battle to get many of them to beat to a different drum. If you've never experienced sound healing or played a drum, this is your time to do so. If you're always pumping yourself with weights at the gym and have never experienced the benefits of tai chi or yoga, this is your chance to try them. Your mind and body will love you for it. If someone offers to invite you to take you out to a drum circle, or a yoga class, say *yes* enthusiastically. When you're trying to use up your vacation days from work, get adventurous and try something totally different than what you normally do. Make a concerted effort to try everything prescribed as indicated and watch how it improves your life incrementally in all facets of soul, body and mind wellness. Life is too short to be stuck in the same box and routine, or flake out after one attempt at doing something new. Try to explore above and beyond your comfort zones and remember consistency is what makes the difference in optimizing and getting results in everything. It is the secret to staying *extra*ordinary.

I DON'T HAVE THE TIME

I don't have the time is a common excuse for those who aren't consistent in practicing the Principles in this book. If this is you, you're revealing your life's not in proper balance. If you've got time to eat, shop, watch television and spend hours surfing the internet or playing video games every day — you have the time to rebalance your life and integrate the *Balance Regimen* I created for you, don't you?

"Don't say you don't have enough time. You have exactly the same number of hours per day that were given to Helen Keller, Pasteur, Michaelangelo, Mother Teresa, Leonardo da Vinci, Thomas Jefferson, and Albert Einstein."

— H. Jackson Brown, Jr.

BALANCE REGIMEN

	DAILY	WEEKLY	TWICE A MONTH	MONTHLY	QUARTERLY
BOOKEND GRATITUDE PRAYER	✗				
I AM REIKI MANTRA	✗				
EXTRAORDINARY ACTION	✗				
GRATITUDE BOTTLE	✗				
MINDFULNESS MEDITATION	✗				
SHAKEY WAKEY! POWER-BOOST	✗				
TAI CHI/QIGONG BODY VIBRATION		✗			
YOGA		✗			
OUTDOOR ACTIVITY		✗			
CREATIVE ACTIVITY			✗		
MUSIC LISTENING	✗				
SOUND HEALING				✗	
READ/WRITE ACTIVITY		✗			
LAUGHTER HEALING	✗				
REIKI/MASSAGE REFLEXOLOGY/ CHIROPRACTIC					✗
DRUMMING		✗			

Balance Regimen Menu

Bookend Gratitude Prayer: This is a five minute prayer and affirmation to say each morning when you wake up and before you go to sleep; hence, a bookend to your day. It's a sample prayer, and feel free to be creative and make up your own. Just be sure to close your eyes, sit in a lotus position and in prayer hands before you start.

"Thank you, God. (Jesus, Allah, Yahweh, Krishna, etc) for this day. Thank you, guardian Spirits and Angels. Thank you, pure light helpers. Thank you all for my good health. Thank you for my peace. Thank you for the abundance. Thank you for the joy. Thank you!" Repeat three times.

'I AM' Reiki Energy Mantra: Reiki, a Japanese form of energy healing is one of the most effective and easiest ways for each of us to connect to our God given life force. If you don't believe me, just try this Healium Way version yourself. Each night I end the day lying down on my back with my eyes closed and two hands (palms down) placed on my chest and silently say to myself my 4 P's healing mantra: *I am Powerful. I am Protected. I am Prosperous. I am Peace.* As I've said before, you can add your own unique version such as I am Good Health. I am Pure Joy. I am The Light. I am Abundance, etc. Create your own mantra and repeat it in your head at least five times. Take at least three long deep breaths (in from nose and out from mouth) into your diaphragm each time you say the mantra. You will start releasing much stress and as you start relaxing, go back to your normal breathing. Within a few minutes you will notice the healing energy radiating from your hands to your heart. It will be warm to hot. It is a powerful healer and will put you to sleep before you know it! The way I see Reiki's power is using simple laws of physics. We are all made of energy and are constantly radiating with it, whether in motion or in stillness.

From head to toe however, that energy is often flowing out quicker at the non-connecting exit points — our hands, feet and head. But what happens if we take one of those outlets (such as our hands) and stop the energy from escaping by directing it to another energy entry point into a different area of the body (creating an energy loop). What we get is a kinetic flow of energy that circulates and radiates onto a targeted area that energizes all the cells it comes in contact with. Thus, producing concentrated healing energy. You can direct this energy to power any area of the body that has issues. It's you being the doctor and the healer for fixing many of your own ailments! When you layer intention with it and some mind over matter training, you can also send long distance Reiki healing to anyone. My wife has done this successfully countless times.

Extraordinary Action: Each morning, make a mental note of your intention to go the *extra step* above and beyond what is required of you. Be it at work, with family, friends, or total strangers. You are going to make your ordinary day an *extra*ordinary one. Then take the action that matches that intention. After you've accomplished that, mention your *extra*ordinary action(s) to a person you know. Not only will you feel good for being *extra*ordinary, but you will inspire and spread this mantra to others to do something similar.

Gratitude Bottle: Take a wine bottle, soak it in hot water and peel off the label. Cover with a base coat of black or white acrylic paint. Let dry and paint whatever design you wish on it. Be creative. When the bottle is dry, spray it with a couple coats of high- gloss polyurethane. Buy a pack of wooden popsicle sticks from a craft store (500). Keep this bottle in your bedroom. Each night jot something nice that happened to you that day on the stick and put it in the bottle. Use the front and back of the stick. At the end of one year, take all the sticks out and celebrate all the good things that happened to you in the year. This is a great exercise to be grateful for all your daily blessings.

Mindfulness Meditation: You can do this anytime of the day, but especially when you are feeling stressed. Find a quiet room and sit in a lotus position. Put your hands on your lap with open palms resting. Close your eyes and focus on your breath. Breath through your nose, focus on your breath moving in and out of your body. If physical sensations or thoughts interrupt your meditation, note the experience and then return your focus to your breath. Your mind will wander but don't worry, it's normal. Just return to your breath. Start with five to 10 minutes per day. Do it for one month. Afterward assess the impact on the quality of your sleep, your anxiety level. Start meditating for 15 minutes or longer per day and make it a habit.

Shakey Wakey AM Power Boost: After eight hours of tossing, turning and sleeping, our stagnant body requires a wake-up power boost to reactivate the mind and body to face the day ahead with passion and vigor. I've designed a simple all-encompassing 15-minute routine that I do each morning for myself. This Healium Way exclusive content will invigorate you within minutes and set a positive attitude for the rest of your day. I guarantee it.

Check out the video Jim's done for U!:

SCAN ME

Tai Chi/Qi Gong/Body Vibration/Organ Toning: Our ubiquitous technology-heavy and passive lifestyles are unhealthy for us. Our organs are being stressed and are stagnant. The idea of body vibration is just not to have cardiovascular exercise for the heart but to activate the internal organs and glands such as the liver, stomach, kidneys, thymus, etc., by cupping and tapping our entire body from head to toe. Studies in Eastern wellness modalities such as tai chi/qi gong, acupressure, etc., have shown the benefits of energy movement, organ toning, controlled breathing and body vibration for maintaining good health.

Yoga: Yoga is derived from a Hindu spiritual and ascetic discipline, a part of which includes breath control and the adoption of specific bodily postures; it is widely practiced for health and relaxation. I strongly recommend that you join a yoga class in your community or learn online how to practice in your home on your own.

Outdoor Activity: Nature is an amazing healer. Use it as much as you can wherever you are to get cardio exercise like jogging, hiking, walking, biking, playing sports, Frisbee, swimming, etc,.

Creative Activity: Make sure you integrate at least ONE fun creative activity per week in your lifestyle. Get creative with painting, drawing, playing music, singing, photography, sculpting and so on. Going to plays, concerts, comedy shows, etc, is also highly beneficial.

Music Listening: Music is our brain's mood-regulating elixir. Try listening to classical, jazz and chill wave music while working or in rush hour traffic. It will calm your nerves and put you in a relaxed and more productive state. Turn on rock, pop and other genres for a more upbeat and danceable experience.

Sound Healing: A sound healing or vibrational "bath" is a relaxation technique and meditative experience during which participants bathe in the sound waves produced by instruments such as crystal or Tibetan bowls, chimes, gongs, drums, rain sticks, etc. I highly recommend that you experience the benefits of this modality for chakra balancing and mental wellness.

Check out a sound healing sample Jim and Donna have done for you:

Read/Write Activity: We are reading and writing less as a society. Technology has intoxicated us with video games, YouTube videos, VR goggles, and so on. This can create a dangerous imbalance which can be easily corrected by taking the time to read books, newspapers, articles, comic books, and so forth. You will expand the mind in a holistic way. Try to write poems, blogs, songs, etc., too.

Laughter Healing: Laughing can relieve stress, increase pain tolerance, and support the immune system, as well as serve several other healthy purposes. It's a proven medicine. Sadly, as adults we seldom laugh. Just try laughing when you are tense, watch how it reverses your emotions almost instantly. *Laughter Yoga* is a health practice where people practice forced laughter as a group — but it can soon turn into spontaneous laughter. The fact is, your body does not know the difference if the laughter is real or fake. Other ideas: Watch funny shows instead of serious news; randomly laugh in the car when commuting to and from work; laugh in the shower; if you're having any pain in your body point to the area and laugh it off.

You'll be surprised how your body starts healing faster and your immune system improves.

Drumming: You don't need any special skills to drum. Hand drums and percussion are the easiest and most fun musical instruments to learn. As a beginner, I suggest investing in an affordable djembe (African drum) or a similar instrument, and start freestyle drumming at home. You can also join a local drum circle in your area. It's the most fun and therapeutic release you'll have!

Drumming circle at Healium Center

Massage: There are many people who've never had a therapeutic massage. To some it is a taboo, and to others it's a pampering luxury. To all those folks, I say; *"You don't know what stress relieving and muscle-relaxing benefits you're missing!"* Get in the groove of getting a massage at least quarterly. Try a sampling of the common types: Thai, ayurvedic, deep tissue, Swedish, aromatherapy, etc. Get the best reviews online and experience its benefits anywhere you are in the world.

Reflexology: Did you know there are vital points that you can press on your body that control all aspects of your organs and ailments? Reflexology, also known as zone therapy, has a way to access and heal each of those points using the feet, hands and ears. It is another alternative medical practice that maps our organs using specific thumb, finger, and hand massage techniques. Get a crash course on this self-care modality to help reduce headaches, backaches, stress and more. As a certified Reflexologist, my wife taught me some basic pressure points for relieving aches and pains on myself, and it's invaluable.

Chiropractic: Americans tend to abuse their backs a lot by doing strenuous workouts, sitting and not stretching enough. As a result, your spine and posture will need periodic alignment and TLC. I'll go see a chiropractor for care of my back once or twice a year; however, you may prefer regular visits based on your needs.

Experiencing a musical concert at Healium

2

The Coronavirus Awakening

"The secret of change is to focus all of your energy not on fighting
the old, but on building the new."
— Socrates

I began this two-part adventure with you at the onset of a global pandemic known as Covid-19 — a deadly novel strain of a coronavirus that was first diagnosed in China in late 2019 (hence the '19'). It gets its viral name from its resemblance to a crown that latches its spiky surface proteins to receptors on healthy cells, and starts its destruction. As of this writing, 5 million humans have died worldwide — making it the world's worst health crisis in this century and 2020-21 a historically f*cked up period for many. It could be debated that this virus was not a natural-occurring disaster, but a man-made engineered calamity on humanity, reinstating our ugly truth about our flawed condition. No matter how the facts unfold and history ultimately records or sanitizes it, Covid-19 will leave an indelible mark on everyone for generations to come. As with any major crisis, the most vulnerable to the pandemic are not just the unhealthy, the poor and the reckless, but the ones who fail to pivot, adapt, rebalance and use common sense. In America, the imbalances that show up in high rates of obesity, cancer, heart attacks, diabetes, etc., can be fixed by bettering our diet and exercise and not polluting the air we breathe. Our poverty rate can be solved by having smarter and more equitable governance and investment in our own people. Our recklessness and stupidity can be fixed by prioritizing our education and human capital. Looking at the bright side, it is my hope that the painful Covid-19 period be seen as a positive catalyst — by waking us up from our comforted malaise. Whether you realized you were being enslaved by your profit over people employer and quit your job for better pastures, filed for divorce from a disempowering and unhappy marriage or took other transformational measures in improving your life — you were part of the *coronavirus awakening.* For me, the coronavirus period did not just allow me to have the time to write this book, but it gifted me an awakening with a loved one that's worth discussing.

I woke up the morning of this writing with a ray of bright sunlight shining through the glass pane in my bedroom window. The sound of chirping birds confirms it's a beautiful day as I say my daily morning, *I am mantra* prayer of gratitude and do my *'A.M. shakey wakey* exercise. I'm blessed and feeling renewed. It's a special day for two reasons: it's my daughter's 28th birthday, and a day my heart feels lighter and less burdened, closing her decade-long open wound with me. It's a day we'll both cherish and celebrate. Although we are isolated from each other due to the harmful virus, we are never more interested in re-connecting to heal our individual mind virus.

In a previous chapter, I told you about the success of initiating my personal *30-day detachment and conflict resolution* exercise to reconnect with my daughter. Using many of the Principles of The Healium Way, specifically the *facing forgiveness* method discussed earlier, I wanted to prove to myself during the writing of this book that I could stitch our emotional wound. I couldn't pinpoint the exact cause of the wound until I got the symptoms under control. But I knew it had to be deep and there was something still lodged inside of her that needed to be released.

In this chapter, I will disclose to you how this flushing out (that freshly occurred during the writing of this book) started as a childhood molehill issue that manifested into a mountain and an eventual destructive volcanic eruption. It's a story that could be a valuable wake-up call in your own personal relationships.

TIT FOR TAT WITH DAD

Just a year earlier, my daughter raged at me and I had no clue as to why. She shouted that she hated me, and then went silent on me for more than eight months. Having seen myself as a great dad, I was somewhat blinded and unaware that I had anything to do with past emotional damage to my daughter. Yet, I knew there was something I needed to do for her to heal.

I employed The Healium Way Principles in baby steps, lowered my expectations and stuck with the intention of reducing the bleeding. And it worked. We stopped the hate, began texting and lightly conversing. But our relationship wasn't back to normal, so I felt the need to unpack more of our mutual stories. One day I texted her to meet me for lunch to have a 'father and daughter' time — to open communication. To my astonishment, she refused. And I was confused. For sure, this wasn't the same daughter who just a few years ago was closer to being my twin flame (mirror soul): with my mannerisms, my altruism, my creative talent.

She even gave me a Bee Gees tattoo on my arm to match hers. We were closely tied — in more than just one way. Sometimes, it was too close for our own comfort and we did not respect each other's boundaries. But there was something else I was overlooking in my role as a protector, provider and parent — the sensitivity and immaturity of the younger generation, especially with a lesbian offspring who was facing social challenges of her own. Lucky for me, my daughter was about to confront me about it. She continued her text by saying she was not ready to meet with me alone. In my eyes, that left the door open a crack.

Was she ready to talk? Or was she afraid of inciting a confrontation? I discussed her text response with my wife, who got both of us to agree to meet for lunch by being our chaperone. For me, this was a significant improvement — for my daughter to meet with me and be ready to unearth her past skeletons. During our lunch together, I put all the tools I've outlined in this book to good use. I imagined being surrounded with white roses (to neutralize negativity) and put myself in her shoes (to have empathy). As an icebreaker, I made light conversation and cracked some jokes to blunt the uncomfortable tension. I also listened more than I talked. I did not raise my voice and was careful not to interrupt her. I tried hard not to judge her many complaints and unfavorable labels of me being insensitive, egotistical, disrespectful, dishonest and so on. My inner voice was calm knowing that much of what she was regurgitating was hot air being released from a boiling source. She continued unleashing and outpouring ill feelings toward me to the point where my wife interrupted and corrected some of her false statements. It was painful to digest, especially when much of the vitriol was a one-way personal attack. All of it was a prelude to something deeper. After roughly 40 minutes of getting punched in the gut and being on the ropes like Muhammad Ali, I was eager for my daughter to stop fluttering like a butterfly and bring on the bee sting. And she did! It was a Grand Canyon-sized emotional crater that had been festering in her own gut for some time.

THE EMOTIONAL PLUNGING

She revealed to me that on one particular day when she was 16 years old, I went into her room, unpinned from the wall her newly created "very personal" self-portrait drawing, made a copy of it and pinned back the original, all without getting her permission. Apparently, I disrespected the fact that it was a drawing that she wanted kept private. She said that at the time she accused me of violating her wishes, her space and her property, but that I sloughed it off, ignoring her pleas and never apologized to her. During this head-jarring moment, I tried revisiting the incident in my mind and remembered it vaguely. At the time, I didn't make much of an issue with it — except that I was excited to show my friends my daughter's new art piece.

My daughter's 'very personal' self-portrait at 16.

I also thought she was overreacting and being childish about it. While she was recounting this story, I felt her unhealed emotions match her uneasy body language.

I quickly realized how this one incident could be the root of all the pain and problems in our severed relationship. In order to confirm this fact, I had to activate more principles of The Healium Way. I did not hesitate to own my irresponsible behavior of the particular incident and immediately apologized for taking her power away and not respecting her feelings at that time. I admitted to her that as a parent I never got a "how to" book to raise children, but that I slept well at night knowing that I was a devoted father who always put the family's interests before my own. I quickly realized while unpacking the incident how a sensitive teenager's life could have been shattered by my improper actions. What seemed like a molehill incident to me quietly built into a mountain of pain for an adolescent lesbian. The incident grew like a cancer in her head destroying the healthy cells (good memories of our relationship) and was supplanted by magnification of the few bad ones. Pretty soon, her entire mind was engulfed with bad blood and corrupted with falsities. In fact, she had given me clues in the past of this condition by drawing this piece of art:

In 2012, my daughter released her pent-up emotions on me by drawing herself as a young angry girl trying to suffocate me with a bag over my head with my arms bound with a seatbelt. She called the art drawing "Daddy's girl" When I asked her what it represented, she told me it was about me being overprotective and having too much control over her. I responded by saying I understood her feelings and loved her. In hindsight, I should have dug deeper into that teenage mind!

As we kept talking, I realized how it was possible for a mountain to slowly form its layers of emotional boulders over the years, using false assumptions and one-way narratives — that eventually fueled the energy of a volcanic eruption a decade later. It wasn't until she had the two back-to-back car accidents that triggered the explosion. So in a paradoxical way, we can thank the accidents for bringing us together, a curse that turned into a blessing in a strange way.

This overdue release was a revelation for me, a cathartic moment for both of us — as we each shed tears. It felt like an albatross-sized lump in our hearts had just been lifted. It was the necessary breakthrough moment for both of us. After talking openly about her feelings, she was a different person without the hidden angst, being bitter or resentful toward me. In many ways the experience reminded me of a plugged-up main sewer pipe that backed up and spewed sh*t on the entire plumbing system, and once we took a plunger to it and dislodged the culprit of the restriction, everything began flowing normally again.

The lesson here is how it took just one unnecessary and harmless (albeit stupid) thing that I did *waay* back in time that could have destroyed our relationship. But it's not an uncommon story. Often little molehills turn into mighty mountains of internal magma that eventually erupt—triggered by a plethora of reasons from a person's immaturity, mental state, environment and other hidden factors. I've heard of many parents who've described similar situations in their family. Unfortunately, many of these parents (especially in the Eastern culture) are old school thinkers who think the adults are always right even when they are wrong. They don't take the unconventional road that I took — to make the effort to get vulnerable with their children and unpack the skeletons in the closet. It takes courage, patience and resilience to do what I did; being the wiser adult. In most cases like this, parents use silence, guilt, shame and even money as a weapon until the offspring comes around. In rare cases, I've seen parents pay for their professional counseling or therapy — but that route can backfire as many young adults are proficient at manipulating the therapist to get their desired outcomes. My daughter was a good example of that. She spent a lot of my money on therapists — yet wasn't able to dislodge the painful truth until she confronted me head on. That is why, using The Healium Way as I did, and having a heart-to- heart dialogue is more effective as an emotional plunging tool than resorting to conventional therapy alone.

Does this story resemble any similar situation in your family or life? Are you ready to bury the hatchet with someone you love? Sometimes the signs are there, but we are not connected to the present to diagnose them. Sometimes we are too sick ourselves (either physically or emotionally) to nurse the issue. Sometimes we've got our heads in the sand or up our ass. Sometimes we're afraid of taking a chance to stick our neck out. And sometimes we just don't give a f*ck. Fortunately, The Healium Way is about staying connected, getting our head out of the dark holes, and giving ourselves a chance *to want to give a f*ck.*

SICK OF BEING SICK

The coronavirus global pandemic period that began in 2020 will be remembered by all of us; for good or bad. From our perspective, it's best to look at it with a more objective lens and see it as a catalyst for positive change for each of us. We got tested on mental, spiritual, physical and economic levels like never before in modern history. Five or ten years from now, each of us will have to look back and ask ourselves what we did during this period. Did we sit idle with our heads hanging in a fetal position and have self-pity — or did we get off our butts, adapt, get creative and forge forward? Did the unhealed take this pause button to activate their inner-creative to heal? Was this virus a Divine message for exposing mankind's own self-induced mind viruses? Was it a wake-up call for reducing our lower-vibrations and getting on a higher ground? As I've stated in this book, everything has a purpose with an accompanying lesson to teach us the importance of balance. And to me, nature is our most powerful truth mirror. The pandemics, wildfires, hurricanes, droughts, floods, etc., offer global humanitarian lessons that reveal imbalances and deficiencies as a species. Just look at the coronavirus spike-shaped cell, it has some eerie connections to our perilous state of relationships. It resembles a crown (you) with spikes (your bad habits or actions) that attach themselves to healthy cells (other people) and cause damage to them. If the cells being attacked are not healthy, the end result is death. It's no different to a dying relationship, a breakup or enmity for someone. Our virulent behaviors are mimicking the virus, most of it from our own enemy — the mind. Indeed, our survival depends on our individual mental wellness and actions. This virus metaphor is a powerful lesson to pave the way for a peace plan for America. But the plan cannot be executed collectively until it is practiced and perfected by each one of us individually.

In the ancient wisdom of the Tao, we are reminded how, "*It is only when we are sick of being sick that we stop being sick.*" Both my daughter and I were tired of having a rift with each other.

We were ready to have her wounds closed and healed as opposed to allowing the relationship to deteriorate and slowly die. Alternatively, both of us could have let our egos and pride get in the way and not make any attempt to mend our broken hearts. The choice was ours to make or break — and the personal power was for us to use or misuse.

We also had to change the way we looked at the pandemic. We could have fallen prey to the prevailing winds of conventionality and stagnation of doing nothing until the virus was under control. But we chose to embrace the winds of change by taking control of our own mental health. When we took self-responsibility for our own f*ck ups, we committed to an intentional shift from being ordinary to becoming *extra*ordinary. But make no mistake, this path of the higher self is always vulnerable to being attacked and hijacked by dark forces, and we must be vigilant in becoming the *roots*-type human and not get uprooted or derailed.

Chapter Takeaway:

What did this chapter do for you? Inspirations, lessons, questions? Looking at yourself, what did you do during the coronavirus period? Did you see it as a death knell to fear, or did you use it as a harbinger of your own awakening? Do you have a similar impasse with someone you love and want to fix or have closure? Think about it in an objective manner and learn from your mistakes moving forward. Because there's going to be more crises and pandemics in our lifetime, and they're all-powerful lessons for our personal growth and transformation. Now meditate for a few minutes before moving on to the next chapter.

Healium Center sits empty during the Covid-19 pandemic.

3
The Detoxing

"By not craving for validation from anyone,
we are starved by no one."
— Jim Peera

Steven was a quiet and shy millennial with tattoos over a large part of his medium-framed body. He came to us by way of another young participant who was a regular favorite at our Center. She had just befriended Steven, a lonely traveling gypsy, and thought that our sanctuary would benefit him. As with everyone, we welcomed Steven with open arms and he said that he especially loved the fact that we were not affiliated with any religious belief system. He made friends with like-minded people and interacted in our freestyle painting room. But at closer look, I noticed this man was not like many others in the room. His eyes were sunken deeper than I'd ever seen of any young person. I suspected that he was a highly disturbed and traumatized white male who was hiding some dark childhood secrets. I noticed that his first painting was executed quite quickly, as if he was eager to release his pent-up emotions to clear his mind. As I looked over his shoulder, I saw a large portion of the canvas covered with a meat grinder with blood-dripping brain parts spewing out of the grinder's holes. When I asked the troubled young man to explain his piece, he just replied; *"It's how I feel inside my brain right now, Jim."* I didn't ask him to elaborate as I wanted him to keep coming back and do more work, judgment free. Steven kept his promise to me and was consistent in participating at our weekly Open Studio events. Each time he opened up a little more with his artwork and about himself. He revealed to us that both his parents were Satanic worshippers who abused him as a child. He recounted how he'd seen some horrific things that had f*cked him up to where he too trusted Satan over God. *"I am a Satan worshipper Jim, what do you think of that?"* he said once. I didn't flinch at his remark or try to persuade him to change his beliefs. I suggested that he keep attending our sanctuary and partake in all the creative and healing activities to help him get on the Divine path. And to my surprise, he did. By the third month, Steven had come to terms with his ugly past and was slowly undoing the toxicity that had consumed him from within. At a certain point he was excited to show my wife and I a new artwork: an image of the sacred heart of Jesus. It was the exact opposite in tone and content of his first piece. We both smiled when we saw it, as it conveyed a classic dark to light transformation that we're used to seeing at our Center. I noticed how Steven had stopped slumping, looked better and was more confident and empowered. Although he often referred to my wife and me as his mom and dad (as many millennials lovingly did), we knew that Steven's personal goal was to return to Florida and find his real father who he hadn't seen for many years. He wanted closure, but was torn and didn't know whether to forgive him or not. When he asked for my opinion, I told him to follow his heart and not to overthink it. I reiterated to him that forgiveness was the ultimate liberation from a dark path.

The awakened Soul mustered a smile, gave me a hug and took off on his *search and find* mission to reunite with his dad. We didn't see Steven for a few years, but then in 2019 he paid us a surprise visit. He said he was in a hurry to be somewhere else, but that he wanted to stop by to thank me and tell me that he did find his father — but that they couldn't get on the same path. I noticed that his eyes weren't sunken like they were during his visit to The Center, but were still sad. I told him that he had done everything he was supposed to do, that he had cast off his demons and was now free to live life to his full potential. He gave me a thumbs up, smiled and waved goodbye.

I know there are many Stevens out there with stories of pain that will convert into some peace thanks to detoxifying truths, forgiveness and personal awakenings. That's what moving the needle towards being *extra*ordinary and living a life without regrets is all about! America can definitely benefit from its own awakening and forging peace on many fronts. The preceding examples of individual transformations demonstrate how each of us has the personal power to accomplish whatever we set our minds to — by our own willingness, thoughts and actions.

JANUARY 6, 2021

Besides the woes of a historical pandemic, America held its most consequential presidential elections since 1864, the year when the nation had a choice to end the Civil War by electing Lincoln or to further divide its people. The 2020 election focused on removing from power a divisive and toxic leader who was on track to shred America's democracy and plant the seeds of white supremacy and autocracy on its soil. It was a scary era of historical significance in American politics. The country was subjected to third world-styled rule as the sitting president threw his usual tantrums and used his bully pulpit to incite more mayhem, subvert democratic voting rights and refuse to give up his throne peacefully.

On January 6, 2021, This demagogue even incited a violent militia-styled insurrection on Capitol Hill to delegitimize a fair election and pour more salt into the deeply wounded and divided nation. What happened on this day will be remembered by historians as an ugly and a serious threat to its constitution. More disturbing was how the Republican party leaders stayed silent amid the chaotic attack to safeguard their individual seats of power.

Thankfully, 81 million Americans (7 million more than Trump) voted for a new pilot to steer their ship: Joe Biden, with Kamala Harris; the first colored woman of immigrant descent as his copilot. To one half of the country, the changing of the guards signified a necessary detoxing that restored a nation's tethered and hostaged Soul, ravaged by four years of "Trumplican" mindf*ck. To the other half, the Democrats' win was seen as illegitimate and unacceptable. For those who consider themselves Libertarian, it offered little solace towards having less government in their lives. Whichever camp you're in, it's important to understand that America is not ruled by its elected officials as much as it is held captive to the whims of lobbyists, special interest groups and powerful corporations — all with profit and power agendas. Some would call that a corporate coup d'etat. It further confirms the fact that we as a people must pay more attention to all the games and tricks our politicians are playing with our financial and mental health — no matter what party they're in. We cannot be blinded by partisanship or fear but must open our eyes and put our thinking cap on to defend common sense, morality and respect for one another.

Alas, only time will tell how the world's most watched and revered democracy holds up — as most Americans are notorious for wanting instant results, avoiding personal responsibility, and enjoy wallowing in their complacency and comforted malaise.

THE FLEA IN THE JAR CONDITION

The fact that millions of Americans are falling into this state of malaise and succumbing to an indoctrinated mindset is a more concerning and toxic condition. At its worst, people become demoralized and trapped in a low-vibrational and scarcity-based loop that they normalize. This unhealthy condition can turn into a self-induced permanence akin to the analogous flea in the jar experiment.

Let me explain. The jar symbolizes entrapment, which is similar to the box metaphor discussed in Part 1 of the book. The flea is put in a jar and the lid is closed. As the flea tries to jump out to escape, it experiences pain from hitting the lid. Eventually, it is conditioned to fly just below the lid to avoid being hurt. However, even when the lid is removed, the flea keeps flying to the same height just below the lid and never tastes freedom. It is comfortable in its prison, and never sees any possibilities in its life because of its self-programmed limitations. This analogous flea normalizes its loneliness, depression, scarcity, imbalance, unhappiness, disempowerment, etc. Ironically, this type of individual is not just the thumb sucker, the victim, the lazy, the hyper-sensitive, the sheeple and the uneducated. But it also includes the super-smart, diabolical and calculated... and everything in-between; the ordinary person! In other words, there are more fleas in the jars that walk amongst us than you may think. What's worrisome is the flea's loss of emotional intelligence and inability to accept many raw truths. That's because this entrapped condition is a product of an unhealed and imbalanced person, regardless of status, race or any category.

You know these folks: the deniers, the cynics, the haters and the close-minded who don't think anything is wrong, can't see or willfully deny their unhealthy mind or state of being. This self-defeating condition parallels a prison guard mindset that fights to protect its situation and even recruit others to join in their shrunken world. After all, misery loves company. When we add a divisional-based population to this phenomenon, it gets even worse. We see people who are eager to knock down others aggressively in tribal fashion. A good example is when overweight individuals band together to mock and hate on those who eat healthy and are in better shape. Without looking at their own Mirror of Truth, putting on a thinking cap and seeking change, these masters of scapegoating, stop short of their self-transformation and stay fearful, angry and divisive their whole lives. Our bar is so low in many aspects — from morality to personal responsibility to personal empowerment, that this flea in the jar condition has become our new normal as individuals and as a society. In fact, you could be in this state and not know it. I see it in many people at The Center and all around our country who are in dire need of some emotional, spiritual, moral intellectual or reality check.

So, America, we're at a critical intersection where untold millions of people are converging: Downtrodden fleas and walking zombies going one way — and mentally agile, awakened people who are willing to correct our unhealthy imbalances going the other. Which group do you want to join? More important, are you afraid of being told that you're the flea in the jar and can handle the truth?

FEAR FEEDS OUR FLAWS

I pointed out earlier that fear is our built-in human flaw. Unfortunately, it is a pesky flame that is in dire need of detoxing as it feeds the fire of hatred for *white fright.* As I've commented on this subject in Part 1 of the book (Camp Divide), there's a convergence of two unhealed camps: A diehard tribe with a shameless obsession of practicing profit-over-people and another that is unabashed about protecting and favoring the white race in America. The latter is about being afraid of losing America's white privileged majority and status, while the former is lured into fearing the false narrative that we're turning away from capitalism to socialism. Neither of these fears have any real basis, but do keep surviving and thriving and expanding the respective camps. What's the explanation? For one, a race-based separatist philosophy flourishes more in laissez-faire runaway capitalism societies due to ascribed freedoms — and America is ground zero for this type of society. But more disturbing is the hypocrisy and double standard for fixing it. No one gets punished in America for spewing racist slurs toward an immigrant or organizing public KKK rallies. Yet you'll be locked up for not paying a speeding fine and foreclosed for missing a few months of mortgage payments. Why is that?

THE GREEN BLOOD SOCIETY

Whether you're ready to blame class warfare or our misplaced priorities for our many ills such as rampant racism, America's ugly truth is that it has programmed itself to be a product of one color: green. It's in our blood. If our runaway capitalist system of profit over people is our downfall, then our green blood in our veins is our toxic companion that hinders our progress. The thing is, we'll use fear as a poison to profit from the propaganda and rhetoric to wag the tail of racism, but we won't cut the snake's head to stop it. Perhaps it all makes sense from an artist's point of view. If the color green is in America's blood, mixing our Divine-derived red blood with our man-made green blood — makes it a brown color blood! From this creative perspective, could it be that America's browning is inevitable? Or that our society's lifeblood and survival depends on us *not* trying to profit from racism or prolong its poisoning? What do you think it all means?

Perhaps we must start looking at some unconventional solutions, such as ticketing people for being blatantly racist or fining corporations for exclusionary treatment of certain groups of people, etc. If not, America will continue to embrace double standards and not get serious about containing the ugly head of systematic racism.

Could that inaction be because racism is highly profitable for the power holders and the corporate media that exploits it? Many fearful, fragile and fickle Americans have been pouring their hard-earned dollars into the coffers of openly racist radical groups and sensationalist media outlets like never before. And that vileness is spreading to other areas of the economy further skewing our moral compass. The decoupling of Wall Street from main street during the pandemic is a prime example. The egocentric financial markets turned a blind eye on America's 99 percent — pouring gasoline on an already inflamed downwardly mobile people. The stock market continued making record highs while record numbers of people suffered from hunger, filed for unemployment, started using food stamps and filled up hospitals. Many of these poor unfortunates were in communities of color. To add fuel to the fire, according to Bloomberg News, the world's top 500 richest people added $1.8 trillion to their combined net worth during the first year of the pandemic. How shameful and foretelling is that?

In order to rebalance some of the inequities, America started printing trillions of stimulus dollars to help its people. But that's not without a cost. They're strings attached that will cause much emotional and economic discomfort down the road. The effect of printing money out of thin air and giving handouts will come to boomerang on us in the coming years, with higher taxation, less freedoms, more inflation and more regulations for ALL of us. It will first show up on a local level with cities and counties stripping our wallets in the form of high property taxes, higher sales and income tax and similar revenue generating measures.

We may think we can relocate to different states to avoid the pain, but that carrot stick will be short-lived, as all states will eventually be forced to balance their budgets and come for your money — as will federally mandated regulations. We won't be able to run or hide from all our problems, but we can get many of them under control by our awareness and making smart choices for ourselves today. Many of the self-improvement ideas discussed in this book will get you in the right frame of mind to strategize, compromise and reprioritize. The smarter path is always a proactive one, where we start planning to protect our freedoms and finances before the sh*t hits the fan and boomerangs on our own face.

We put on our masks and our 'I Voted' buttons to get rid of two viruses in America in 2021, the first that almost destroyed our democratic institutions and the second that damaged the lives of millions. But we better keep those boxing gloves on hand and be prepared to fight a virus that has been engulfing our society for many decades — the virus that comes in all shapes, sizes and colors that flows in our veins — the virus of greed!

"All Mine"

(Mixed Media Clay) Artist: Jim Peera

4

Four Weeks to Unf*ck Yourself

There's a difference between being a f*ck up and f*cking up. The latter is a temporary condition that all of us have experienced in some form or fashion. And when this condition is not remedied in a timely manner, it manifests into the chronic state of turning into a flea in the jar or even an outright 'f*ck up', which we all must avoid. The Healium Way of self-transformation instructs us that we've all contributed in some manner to our *f*ckening* (the condition of f*cking up repeatedly). As flawed beings, the hard part of unf*ckening of ourselves is putting aside our pride, hypocrisy and ego and getting to a state of *reckoning*. It is at this awareness stage where we are presented with the opportunity of learning our life lessons and discovering our personal *awakening*. Don't think of this as an *awoke*-ning where we rage at anyone we find fault with, but a more objective and balanced prescription that brings a needed self-realization — no matter how painful. The Healium Way inspires us to get there by being serious with a goal-oriented approach of putting a four- week time limit to accomplish our mission.

By having our *hierarchy of expectation* at the highest level for ourselves, we can keep our own bar from being lowered. The time for self-improvement and unf*ckening is fleeting, however, and Americans of all demographics must look at their country's current state of being as an S-O-S condition. Without sounding self-righteous or condescending, I want to get off my chest this emergency affirmation that has been ringing in my head and ears for a while and is valid for the critical times that we're all facing:

Jim's S-O-S affirmation to save America's Soul:

The truth hurts — but it heals. Once we understand how **SPOILED, SELFISH** and **STUPID** Americans have become, we can admit to our inability to **SACRIFICE** and make **SENSIBLE** decisions as individuals and as a people. We must know that this condition is not **SUSTAINABLE** for our **SANITY**. We must find **SMART** and creative **SOLUTIONS** to **SAVE** our **SOCIETY**. Let's **START** by not **SCORCHING** our open wounds, but by **STITCHING** them back to mend our **SEVERED SOULS**. It is un-American to keep **SEPARATING** and **SUFFERING**. Consider this your individual and collective **S-O-S** call to action.

TIME TO GO TO WORK

If you're in some agreement with this affirmation — you're ready to unf*ck some things about yourself. Each of us has some form of undesirable characteristic, deed or mistake we can pinpoint that is weighing us down. The beautiful thing is, once we unf*ck ourselves, we stop having the urge to f*ck others, physically and emotionally, which is a win-win for everyone on our path to upliftment and peace, individually and collectively. In order to begin the self-improvement reconstruction, we need to repudiate our ills and moral deficiency as a people first. It's important that we put aside our respective red, blue, white, colored and other labels, and see each other simply as a quilt of multifaceted humans. The task at hand is to defy hate and division and set the intention to practice the activities during this four-week program to better your chances of transforming into a more grounded *roots*-type being. In order to best prepare for this four-week challenge and do the work, you'll need to identify and purge some unhealthy influences from your life. Removing these dead weights will help your mind work more efficiently and make it easier to stay the course. Let me elaborate on a couple of these influences.

PURGING THE EXPLOITIVE MEDIA

There is very little breadth in mainstream information channels or social media platforms in America today. The shallowness is cleverly engineered to mirror and satisfy our superficial needs. Think of it as the 'dumb to dumber' phenomenon that profits from your ignorance, naivete and stupidity. If you don't already know it, they're making you more mule-brained by presenting a biased version' of the facts by the so-called "experts" who are carefully groomed to spin and recycle information into agenda-based opinions, infotainment and even disinformation. The Healium Way solution is not to stop consuming news content, but rather to *expand* your outlook and knowledge across the entire information and media ecosystem — no matter how difficult or uncomfortable. By plugging into diverse news feeds from around the world, you're able to make your own decision on what information is fact, fiction or propaganda. If not, you'll be hooked to a particular pattern of news consumption due to *confirmation bias*; a tendency to search for content that supports your predisposed values or beliefs. That practice is counter to a healthy balance, as you never get to explore any other viewpoints outside of your own little box of beliefs. It's common in authoritarian regimes, but has become pervasive in America today and is our self-induced mindf*ck.

Therefore, be aware of your attachment to any single source of news, including podcasts and online channels hosted by famous people.

Ditching traditional news media for social media is also not the answer, as you're just swapping one dirty underwear for another. That's because social media is a more dangerous form of confirmation bias and behavioral engineering. Most platforms use AI and smart algorithms to hook you with every click — without your knowledge or permission. They know exactly what you like, what you hate and how to feed you more of the same by throwing you into deeper biased territory — often negative. If you make a post about hating someone, you'll be bombarded with propaganda, hate stories and matching merchandise about that person. Never discovering the flip side of them to construct a more objective profile. Think of it as a fancy shovel gifted to you to dig your own grave. It is a big reason why we're so myopic, polarized and divided as a nation. If you absolutely have to communicate via social media, just make your post and forget about it. These sites not only make us crave for constant validation, but they bombard us with targeted ads and shamelessly sell our private profiles. So don't keep checking to see how many likes, dislikes or comments you got or didn't get. It's irrelevant to your mental wellness. In fact, it will actually exacerbate your mental instability and illness. You made your post — your point — and you got it out of your system. Why do you have to rationalize it, defend it, or want validation for it? It's not important what others think or don't think about your post. Stop satisfying your egotistic itch and dopamine hunger. It will make you feel good when positive things are said about you, but make you sad and angry when the lies and sh*t come your way. So why fall into that trap? Social media does not make you more or less valuable as a person. If you do have to get your message out to your community, use the neighborhood-powered and closed group sites to reduce the idiots, the crazies and the fragile minds that troll the Word Wide Web 24 hours a day. In a paradoxical way, similar to Trumpism, all these platforms are a mirror onto yourself; they're not so much the cause of our societal ills as they're a symptom — revealing our own imbalances such as insecurity, narcissism, materialism, mental fragility, loneliness and so on. Although it's easy for many people to get sucked into these toxic digital boxes, it's vital to look at the forest from the trees and deploy a "digital detox" habit into your lifestyle. Using nature as our healing partner, we can discipline ourselves by spending quality time outdoors connecting with the flora and fauna, water and nature spirits and fresh air to find a healthier balance. Just take a baby-step approach, do it consistently and stick to it.

UNFRIENDING THE 'ACT'

The second purge in our march toward our unf*ckening is to fake attachments and acquaintances in your life, i.e., our circle of so- called "friends." In order to understand the value of The Healium Way, we must practice each of the Principles and exercises with *real* people in real situations at work, home and social gatherings. Many of these people are your true *friends*. But who are your friends and what is our definition of a "friend"? You'll be surprised to discover some hard truths. In the West, we conflate friends and acquaintances. In a profit-over-people and overworked lifestyle model, people don't really have time to get too close to others. What we have in America today is a superficial and agenda-based relationship with people.

Often it's a deliberate choice of having acquaintances that we falsely label as friends. I call it our *ACT*: *Acquaintances for Convenience and Transactions*. We're all guilty of it, particularly in the West to a certain degree and it's difficult to admit — but it's the truth. Very few of us have close and true friends who we can rely on and totally trust with our deepest secrets or problems. Most people I know have a closer relationship with their cats and dogs than they do with people. That fact in itself reveals a lot about ourselves. Many individuals cannot handle intimate or conditional relationships with other humans, and as a result choose loneliness or unconditional animal love instead. People also learn to use others as needed, and shove them aside once they're done transacting their business or fulfilling a selfish purpose. Keeping our distance from people gives us the alibi to stay connected without having the responsibility to be aligned on a heart and Soul basis. That's the price of living in a fast-moving capitalist society and a disillusioned reality. The TV show "Friends" was very popular because it showcased an idealistic version of Americans. That level of closeness, camaraderie and intimacy doesn't exist in real life. At least, I have not witnessed it in my four decades living in the country! Everything I see when it comes to friendship appears superficial and transactional. Often it takes on a more sinister condition where the "C" in the ACT stands for competition and comparison, typically related to status. In this mode, you're either there to make the other person feel better about themselves and stroke their ego (because you've got less money than them), or make them feel bad and be jealous of you (because you've got more money than them). It's all a mindf*ck. Many of my real estate "friends" belong in this category; they never stop talking about money and try to size you up against them. Be aware when that happens to you; that's an unhealthy relationship that merits a total disassociation or at least reducing time spent with those people.

Not surprisingly, our ACT is a by-product of our *individualistic culture* that pairs dangerously with our *disposable society*. This awareness is necessary for us to make a healthier shift toward building better relationships. We'll attract needy or self-absorbed people when we're putting on an ACT. Therefore, during the four-week action plan, don't surround yourself with users, flakes or enablers. If all you have among the people you call friends fit this definition, take the time to reevaluate your close circle and reach out to others who might be better choices for you. How about spending less time on your phones and computers engaging with robots and narcissists — and engaging with like-minded humans? People capable of being good friends are getting rarer, but they do exist, if you're willing to do some work to seek them out. This is also your time to turn the mirror on yourself and see if *you* are putting on an ACT with your own circle of friends. After all, you don't attract what you want, but who you are.

THE ACTION PLAN

By reducing our addiction to news & social media sites and trimming our stock of fake friends, we're well positioned to tackle our unf*uckening. I've handpicked four Principles of The Healium Way to align with the four-week challenge: 1) Principle #8, *Honoring your emotions; 2)* Principle #2, *Removing our resistances;* 3) Principle #5, *Mastering detachment and resolving conflicts. 4) Principle# 19, Being an instrument of peace.*

Notice how all of these Principles are interrelated in some manner. Collectively, they provide us with the fuel for lifting us into the higher and *extra*ordinary realm. The purpose of our mission is to devote one week to each of these Principles. Each day you will test out the lesson of the respective Principle with your guru, your doctor, your life coach and your therapist: YOU.

You will do this by reducing unhealthy distractions and staying allocentric or inward focused. By the end of each week, you will have moved the needle of positive progress with relative confidence and ease. First, you'll have to identify your particular f*ck up in detail.

Is it a bad relationship, an infraction with someone you love, a mistake you made with your finances, a bad decision you made as a person in power, etc.? You may have a lot of these regrettable choices that are comfortably stored in your subconscious mind. But only pick ONE from your list to activate the conscious mind and take the challenge.

My suggestion is to pick the one that is weighing you down *the least,* as your first practice piece. If you're bold, pick your worst one and go for it!

Week One *Honoring your emotions:* Once you've chosen the particular f*ck up as your template, start the week by paying attention to your inner voice. Specifically the one that you've been too busy to listen to — your higher self. Using Principle #8, the goal by the end of this first week is to go from your *f*ckening,* to an honest *reckoning* with the issue. The example we're using for this exercise is a f*ck up of an unpaid debt with someone. In fact, it's become your *f*ckening* because you have a track record with creditors and people of not paying your obligations on time. This creditor/lender (person, entity, landlord, etc.) has lost trust in your ability to honor your obligations, while you've decided that your payment delay is justified. That's your ugly, lower-vibrational self in action. Now take this IOU, lease, promissory note or loan that you signed, and place it on your chest. Feel the energy of the burden on yourself. What emotions are you going through? Do you feel anger, fear, sadness, disgust, guilt or any shame? Don't try to influence your emotions, as much as *honor* them as they present themselves. Use the entire week to befriend these emotions as you make your truth serum in getting you to a place of reckoning. Each day you'll want to use the creative and healing tools we've discussed throughout the book to help you release your emotions and expose truths. Remember, the convenient justification tools of denial, victimhood, entitlement and pride are your enablers and defense mechanisms. This is a good time to put yourself in the creditor's shoes and imagine you were owed the money. During this period, you realize the importance of being responsible for your own actions. If you do this correctly, your stress levels and anxiety about repaying the debt dissipate. By the end of the week, you should have dismantled many of those excuses for not living up to your obligations.

Week Two *Removing our resistances:* In this week, you will be using the tools in Principle #2 to further come to grips with some truths about your f*ckening. There will be lies that you will tell yourself about it, but that is your resistance from your higher self.

During this week, you solidify your *reckoning* which turns into an intention, a healthy signal that you are ready to act to unf*ck yourself by having a plan to pay back the debt. By the end of this week, you will no longer see the debt as a burden, as the underlying weight of your resistances such as fear, ego, judgment and pretense are not tempting or misleading you.

Week Three *Mastering detachment and resolving conflicts:* In the third week, Principle #5 kicks in to help you detach from any negative or predisposed outcomes that may still be lurking inside you. You're now fully open to paying the debt and are in the damage-control phase where you have to connect with this creditor/lender to smooth over the f*ck up. You accept that you will not go unscathed, as there will be fees, penalties, buyer's remorse and distrust coming your way. But you're OK with it all, because you now own up to your f*ck up and take responsibility for your actions. This is the week where you enter the *awakening* phase and prepare yourself mentally to deal with the fourth and final week of your transformation.

Week Four *Being an instrument of peace:* In your final and most empowering and satisfying period of your four-week path to becoming a better person, you start the week by having one goal: to pay your debt — either in full or by making an automatic bank draft payment plan (so you cannot renege on your word). You'll need to visualize this outcome in your head each morning when you wake up. That's your payback affirmation, so you don't flake out. Use the tips in Principle #19 and forge a path to your action plan. Reactivate the tools prescribed in this book to get you to a place of inner peace, free of any guilt, hesitation, resistance or regret. This is your week of *awakening.* You will feel lighter in the chest now, free of the emotional baggage that held you hostage by your low-vibrational condition. You are ready to come to the table and connect with the creditor/lender you f*cked. In fact, you are eager to not just apologize but are prepared to face punishment or consequences.

Nevertheless, you now feel liberated, empowered and reinvigorated because you are operating from a place of strength, not weakness; and light, as opposed to darkness. Your awakening is powerful and has just elevated yourself from an ordinary to an *extra*ordinary person, who is a step closer to being a *roots*-type human being.

Once you've successfully come to terms with *unf*cking* yourself with a particular issue, you will be able to repeat this same four-week technique with other self-induced burdens and problems. What's more, this exercise will have a positive snowball effect on everything that you do from that moment. You'll be able to sit on the same table with an opponent of differing views and maintain a peaceful dialogue. Your productivity will increase at work, as you'll have higher self-esteem and enjoy a better home life. Obviously, each person will have varying results and will implement the Principles differently. Some of you will be reluctant to engage in art exercises as much as others. But it's important to stay the course, to make small consistent steps to accomplish big things. That's how we shift from the low-vibrational self of our *f*ckening* to a place of *reckoning* and experiencing an eventual *awakening* of our better and higher self.

"Untitled"

For YOUR interpretation!

(Pen on Vintage Paper)
Artist: Haseena Peera

5
Unconventional Wisdom

From the very beginning of The Healium Way, I've tried to instill in you the importance of valuing unconventional wisdom. With this philosophy, I've been able to not only survive, but thrive — especially by understanding the power of our Divinity that resides within each of us.

THE BLESSED CURSES

I've given detailed examples throughout The Healium Way of how my own life's stories have shaped the narrative of my *blessed curses*. Painful events that seemed like curses turned out to be powerful lessons and blessings. From the time of my childbirth survival to today, I've learnt to respect and trust my maker as the captain and pilot of my life's wild rides. It is with this truth and belief that I feel we begin improving our own reality and our own future. Instead of looking at all our sh*t and f*ckups as curses, let's look at them as Divine signs and welcomed blessings. Even earthshaking events like Covid-19, global warming, institutional racism, rising economic inequality, terrorism, and Trumpism can be Divine signals — for our transformation. This shift in perception requires us to think in unconventional ways on our path to become more creative, more courageous and more compassionate. Let's start on that journey by taking a healthy pause from the day-to-day grind that is clouding our judgment and foresight.

THE HEALTHY PAUSE BUTTON

Unconventional wisdom teaches us to recognize the benefit of a pause button. Whether it's the metaphor of the mountain or the ladder, each of us wants to climb to the top and have financial freedom and happiness. The paradox is, the top is an illusion and most of us have been programmed to not stop climbing. Trying to attain financial freedom is oxymoronic if you're trapped inside an egotistic and dissatisfied mindset. Sure, enjoy the ride up but learn to switch from pressing the "next" level button to the "pause" button — and appreciate your moment of individual success. Sometimes the pause is forced upon us (or appears to be) by illness, tragedy, war, ordeal or a pandemic. These actually become signs for us to reassess our paths. Sometimes the pause is more deliberate, as I chose to do when I opened Healium Center and put my highly lucrative real estate career on indefinite hold.

DON'T SWEAT THE SMALL STUFF

Because everything in life is situational and relative, it makes sense not to get caught up in making mountains out of molehills, which can easily erupt into volcanoes. You may be having one of the best days of your life and some jerk can ruin your whole year by crashing into you at a busy intersection. Instead of stressing about why a person did or didn't do something, spend your energy on what you *can* control and take the steps to improve your own condition. The majority of things that we worry about never materialize. As the saying goes, *"Don't cry over spilled milk and go milk another cow."* Stress is part of life, so learn to manage stressful situations before they snowball into chronic health issues. When we stop sweating the small stuff, anxiety and depression levels are reduced significantly. By decreasing our valuable energies on stuff that is soul-sucking and mind-weakening, we're able to focus on the things that really matter — our own wellbeing and our family.

EMBRACE THE MYSTERY

There's a reason our Creator made us all different in skin color — to figure out how to get along. There's also a purpose for not knowing all the answers to our existence. As the Tao says, *"The mystery is the doorway to all understanding."* It is where our knowing ends and we embrace the mysterious. This unseeable, unknowable, powerful realm that is invisible keeps us grounded — and on the edge. That is the Creator's intention. Unlike a conventional mindset of trying to make sense of everything, how about we simply stop asking fortune tellers to predict our next best move or relationship? Astrology, numerology and all the metaphysical tools of foretelling our future are cool and have their purpose, but the actual mystery is more exciting. It's all going to happen in Divine order anyway. Just relax, let go, allow and enjoy your temporary visit here with passion and vigor. You'll have less stress and a fuller life if you don't give in to that impulse. When I deploy this unconventional way of looking at my own life, I become less anxious and worried about what might or might not happen tomorrow. This way, I'm not afraid of death and I trust in the Divine order to let the chips of life fall where they're supposed to.

UNDERSTAND OUR PARADOXICAL NATURE

I've alluded to this phenomenon throughout the book, but now let's put it to the test from your own perspective. Yes, everything about our existence is open to interpretation, and here's the mindf*ck: life in itself is a paradox, a self-contradictory statement which can only be true if it is false and vice versa. *"Everything makes sense, and nothing makes sense,"* as I put it. Essentially, fake news is a paradox, as news is not supposed to be fake. Yet as we've come to know recently, it can be. The existence of God is also a paradox, as it cannot be proven but we know that a higher all-knowing power exists. Now add to this phenomenon the condition of duality — where two opposites are like two sides of the same coin and together make a complete coin. Let's go on with this analogy: good/evil, light/dark, material/spiritual, male/female, destruction/creation, yin/ yang, etc. Using this paradoxical and dual nature of our existence, you can make a case that perhaps the low vibrational conditions that we're trying to avoid such as tribalism and separation is a pie in the sky idealistic mindf*ck that is our species comfort/default position. That people prefer to gravitate towards their own color and kind — rather than understand and assimilate with people who are different. We've found good evidence of this truth at our Center. You can also label all the Principles of The Healium Way as nonsense and unnecessary, if you wish. You have the universal license to do that. I just told you why and I won't be offended if you do.

So let's test this paradoxical theory just for fun. You could argue that the three ugly truths we revealed earlier in the book (Part 1) don't have anything to do with you. The ugly truths are 1) *We are flawed beings; 2) Each of us is unique but not special* and *3) We all harbor some unhealed scars that are keeping us from operating at our higher vibration.* You argue that these ugly truths are truly disempowering and constrictive to your growth and transformation. You'd rather skip reality and see the possibilities through an idealistic kaleidoscope lens by preferring to take the opposing view. By seeing yourself as a sound and perfect being, you will trick and condition your mind to behave in tandem with this renewed idealistic condition. By looking at yourself as a *special* human being, you actually manifest that character and start doing special things in life. By not visiting the skeletons in the closet and the unhealed scars of the past, you bypass the dark emotions and forge fresh new synapses in your mind that take you on a path of enlightenment. In other words, you attain higher consciousness by thinking, breathing and living in that Divine ecosystem without having your low-vibrational man-made realities get in the way. I know many of you who live by this philosophy, and I respect it – even though I disagree with the premise.

But if life's rainbows and butterflies perception of the world works for you, the more power to you. I'm not going to stop you, if you think it will work better for your personal growth and not make you hibernate in your fear-induced bubble by replacing human contact with a dog, a cat or a robot. It's possible that this thinking could be the exact placebo effect that you need to move the transformation needle towards the center of the dial for you. Our goal should be to get on a path that liberates us from many constrictive boxes and be in a healthier balance today than what we were yesterday — no matter how we each get there.

WRITTEN IN THE STARS

Alas, though, a word of caution to all my idealist brothers and sisters; don't expect the world around you to match your reality. It won't. There are a lot fewer idealistic fantasists in our real world. And you may be setting yourself up for disappointment, as we're far from unf*cking our self-defeating ways and understanding the power of oneness. So as flawed beings, remind yourself of the *hierarchy of expectation*, and get used to our species' destructive ways by lowering the humanity bar (to the lowest position) for your own sanity. It will make life a lot easier to enjoy and live. I make it my default position every day and I recommend you do too!

Actually, this dynamic is clearly written in the stars. Since we've established that we originate from the stars, we can better understand our own characteristics. Being that stars are made of much chaos and destruction that make them burn so bright, why should we, as star-children expect to be any different? In this universal phenomenon of order and chaos, just think of our species mimicking the duality and unpredictability of the heavens in order to exist and evolve. It's our universal karma to own, understand and live with.

6

A Peace Plan for America

"Those who are hardest to love need it the most."
– Socrates

THE PARTNERSHIP

Throughout the book, our journey together has been planted around harvesting our common life-sustaining crop; peace. Therefore, a peace plan for America is only possible when Americans experience some form of it within themselves. Once you've tasted the sweet nectar of inner peace, the temptation of being attached to a bitter or sour elixir of hostility is significantly diminished. The Soul, body and mind will reject any unsavory intrusion and work hard to protect its preferred palette and balance. It's the Law of Attraction at play, and a good reason why we've spent many chapters trying to improve the self. America's unsavory intrusion (internal or external) can be rejected by the intentions and the follow-through actions of as many people as possible — in *partnership* with each other. We're not going to convince everyone to get on board and don't have to agree on anything except one thing; the desire for individual and collective peace! That's the high bar that we cannot afford to lower. We may not always reach it, but we'll manifest it better being aligned with it and protecting it. It's also something that cannot be outsourced to elected officials, advocacy groups or smart computers, but by joining hands with our multifaceted human demographic; the 'haves' and 'haves nots', private and public enterprises, coloreds and whites, democrats and republicans, young and old, vegans and carnivores and so forth. Moreover, in the spirit of The Healium Way, it must be undertaken using an unconventional approach where creative and innovative ideas are openly shared and tested first on a community level. Many novel suggestions have already been offered throughout the book, so in this chapter I'll go deeper into our *collective* (political, social, economic) responsibilities for peace. Obviously, I don't have all the answers but will share some more ideas here from my own perspective as an immigrant, an artist, a world traveler, an entrepreneur, a healing-arts director and a peacemaker. I encourage you to present your ideas in the various forums where this book is hosted and discussed.

THE LOVE INSIDE

While we've made tremendous progress as a nation in many areas since the turn of the century and are smelling a lot of roses, we've simultaneously added a lot of sh*t on ourselves that needs to be cleaned up. Our modus operandi so far has been to wallow in our own sh*t and wage war with those who refuse to enable our sh*tty selves. With this attitude, it's obvious Americans don't value or love themselves on the inside — as much as they love keeping appearances on the outside. But loving ourselves is an inside job. Unless we Americans fix and rebalance this problem, start respecting each other and stop pitting one against the other — this current period will look like a lost decade of couldas, shouldas, wouldas to our kids and grandkids. And it's been a long time in the making. Entering 2016, Americans were already mentally fragile and disconnecting from their higher self. The prospect of a black man with a Muslim name, Barack Obama, becoming America's 44th president ruffled a lot of white feathers and fed into the dark minds of the unhealed. Yet we ignored those signs, and subsequently saw the rise of violent radicalism and domestic terrorism that came close to overthrowing our democracy. But there are no innocent parties here. A divided people are a weakened people who will have a lot less success defending and overcoming wars and disasters on America's turf, be they natural or man-made. There will be more global pandemics, germ and cyber wars, cybersecurity attacks, computer hacks, climate-change disasters and military wars in our future. But nothing is more shameful than to have Americans terrorize and harm Americans with a radical and vitriolic mindset. That's really dumb and self-defeating. How are we going to survive any crisis as a nation and as individuals if we are constantly hating, battling and pointing guns at each other? We may not be able to stop our enemies such as Russia from compromising our national security or competitive threats like China from outsmarting or out-competing us, but we can stop our own enemy (the mind) from destroying our own health and welfare. We have to get outside that mental box that spews fury, gaslights, or fans the flames of fear and ugliness on others in their boxes. We're all breathing the same air, so let's not choke ourselves with rage and get to a state of loving ourselves... from the inside out.

FIXING OUR KARMA

Peace requires a cool head and our better angels tell us to have open arms instead of tightened fists. The Healium Way is all about taking incremental steps fixing America's various inequalities and societal ills, cut big government, reduce the corporate stranglehold, elect smarter and honest leaders and leave a better future for our kids. We must also fight against having America become more empirical, weaponized and disconnected from its people. Otherwise, we will keep self-loathing ourselves, lose our personal freedoms and be hated around the world where our reputation already suffers from our self-serving failed policies and actions in many trouble regions.

But that's already happening you say! Why is that? It's to do with reaping what we sow by being hypocrites and bed partners with corrupt regimes. Our foreign policy is tainted with self-serving agendas, that eventually whacks our own ass at home. I can site many examples but the most obvious is not being an honest broker in the Middle East and not doing more to address human rights abuses of occupied Palestinians in the Jewish state of Israel. How can America expect its own radicalism, injustices and racism be tamed on its own soil if it turns a blind eye on Israel; its adopted child with its well-documented crimes against humanity? When we feed the belly of any beast with cruel intentions that oppresses other humans due to their beliefs or religion, we're in fact setting up karma for our own people. It's our payback.

This one-sided humanitarian hypocrisy is our downfall as it boomerangs on our own fate as individuals and as a country. Extremism has been festered by our overt flirting with our dark faculties as we deviate further from our morality. In just five decades, we went from a president who sent a man to the moon to electing an unhealed authoritarian who mooned America's allies, its institutions and its own people. How in the world has that worked out for the United States of America? It's time to fix our ways and reverse our bad karma folks. Or we won't manifest peace for ourselves. It's the raw and simple truth.

REDEPLOYING OUR DOLLARS AND SENSE

Thankfully, The Healium Way reminds us that humankind flourishes when each human extols the virtues of kindness, collaboration, cooperation and friendliness and suffers in conflict, competition and chaos. It's the more sustainable way and our only way out of a quagmire we've created. Instead of looking at a centralized authority in Washington D.C. to fix all our disparate societal ills with more laws, regulations, inefficiencies and conventionality, we believe an unconventional and grassroots approach that brings fresh ideas to reinvigorate Americans is the better way. Because the bureaucratic red tape seals the fate of creativity and positive action. In order to do this correctly, we'll need to put politics, egos and our convenient power plays on ice for a minute. Let's re-engage by temporarily disengaging from pushing everyone's hot buttons to score "brownie" or "white" points— and get to the point. Since our various ideas on fixing America require money, we must zero-in on how a partnership in peace can be funded by recycling our fiscal waste. Let's take the lowest hanging fruit by cutting the biggest corruption and waste in America's black hole; The U.S military defense budget.

I see it as a guaranteed annual winning lottery ticket for the Pentagon — compliments of American taxpayers. Approaching a whopping $800 billion per annum, as of this writing, the U.S spends 12 times on militarizing itself as the next largest spenders combined. The term 'defense budget' itself is misleading and oxymoronic. It should be called an offensive budget as we waste more taxpayers' money hastily attacking and occupying other countries rather than investing in our own people. Even sickening is that there's no oversight or conditions attached to this free-flowing government waste. We're being hoodwinked y'all! How about not squandering those taxpayer dollars on offensive weapons of destruction and deploying a small fraction of that towards reconstructing our Souls — with fresh and unconventional methods. I'll give you a couple of suggestions to get your mind churning in the right direction.

We're entering a phase in America with two back-to-back toxic viruses that have mindf*cked us from the inside out: Trumpism and Covid-19. Both are catalysts to start prioritizing our mental health. I'm not talking about diagnosing it with fancy labels and solving it with pills and conventional therapy, but by changing the social metrics that shape our daily environment. This is a forest from the trees idea. And smart leaders in government can help instigate it. Instead of our government measuring our Consumer Price Index (CPI), how about we start measuring our *Mental Health Index?* Instead of gathering data on how much we spend, we'll focus on measuring social factors and influences that *contribute* to our mental illness and wellness. This valuable information will help us adjust and shift to a healthier balance. We'll fix and prevent our many social ills related to mental health such as homelessness, suicides, drug abuse and violence in this way. This is where we can use modern technology and apps to track our progress, give us feedback and get us on a proactive path. Implementing this type of index can shift our entire social ecosystem. For instance, rather than being bombarded with drug commercials, we'll be treated to organic food and plant medicine ads. Our runaway capitalism will be rebalanced to a workable form of human capital-based social good that helps lift ALL boats, not just the big ships. Instead of being fixated on the corporate news media channels, people will get out and start reconnecting with their neighbors, their community and start making their own newsworthy stories of positive change. In the place of daily conflicts, the reporters will give us stories of courage and hope. Instead of repeated updates on the daily stock market, radio stations will provide updates on acts of altruism, progress and generosity in their city. Rather than listening to inflammatory and divisive AM radio shows during our long commutes to and from work, we'll be inspired to listen to uplifting music or just enjoy the silence and reconnect with ourselves. Our phone usage will diminish as we'll spend more time dialoguing and engaging with real people. Imagine the lead item on the news is America's renaissance, not its demise. All that would make for a positive reading of the Mental Health Index (MHI). This is the power of operating from an unconventional and non-indoctrinated mindset. What do you think of this idea?

Another idea is having non-traditional community nonprofits and for-profit companies that are *disrupters and innovators* in their field join forces with a social enterprise mission. We don't want the conventional and the stale, but the fresh and out-of-the-box movers and shakers. As a good example of such an idea in the wellness field, Healium Center has showed good proof of concept in just one small community in a short span of time. Imagine how much difference we could make with more collaboration and funding from more supporters spanning multiple locations across America. I bet there are dozens of viable game-changers in your community that would benefit from such a collaborative model. Once again, the redeployment of existing financial resources is necessary. How about building less shopping places and fast food joints and taking a sliver of the misappropriated defense budget to build more healthy and creative/spiritual public indoor and outdoor spaces to improve our wellbeing? For sure, there will be challenges, naysayers and haters as we've encountered at our Center, but the payoff is worth the sacrifice.

THE AMERI*CAN*

A peace plan is also about redeploying our own personal time, energy and resources toward fixing America. President John F. Kennedy refers to it quite eloquently in his inaugural speech in 1961, the year I was born. The phrase remains one of my favorite messages by an American president: *"Ask not what your country can do for you, but what you can do for your country."* It is a call for people power, true patriotism and unity that we seem to have forgotten. In the 60 years since JFK's iconic words, we've slipped into a habit of scapegoating and outsourcing our personal power that makes that statement seem out of reach. President Obama refreshed it for us with his "Yes, we can" slogan (borrowed from Cesar Chavez) during his campaign and tenure, but it got diluted in bipartisan politics and tribalism. The reality is, before you can even try to help to fix your country or believe in its potential, you must first fix yourself and be willing to do the necessary work. President Kennedy's words for today's world need to be supplanted with; *"Ask first what YOU need to do for yourself."* Then, once we remove all the distractions and excuses that cloud our judgment, we can go from being an ordinary American to an *extra*ordinary version of ourselves; the Ameri*CAN*.

This shift is about understanding that the longer our unhealed Souls keep feeding and sowing chaos, division, ugliness and hatred, the more difficult it will be to reverse its momentum. Can you imagine a future in America that resembles authoritarian regimes of falsehoods, thievery, corruption and dystopia of the kind unparalleled in American history? We should all be concerned that our self-induced tribalism and imbalances if unattended, will manifest into a 'class and culture' revolution that ferments more racism, domestic terrorism, economic inequities, drug addiction, street riots and an out-of-control mental crisis on Americans. At this juncture, we're on a dangerous edge of such a possibility. So let's take is seriously.

Let me plant one probable scenario that could tip us into such a spiral; a clash between the elite-driven powerful corporate monopolies and the American working class. Instead of tamping down on greed and spreading some of their wealth with employees by offering higher wages and profit-sharing, what if many of our profit-over-people companies doubled down on making *more* profits (to please shareholders and top management)? The obvious reaction from most workers not willing to work for cheap would be to quit or threaten layoffs and strikes, correct? But what if it didn't matter what the workers did? What if the corporations had the "f*ck you" button to press by substituting not just robots, but as many human workers they needed from a hungry pool of ready, able and willing hard-working people; America's undocumented immigrants? American corporations sold American workers out decades ago to outsourcing. What's stopping them from doing the same by *in*sourcing from America's growing non-entrepreneurial immigrant workforce? Some of this reality is already taking place in construction, technology and agriculture, but what if it spreads into other industries, leaving millions of black and white low-skilled workers in the dust? In order to keep inflation and unemployment numbers down and corporate lobbyists happy, our leaders could concoct a creative backdoor policy to loosen immigration laws and re-engineer our new economy. Add to this the growing cancer of Trumpism, and a prospect of a modern civil war fought with automatic weapons, becomes a scary reality.

A TIME FOR RE-PAIRING

Instead of waiting for such an ugly outcome, perhaps it's time we start fixing our profit-over-people imbalance NOW. Our initial repair must be mutually undertaken without excuses by *each* of us. Since it takes *two to tango*, let's see that repair as re-pairing: one person reaching out to a total stranger with kindness and civility. A starting point can look like a peace offering with a common denominator that we all understand: food.

Previously, we've determined that every problem has a creative solution. Now let's return to an earlier example of the biscotti and biscuit analogy we made in Part 1 of the book. What if the biscotti/soy latte person did not ignore or judge the fried chicken biscuit/ice tea person? The Healium Way approach would be to get each individual to taste a sample from each other's plate and/or simply talk about the food (staying away from controversial subjects such as politics and religion while at the table), until they're better acquainted with each other. Using this one-on-one pairing approach as an example, it becomes possible for each person to appreciate and respect the other's unique food preference and palette, without imposing or judging it. As each person gets comfortable with the other, resulting in a fried chicken biscuit-eater agreeing to taste the biscotti and latte and the biscotti-eater sampling the fried chicken and ice tea, we can begin making some progress. This *sharing* begins the process of dialoguing, adapting and bonding — all important conditions for peace and seeing people as humans; not to dismiss, misuse or abuse — but to respect, appreciate and value. Such a proposition takes mutual intention and cooperation; with one person usually taking the bold initiative. But it is highly effective and rewarding when it works. Can this person be you? Can you see yourself taking the *extra*-step and reaching out to someone you find to be different or out of your realm of comfort? Take a few seconds to visualize this positive *extra*-action on your part and then approach a stranger with a smile and an open heart.

Adding some humor will help break down people's defenses and not invite an awkward look. And if you do it with respect and kindness, you will make a new friend. This kind of out-of-the-box thinking transforms you from your ordinary self and to your *extra*ordinary self. Without much effort, your *extra*ordinary action now inspires that person to interact with you with newfound trust. When we layer in art, music, dance, sound healing, drumming (even some adult beverages or plant medicines) to this re-pair setting, we start opening a more substantive dialogue — and even have a fun social experience without hating or harming each other, regardless of all our differences. Eventually, this *extra*ordinary pair of Americans spreads the benefit of their positive interaction with other people, groups and eventually into whole communities. It's a powerful exercise in creating and expanding a contagion for peace and mutual respect — without involving money. Eventually this condition influences the movers, shakers and leaders who can help rebalance the corporate profit over people ecosystem.

The above simplistic but powerful example is based on a proven model that has repaired and brought together adults from all walks of life with great success at our Center; the Truth Lab. It is this type of unconventional *sharing* practice that America desperately needs, to bring broken people back together again. Opening your mind, your hands and your door to people you disagree with or don't understand. These ideas are not pollyannish as they're executable by each of us seeking an America that breathes *in* peace and breathes *out* harmony.

ALIGNING WITH THE GOOD NEWS

The good news is that we have the capability *to* live harmoniously and peacefully with our flawed and unique humans, if we really want to. An alien invasion may not be necessary to bring us to our senses. Perhaps we're seduced by our low-vibrational selves because we choose to relish the bad news, thrive on enmity and partner with fear. I don't recall a time in our history when the American mass media reported that one out of two Americans hated each other, as it does today. The idea that one half of us thinks of the other half as being either stupid or as the enemy is quite a head-scratcher. How about you, is that how you feel? Indeed, friends and family members have been torn apart in ways not seen since the Vietnam War. While some smart Americans are selling their Souls to the temptation of greed and power, others not-so-smart are inciting radicalism and domestic terrorism. But looking at the forest from the trees, America has always had a double standard when it comes to seeing things to suit our own needs. Looking in our rear-view mirror of the past, the country has been mired in much worse racism, economic depression, greed, wars and social ills in relation to our problems and challenges today. So is it possible that America's optics look disproportionately bad to the younger generation due to our technological interconnectedness, information overload, search engines and agenda-based talking points that guide our thoughts and actions every second? Is it possible that we are not as divided as the profit-over-people news and social media are broadcasting?

Since bad news, crap and sensationalism sells, the more glued you are to its purveyors, the more advertising dollars flow into their coffers. It's definitely not in today's news media's interest to give us a positive picture of America, let alone put out stories of hope, progress, community building and peacemaking. If what the media is reporting about our current divisive society is accurate, it means that half of Americans are unhealed by succumbing to unhealthy distortions and misguidance from extremist views and media propaganda. And at its worst, this sobering fact could be a self-fulfilling prophecy that spreads its dark plumes of doom and gloom onto the larger segment of the nation, furthering our malaise. But since we have a lot more beautiful commonalities than we have irreconcilable differences as Divine beings, we just have to walk on that path and focus on fixing ourselves first — being aligned with more of the good news for a change!

SWINGING THE PENDULUM TOO FAR

A peace plan for America also demands putting a stop to the classic condition of America swinging its pendulum too far, too quickly and too hastily — all the time. We see this each time we change party leadership in the White House, as the party in control often flaunts its ego and power by rushing to reverse course and dismantle the agendas and policies of its predecessor. Perhaps it's provoked by our short-term election cycles and the two-party system — but it's self-defeating. We don't have to strangle our free market systems, overregulate ourselves, take away people's personal liberties or mandate other extreme measures to get to a more egalitarian and healthy balance for all Americans. Since we've seen that most of our unhealthy habits, issues and imbalances are formed over a protracted period of time, why should we expect our individual or collective fixes to be speedy or forcefully imposed? It's best to take small *incremental* steps toward any sustainable solution.

If we don't get this lesson right in our governance, we'll always keep changing guards in Washington D.C., vacillating from one extreme to another, dividing and fighting bitterly. This political see-saw phenomenon is also why many Americans increasingly distrust our government, become partisan, practice polarization, act tribal, not vote, despise the wealthy and attach unsavory labels to each other. Let's make common sense, compromise and consistency our personal responsibility to combat our dysfunctionality. We know from past experience and throughout our history what happens when Americans are hasty and quick to draw the lines in the sand or pull the trigger too fast. We go from finger-pointing and perpetuating unnecessary wars and enacting bad policies to being too proud and arrogant to own up to our f*ckups. Why repeat this history?

LESSONS FROM THE AFRICANS AND THE CHINESE

It's not just America's history that has suffered from this short-sighted and *swing for the fences* philosophy. I know from my family's experience of the African dictator Idi Amin's expulsion of all Indians from East Africa in 1970 that the swift and harsh experiment in radicalized black African nationalism failed. In fact, the collective countries of Uganda, Kenya and Tanzania had a brain drain that collapsed their economies, which took a generation to restore. They realized they had made a terrible blunder, but it was too late. By that time, the Chinese saw an opportunity and infiltrated the failed states with predatory investment loans that the Africans could not repay. Today, many African countries are heavily indebted to China and have been forced to relinquish their precious resources and assets as a result of fear-based policies, factions, greed and corruption.

You can say that today China owns Africa. Now, America is not Africa, but it's still highly dependent on Chinese exports and investment. From a real-estate perspective, it is scooping up prime properties and land across our nation like never before. Add to this our unhealthy divisions and torn people, and in many ways there's a warning sign of a serious reckoning ahead. We can learn a lot from the Chinese. While the Chinese have spent the last two decades laser focused on advancing their economy, infrastructure, education, health, technology and wellness of its people, we Americans simply squandered the valuable time and regressed to easy feel-good, thumb-sucking choices and divisive behaviors. So shame on us. And that's why I believe an overhaul of our fundamental character and values is overdue. The blame game led us here and it hasn't worked out so well for the majority of Americans. The mirrors of truth reveal that we ALL bear some blame for our society's f*ck ups. So that's where *you* come in. You, not one leader or a political party, are part of the solution to rebuild our communities with judgment-free awareness and creative-based solutions. Think of it as your patriotic duty to plug your own holes in your life to help our collective vessel from sinking. This will not be easy or quick, but true freedom and success comes from hard work, sacrifice and patience. It's our test to get *our* own house in order — and be our own good Samaritans.

THE GOOD SAMARITANS

Back in 1997, I took a wildlife safari trip to Tanzania with one of my brothers. It was a wonderful and eye-opening experience that I will always cherish. One day as we were riding in an open Land Rover inside the Serengeti National Park soaking in the jaw-dropping sightings of water buffaloes and hyenas chasing zebras before a picturesque sunset, we had a scary tire blowout. It was the kind of moment I'd only seen happen in movies, but this sh*t was for real. To make matters worse, the spare tire on the vehicle was defective. We were at the mercy of time with dusk approaching as the sounds of hungry wild lions echoed all around. Our driver kept a calm demeanor and assured us not to panic, informing us of a nearby Maasai village that would provide urgent assistance. We quickly hunkered down in the vehicle while he sent an assistant to run to the village for help. Within a short period of time (that seemed like an eternity), we noticed a group of young Maasai warriors run toward us chanting and singing while rolling a usable tire. My heart resumed its normal beat, and we were all relieved and ecstatic. As we sat anxiously in the car, all the men banded together to change the tire and completed it just before dusk. I remember two of the men smiling at me with the whitest set of teeth I'd ever seen beautifully contrasted on their shiny ebony skinned faces. I smiled back, gave a thumbs up and in a gesture of gratitude. I took my wallet out and removed some money to tip them for their swift work. *"Bwana, stop! ... Put that money back in your pocket"* exclaimed our driver in an angry tone. I looked at him wide-eyed in confusion and retraced my hand filled with a few dollars. *"This is not America, you do not do that here, sir."* He scolded me, as he thanked our saviors who waved goodbye as we sped off. Our driver went on to explain: "*These villagers understand the principle of being Good Samaritans. They help us and do favors for us without expecting any compensation as we return the favor for them when they need our help. If you give them money, you spoil them and they will expect it every time. This is not how we Africans want to start doing things here — like you people do in America.*" Whoa, the guy made a lot of sense! Having lived in a capitalist society for most of my life, I had forgotten what unconditional kindness looked like. Nothing is free in America anymore. Not even clean drinking water. Everything has a price tag with strings attached. And it doesn't help when our own government encourages incentive-based policies by paying people to take some agenda-based action. Examples of this type of 'bribery' include dangling cash and gifts to people to vote, enlist in the army, get vaccinated, etc. This sort of thing only happens in third world countries and is a terrible example for America to deploy on its own citizens.

The African driver was afraid of importing America's unhealthy profit-over people habits into his country – as he should be. Indeed, this is the undeniable power of American culture and influence in the world. What we do or don't do on our turf, ultimately seeps into the soil of greater humanity and affects other gardens. So the stakes are high for America to get its act together. That African incident was a valuable lesson for me and it underscored the value of reciprocity and generosity without monetization; a model for reclaiming America's future.

THE BAD SAMARITANS

Can the Maasai model of the Good Samaritan-type unconditional generosity be the ticket to our own necessary rebalance? Or is America's brand of exporting win-lose capitalism too far along in corrupting other cultures — and it's too late? For sure, the *money talks and bullsh*t walks* American model is infecting exchange protocols all over the world. Americans are being perceived a lot differently today than were just a few years ago. We have degraded ourselves from the "generous and compassionate" image to a "divide and conquer" and "f*ck y'all" image.

Can we start giving our time and service to others, and perform random acts of kindness without always seeking some form of monetary compensation? I am not thinking about Mother Teresa-type goodness. Nor am I encouraging you to enable freeloaders and thumb suckers. What I am asking you is to simply operate more humanely with your fellow humans. We can surely all do that. From that safari experience 24 years ago, I came to value the parable of the Good Samaritan and saw the results of it displayed in that selfless act in East Africa. But I can't help but think how our Western lifestyle stands out in sharp contrast to that essential goodness. It could explain why many Americans choose to sit idle and do nothing to be of service. It is our lesson to remind ourselves and instill in our next generation — not to be the Bad Samaritans.

THE HOPEFUL UNDERDOGS

Our peace plan cannot be undertaken without looking at the glass half full for America's younger generation. I believe they will rise to meet the occasion before us. These underdogs are our hope for the future, the ones in the Divine order who will find creative solutions to equalize America's unequal playing field. Being an underdog all of my life, I can relate to a generation that feels dogged, marginalized and jerked around by powerful corporations and the elite class. But their time is on the horizon, and with instant access to information and technology at their fingertips, I'm hopeful they will find smarter solutions and provide the necessary reset we need as a society to thrust America on a better path. They will have to. From our own experiences at The Center, we find the Gen Ys and the Gen Zs to be less racist, less greedy, less divisive, more adaptable, more creative, more climate-conscious and definitely more open-minded than the baby boomer generation. For sure, they have their share of imbalances and problems. Their idealism, low-attention span, victim/entitlement mentality, deficient social and financial skills, and obsession with mindless online content can pose a real threat to their greatness. But they're also freedom fighters, dynamic and hardworking in their own ways. These are our future movers, shakers and peacemakers who just need a fighting chance, higher living wages, subsidized high-quality education, free health care and a corporate environment that doesn't enslave them. We must partner with them — not be pissed off at them, or they'll piss away America's future and leave a sh*thole for our grandkids to inherit.

For this reason, I am always listening to my millennial kids and learning from them — rather than just blindly imposing my boomer self-righteous ways on them. They've educated me on cannabis, psychedelics, digital currency, LGBTQ rights, rap music, the green economy, social media marketing, vegan & gluten free food, NFTs (non-fungible tokens), social enterprise and so on. In exchange, I impart my wisdom and encourage them to take the high moral ground, stay creative, take risks, have courage, save more, stay in healthy balance, and practice gratitude — all ideals of The Healium Way. Now, if we could only get the old farts and the rigid power-holders to step aside and allow these young bloods to re-energize America with new ideas and fearless possibilities; we'd all be in better shape. Handing over the torch to the new generation is a win-win proposition if it's done with tact and trust.

The young generation is ready and to take responsibility for their own future, while the old generation can take a well-deserved timeout to relight their dying flames by living life and having fun in the golden years. But that power shift entails an unconventional thought process of opening a sea of tight-fisted hands with the resources and money to join hands with another. That's how we can redeem and rebuild an America that works for everyone. And it doesn't have to take a village; it can start with one person: YOU.

7

Counting My Blessings

W e are only as good as the thoughts we keep, the choices we make, the actions we take and the people we surround ourselves with. Most important, we are always connected to our higher power that is navigating our destined path. For this reason, I always count the blessings each moment that I'm alive.

LIVING OUR LEGACY

I know as a tail-end baby boomer that I am personally walking my talk and spreading my blessings by investing my time, money and energy in making a better world. Alas, I may be in the minority. But as you're discovering, The Healium Way is a prescription not only for Americans — it has universal applications for *every person* to better themselves in their flawed human vessel. It's up to all of us to invest in our present dysfunctions and not screw up our future generations by harnessing our positive karma. By undoing our negative ancestral programming and being vigilant in planting new and better habits, we forge a healthier path for ourselves and empower our children. I am able to do this by practicing what I preach — our Principles on a consistent basis. By healing my emotional past wounds, I can stop being a pain in the ass to myself and others. By not being egotistical, I am a humbler individual. By respecting myself, I can respect others. By seeing others in me, I can be more empathetic. By not worshiping money, I have become a more generous and altruistic person. By noticing the beauty around me, I can see the beauty within me. By not taking life too seriously, I am able to laugh more. By staying young at heart, I don't feel old. By being in a constant state of gratitude, I am abundant. By not being attached to anyone or anything, I am seldom disappointed. By not outsourcing my power to others, I become more self-empowered and autonomous. By always finding creative solutions, my problems are never unresolved. By striving for a life of balance, I am well-adjusted and in great health. By aiming for the light, I don't succumb to the dark. By constantly feeding my Soul, I never stop growing. By being the best and real me, I bring out the best and the authentic in others. By having peace within, I can give peace out. By loving myself, I can love others. By not being f*cked up, I stop f*cking others.

All this happens by starting out as an ordinary being and trying to go the *extra*-mile and becoming an *extra*ordinary human, one step at a time. When you purposely live a life in balance and without time for regrets in this way, you're essentially shaping your legacy while you're still alive. We now care less about the pressures of 'leaving a legacy', but more about *living our legacy* —emulating the vibration of enlightened beings. Your work and good deeds while being alive become your life's karma that may survive generations. Once you're a *roots*-type person, you're also not concerned about buying your way into history and having anything named after you — that's your ego beast to stop validating. Why not let the world decide after your exit if you deserve any accolades!

That in a nutshell is the simplicity and beauty of The Healium Way. It shows us how far we are deviating from our Divine Source — but more important, how the reconnection is achieved by detaching from the man-made transgressions and distractions that don't serve us.

THERE ARE NO COINCIDENCES

Looking back at that earthshaking calamity that forced my family out of our African homeland a half-century ago, I can only look at the glass half full and say that what seemed like a curse at the time turned out to be a Divine blessing for me. It also wasn't a coincidence, happenstance or fluke. The universe is more intentional than that. Thanks to Idi Amin's wrath, I met my life's Soul partner in an exciting new frontier of opportunities called America. At the rate my family's fortunes were climbing in Tanzania, we would have never left our homeland, and who knows what my life would have looked like. Perhaps our family would have been more grounded, healed and united. But destiny had a different plan. And my wife has taught me a more ethereal way of looking at life as a whole. As a modern Shaman healer, her spiritual and instinctual gifts have given me a deeper understanding and appreciation of our Divinity and the unseen realm, including our world of dreams, Spirit guides, guardian angels and ghosts. I'm not sure how this came to be, but I went from being a skeptic to a believer regarding the awesome power of metaphysics. A good example is the power of distant energy healing, which she often does with great success with her clients. That stuff works! She's also taught me to recognize and to learn the value of serendipity and a Divine plan. Unbeknownst to me, it was this belief that connected both of us back in 1981 at a community cultural event in Tucson, Arizona.

It was a beautiful Saturday evening in June and my hot Mexican date stood me up at the last minute. I was furious, as I was all prettied up in a tightly fitted polyester shirt and bell bottom pants—with no backup plans for the night. As a comforting gesture, my brother insisted that I follow him to the Filipino Club dance and banquet event where I could meet girls and eat Filipino food. He asked me to take some videos of the cultural dance performances for him, and I was starving for some good food so I grudgingly agreed. Carrying a clumsy Betamax camcorder on my shoulder, I proceeded to film the girls on the wooden stage. My camera lens was fixated on an 18-year-old girl who was wearing a green sequined two-piece outfit while doing a traditional cultural dance. She was gorgeous, and my brother said she was a mestiza, a girl born to an American father and a Filipina mother. What an amazing and fiery combination! I immediately had impure thoughts and hungry eyes of making out with her in the backseat of my turquoise blue Chevrolet Chevette. But this girl was not an easy fish to hook.

Behind her beauty queen stunning looks was a shy and studious gal who had never dated anyone and was chaperoned by strict parents and brothers. *"You've got no chance with that girl,"* I heard my family and friends tell me at that party. To me that *"No"* meant *"I've got nothing to lose — Yes!"* I quickly turbocharged my charms and persuaded her father to permit his only daughter to dance with me that night. He reluctantly agreed — and I was elated. After the short and timid slow dance that had both of us nervous, I knew I had someone unique with higher vibration energy. My eyes never left her sight and two short years later as a 21-year-old, broke-as-f*ck college student, I mustered up $45 and bought her a cubic zirconia (faux diamond) ring from a pawn shop and proposed to her. Lucky for me, she didn't fuss about the ring and accepted the marriage proposal. I knew right away that the girl was not materialistic and could be trusted with money matters — my type of woman! We both took a leap of faith that day, got married against both of our families' wishes and eloped to California to pursue my fashion design career.

Our makeshift wedding sucked, and my wife often reminds me of how bad it was. But we never looked back or regretted that life-altering decision. Most of my family thought I'd lost my head and gave the marriage a six months post-honeymoon shelf life. Meanwhile, my in-laws' family & friends thought she'd end up beheaded somewhere in the desert of Saudi Arabia. Obviously, everyone was proven wrong and we're here to tell our story — with both our heads still intact. I made margaritas out of lemons that fateful Saturday night, and thanked the invisible forces for their Divine assistance. These invisible signs are our spiritual connection and teach us that *there are no coincidences in life.*

PAYING IT FORWARD

As we've seen in this book, these Divine signals have played an important role in my life. From my survival story at birth to today, I find clear evidence of its undeniable power, and have great respect and trust in it. Being that everything has some underlying higher purpose, we often look at things as being good or bad. It's our man-made default position. However, in the spiritual realm of universal higher consciousness, we have to believe that it's all good — whether we agree with it or not. As a recipient of this cosmic synchronicity, I met the love of my life, produced two great children, provided an above average life for my family, made history fighting the dark forces in Alabama, and created a pioneering healing arts sanctuary to uplift America, to name a few accomplishments that my maker envisioned for me. Conversely, if I had ignored the signs, I could have missed out on many of those life-altering opportunities. In an egotistic and typically Western way of looking at things, you could say that I'm a product of my own making — by navigating my path, choosing my environment, making good choices, being creative, working smart, being educated, applying my skills, and having good timing. But that man-made view is only true on the thinnest of surfaces. I see everything through a spiritual and higher vibrational lens. Perhaps that fact has nothing to do with my life to this point. Maybe, I've never been in control of my life or any of my accomplishments since I was born. Could life simply be a grand illusion, where our paths are already planned before we begin the journey? Could it be that all of the trials and tribulations, lessons, achievements and blessings were destined from the start, and we just go through life as an exercise in futility? Could we be an experimental species that is being controlled by invisible extraterrestrial life forms that we conveniently label as God? It is definitely all possible, and the best part about it is — that we'll never know!

In this context, if you picked this book up (or were handed it by someone), and have interacted with it, perhaps it wasn't a happenstance but rather a Divine purpose for you to have it. It is now up to you, to either stow it away to gather dust on your bookshelf, or re-read it and use it as a tool to rebalance yourself toward becoming a better human being. If the book has benefited you, pay it forward and donate a copy to a friend, a neighbor, a family member, a co-worker or a total stranger. Now you'll have someone to share your renewed self. Eventually, each of us will operate from a place of love and light and connect with one another to spread the contagion of hope, unity and peace universally. Perhaps this body of work has inspired you to write your own story and make a difference in the world. So just do it! Don't die with the message still in you and have any regrets. I wrote this book to inspire others, and leave something for our next generation to build on and to do it better than me. Just tell your story and do it without reservation. You never know whose life you will help transform and save.

In the Healium Way of seeing things, it is U who holds the key to open the door to the gates of eternal paradise when you return to your mothership. There won't be any awards, medals, reward points, 'like' buttons or virgins waiting for you. It will just be you, carrying your immortal Soul and devoid of any man-made bullsh*t. We're not exactly sure who'll be on the other side of that door, but you can bet that your maker is interested in seeing you again. This Source that you've *out*-sourced to man-made trappings is curious about your adventures down here, as much as you're anxious about your afterlife up there. You can enter through this gatekeeper's doors, slumped over and hanging your head with a long face, full of disappointments — or by jumping up in the air with joy, carrying a big smile and having absolutely no regrets of your temporary visit down here. The choice is always yours, and may determine what this maker has in store for you.

Peace, love and respect,

Jim Peera (aka: Jim Healium, Azim Peera)

THIS KEY I HOLD

THIS LIFE FEELS LIKE I AM LOCKED UP IN A CAGE, AND THERE'S NO KEY.
IT'S NOWHERE TO BE FOUND AND SO I'LL JUST LET IT BE.

THE PATH I WALK IS LONELY AND DISCONNECTED.
I LOVE THIS CELL, MY INTERNET, BEING BITTER AND INTROVERTED.

THAT BLANK CANVAS INVITES ME TO SOAK MY TEARS OF PAIN.
I'D RATHER DROWN IN A COCKTAIL OF PILLS TO STAY SANE.

THE DUSTY GUITAR LAYING ON THE SHELF STARES AT ME INCESSANTLY.
I CHOOSE TO LIVE DYING WITH THE MUSIC STILL IN ME.

THIS WORK I DO HAS TURNED INTO AN ADDICTION TO STAY BUSY.
IT FOLLOWS ME EVERYWHERE AND SHOWS NO PITY.

THE MASKS I WEAR NOT TO APPEAR SO LAME.
THEY HIDE THE SHADOWS OF MY CHILDHOOD TO BLAME.

THIS FACE CONCEALS THE WRINKLES OF MY LIFE'S SHOULDA WOULDAS.
THE SCARS BENEATH REVEAL THE PATH OF WHAT I COULDA.

YOU SAY I BUY INTO A STATE OF ANGER AND FEAR.
THE PRICE OF JOY AND FREEDOM MY FRIEND, IS TOO DEAR.

THAT PORTAL OF INFINITE AND ABUNDANT POSSIBILITY.
I LIKE IT SHUT AND DISTANT AS I DO MY SOUL AND DIVINITY.

THIS PRISON I LIE IN HAS NO BARS, CHAINS OR DOORS YOU SEE.
I MADE IT UP IN THE HEAD TO FIT MY REALITY.

THERE'S NOTHING TO LOOK BACK IN VAIN OR REGRET.
MY LIFE WAS PREDESTINED THIS WAY I BET.

HOW TIME HAS FLEETED NOW THAT I AM SIX FEET DEEP IN THE HOLE.
MY HANDS STILL TIGHTLY CLENCHED, DRY, BRITTLE AND OLD.

TO KNOW THAT I HAVE HELD THIS KEY IN MY HANDS ALL ALONG.
WHEN WILL I EVER LET GO, AND USE THIS KEY I HOLD ?

JIM PEERA

This Key I Hold

Body Art Installation at Healium Center

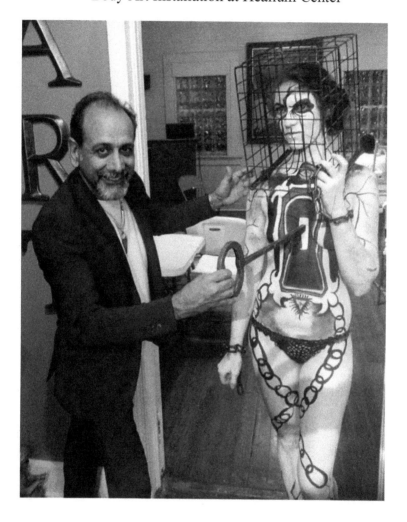

Scan to listen to the "Power of Love" poem by Jim Peera dedicated to his wife, Blue Thunder:

(Left to right) Visionary Artist Toni Taylor, Jim Peera, Donna Peera (Aka; Blue Thunder) unveiling their Spirit portrait; POWER OF LOVE

UPLIFTING YOU WITH THE ARTS!

CONNECT. UPLIFT. EMPOWER

www.HealiumCenter.com

Epilogue

Our Common Bucket List

As all the sages, wisemen and ancient writings teach us that our common shared human experience is living up to our truer and higher self. The way we stay steadfast on that path is to understand that anything less is a result of our own man-made attachments, choices and actions. Our high bar therefore is to exit this earth having lived a full life doing *extra*ordinary things and having no regrets. With this in mind, nothing would give me greater satisfaction than to turbocharge spreading the message of peace and The Healium Way across all our communities and into the world at large. Specifically, I would love to see a Healium Way sanctuary in The White House, no matter what political party occupies it. This is on my bucket list — and perhaps you could help me make this more than a pipedream, but a reality. And we can get there together. Can you imagine being able to get our leaders in power to press a *pause* button on making any hasty moves or attacking any nation, by taking a couple hours to chill out, release and recharge by painting, drumming, jamming, dancing, laughing, hugging, meditating, and addressing pent-up emotions in a fun and healthy way? It could be highly beneficial to the entire White House staff to connect, uplift and feel empowered. If there's a designated Situation Room at the White House to strategize a military action to go to war, surely, we can have a designated Healium Room to activate creative actions to fight for peace. If there are powerful lobbyists buying politicians to protect their self-interests, for sure we can sell the idea of protecting our individual sanity and our collective humanity to our elected leaders. We already know of one president in our modern history who came pretty close to this reality.

President Jimmy Carter, known as the Rock 'n' Roll president (due to his love of music), was proud to have never fired one missile, attacked any nation or dropped a single bomb on enemy soil during his time in office. But in the eyes of most Americans, Carter is not celebrated as a peace leader, but as a weak statesman, who wasn't exciting, tough and mighty enough for America. As an unconventional thinker, peacemaker and a humanitarian, he definitely earns my respect. During the 1979-1981 Iran hostage ordeal that lasted 444 days, Carter could have easily bombed Iran and been hailed as a hero and a strong leader in the eyes of America and the world. But his goal was to resolve the situation peacefully and return the hostages in one piece. A military strike could have cost the lives of all 52 American hostages.

The Georgian peanut farmer turned president recalls how he found personal solace by retreating into a room at the White House listening to Willie Nelson and Bob Dylan songs. Music gave him peace, upliftment and solitude in his hours of stress and burden. As a God-loving man, he selflessly activated his Divinity within and earned a Nobel Peace Prize for doing godly things across the globe.

Although leaders must protect us from enemy attack or aggression, we must also only use force as a last resort. Instead of having our reptilian brains fire in haste and our egos stroked, we could calm the mind and rethink our actions more creatively. I am certain we would avert many unnecessary wars and learn to dialogue and disarm our internal and externalized hostilities. After all, I have just proved to you in these pages how art heals. Now let's save lives with it!

"Warrior of Peace"

(Oil on Canvas) Artist: Toni Taylor

Acknowledgments

It's been my honor and pleasure writing The Healium Way (Part 1 & Part 2). I must say, it has been one of the most therapeutic journeys of my life. First and foremost, I'd like to thank my Creator and my Spirit guides for keeping me safe during the course of this writing. This invisible force has been my collaborator and partner since I was born and helped me write this book. I wrote my first words at the onset of the Covid-19 pandemic, and with each day I prayed to the higher forces to protect and empower me to complete this important body of work. It was not conceived as a 2-part book, but Spirit took over and the words just kept on flowing, often waking me up in the middle of the night to write. I was blessed to have my wife, my daughter and my son to inspire me to empty the contents of my brain every day onto paper and tell my story, without holding back.

My wife Donna (aka Blue Thunder) and I shared many deep conversations as she helped me put into perspective some important moments and stories of our personal adventures together. She was a co-conspirator on this journey and I can't thank her enough.

You can visit her at:

Bluethunderhealing.com

" Blue Thunder "

(Oil on Canvas) Artist: Toni Taylor

My kids were also supportive during this writing process. Although my son was in self-lockdown the entire period, he and I shared some beautiful and important phone conversations during many late nights and wee hours of the morning. As an expert in the plant medicine business, his high-quality artisanal hemp products helped me invaluably during this writing!

You can visit him at:

Upliftingartists.com

My daughter was a true trooper who helped make this book more gripping and relevant. By giving me the opportunity to help unearth and heal her emotional teenage wound with me while I was writing this book, she further validated the value of The Healium Way as a transformational guide. One of her most captivating compositions that inspired me during the Covid-19 period is called *"Within."* She put out a demo version in hopes to get the music or film industry to recognize it and make it a hit song. You can check it out here as well as her portfolio of work:

Portfolio **Within**

This book would also not have been possible without the stories of all the Souls that entered through the doors of Healium Center in Atlanta, Georgia. Therefore, whether I've used your particular experience in this book or not — you've all contributed to this writing in some way and I am grateful to all of you for your love, support and presence — even if we didn't see eye to eye on some things. As a transformational guide without excuses, The Healium Way could not be written without intentionally ruffling some feathers and being an equal opportunity critic. It's only by provoking, disagreeing and re-engaging, that we have the opportunity to become better human beings. In conclusion, although I lost two of my family members to the pandemic, this book could not have been possible without Covid-19. Looking at the glass half-full, the historic crisis that claimed millions of lives worldwide was in a strange way less of a curse to me as it was a blessing. It helped me go within and dedicate the time to write this exciting human adventure story for you!

MANGO SALSA FISH DINNER
30 Minute Flexitarian Recipe

Serving size: 4 people
Main Ingredient: Fish

Morning Prep: (10 mins)

Thaw filet of fish (steelhead trout, red snapper, grouper etc)
Prepare mango salsa: chop and prepare before going to work.

Mango Salsa:
1 diced and chopped medium onion
1 medium tomato or half pint grape tomatoes -
1 large not too ripe mango - peeled and diced
1/2 teaspoon ancho chile powder
1 pinch of sea salt (and/or capful lemon/lime)
Mix in bowl and refrigerate

Evening Prep (20 mins)

Fish Preparation
Use filet of fish with skin on bottom side of pan
Coat non-stick pan with 1 to 2 tablespoons of olive oil
Preheat oven to 350 degrees fahrenheit

Dry rub for fish

Compliments of Donna Peera (Aka: Blue Thunder)

2 teaspoons garlic - granulated
2 teaspoons cumin powder
2 Tablespoons dry bbq rub
2 teaspoons ground thyme
2 teaspoons ground turmeric powder
Use pinch of sea salt if bbq rub is unsalted
Apply liberally with hands and coat on top side of fish (unskinned)

SCAN ME

1. Bake seasoned fish for 15 minutes.
2. Stir fry Mango Salsa in 1 to 2 tablespoons of virgin olive oil in a frying pan for 2 minutes.
3. Stir fry on medium flame a quart of ready sliced mushrooms in 2 tablespoons olive oil and 2 tablespoons ground cumin for 10 minutes until mushrooms are soft.
4. Prepare mashed potatoes in a pot. Use 2 cups instant dried mash potato, add 1 cup water, 2 cups non dairy milk, 2 tablespoons non-dairy sour cream, 2 tablespoons minced onions, 2 tablespoons garlic powder. Add a pinch of sea salt to taste. Stir well and put on medium flame and heat slowly for 5 minutes until creamy.

Pour mango salsa over fish and serve mashed potatoes and sauteed mushrooms on the sides of the plate.

There you have it...a healthy meal in 30 minutes. No dairy, no gluten & no eggs. Enjoy!

CPSIA information can be obtained
at www.ICGtesting.com
Printed in the USA
BVHW021339231121
622333BV00022B/671